Y0-BSF-727

MEDIA,
ELECTIONS
AND
DEMOCRACY

*This is Volume 19 in a series of studies
commissioned as part of the research program
of the Royal Commission on Electoral Reform
and Party Financing*

MEDIA,
ELECTIONS
AND
DEMOCRACY

Frederick J. Fletcher
Editor

Volume 19 of the Research Studies

ROYAL COMMISSION ON ELECTORAL REFORM
AND PARTY FINANCING
AND CANADA COMMUNICATION GROUP –
PUBLISHING, SUPPLY AND SERVICES CANADA

DUNDURN PRESS
TORONTO AND OXFORD

© Minister of Supply and Services Canada, 1991
Printed and bound in Canada
ISBN 1-55002-115-X
ISSN 1188-2743
Catalogue No. Z1-1989/2-41-19E

Published by Dundurn Press Limited in cooperation with the Royal
Commission on Electoral Reform and Party Financing and Canada
Communication Group – Publishing, Supply and Services Canada.

All rights reserved. No part of this publication may be reproduced,
stored in a retrieval system, or transmitted in any form or by any
means, electronic, mechanical, photocopying, recording, or
otherwise (except brief passages for purposes of review) without the
prior written permission of the Minister of Supply and Services.

Canadian Cataloguing in Publication Data

Main entry under title:
Media, elections and democracy

(Research studies ; 19)
Issued also in French under title: Médias, élections et démocratie.
ISBN 1-55002-115-X

   1. Mass media – Political aspects – Canada. 2. Communication in politics –
Canada. 3. Electioneering – Canada. 4. Canada. Parliament – Elections.
5. Democracy. I. Fletcher, Frederick J. II. Canada. Royal Commission on
Electoral Reform and Party Financing. III. Series: Research studies (Canada.
Royal Commission on Electoral Reform and Party Financing) ; 19.

P95.8.M43 1991   324.7'3'0971   C91-090531-2

73416

Dundurn Press Limited
2181 Queen Street East
Suite 301
Toronto, Canada
M4E 1E5

Dundurn Distribution
73 Lime Walk
Headington
Oxford, England
OX3 7AD

CONTENTS

AUGUSTANA UNIVERSITY COLLEGE
LIBRARY

FIGURES

TABLES

FOREWORD

THE ROYAL COMMISSION on Electoral Reform and Party Financing
was established in November 1989. Our mandate was to inquire into
and report on the appropriate principles and process that should govern the election of members of the House of Commons and the financing of political parties and candidates' campaigns. To conduct such a
comprehensive examination of Canada's electoral system, we held
extensive public consultations and developed a research program
designed to ensure that our recommendations would be guided by an
independent foundation of empirical inquiry and analysis.

The Commission's in-depth review of the electoral system was the
first of its kind in Canada's history of electoral democracy. It was dictated largely by the major constitutional, social and technological
changes of the past several decades, which have transformed Canadian
society, and their concomitant influence on Canadians' expectations
of the political process itself. In particular, the adoption in 1982 of the
Canadian Charter of Rights and Freedoms has heightened Canadians'
awareness of their democratic and political rights and of the way they
are served by the electoral system.

The importance of electoral reform cannot be overemphasized. As
the Commission's work proceeded, Canadians became increasingly
preoccupied with constitutional issues that have the potential to change
the nature of Confederation. No matter what their beliefs or political
allegiances in this continuing debate, Canadians agree that constitutional
change must be achieved in the context of fair and democratic processes. We cannot complacently assume that our current electoral
process will always meet this standard or that it leaves no room for
improvement. Parliament and the national government must be seen
as legitimate; electoral reform can both enhance the stature of national

political institutions and reinforce their ability to define the future of our country in ways that command Canadians' respect and confidence and promote the national interest.

In carrying out our mandate, we remained mindful of the importance of protecting our democratic heritage, while at the same time balancing it against the emerging values that are injecting a new dynamic into the electoral system. If our system is to reflect the realities of Canadian political life, then reform requires more than mere tinkering with electoral laws and practices.

Our broad mandate challenged us to explore a full range of options. We commissioned more than 100 research studies, to be published in a 23-volume collection. In the belief that our electoral laws must measure up to the very best contemporary practice, we examined election-related laws and processes in all of our provinces and territories and studied comparable legislation and processes in established democracies around the world. This unprecedented array of empirical study and expert opinion made a vital contribution to our deliberations. We made every effort to ensure that the research was both intellectually rigorous and of practical value. All studies were subjected to peer review, and many of the authors discussed their preliminary findings with members of the political and academic communities at national symposiums on major aspects of the electoral system.

The Commission placed the research program under the able and inspired direction of Dr. Peter Aucoin, Professor of Political Science and Public Administration at Dalhousie University. We are confident that the efforts of Dr. Aucoin, together with those of the research coordinators and scholars whose work appears in this and other volumes, will continue to be of value to historians, political scientists, parliamentarians and policy makers, as well as to thoughtful Canadians and the international community.

Along with the other Commissioners, I extend my sincere gratitude to the entire Commission staff for their dedication and commitment. I also wish to thank the many people who participated in our symposiums for their valuable contributions, as well as the members of the research and practitioners' advisory groups whose counsel significantly aided our undertaking.

Pierre Lortie
Chairman

INTRODUCTION

THE ROYAL COMMISSION'S research program constituted a comprehensive and detailed examination of the Canadian electoral process. The scope of the research, undertaken to assist Commissioners in their deliberations, was dictated by the broad mandate given to the Commission.

The objective of the research program was to provide Commissioners with a full account of the factors that have shaped our electoral democracy. This dictated, first and foremost, a focus on federal electoral law, but our inquiries also extended to the Canadian constitution, including the institutions of parliamentary government, the practices of political parties, the mass media and nonpartisan political organizations, as well as the decision-making role of the courts with respect to the constitutional rights of citizens. Throughout, our research sought to introduce a historical perspective in order to place the contemporary experience within the Canadian political tradition.

We recognized that neither our consideration of the factors shaping Canadian electoral democracy nor our assessment of reform proposals would be as complete as necessary if we failed to examine the experiences of Canadian provinces and territories and of other democracies. Our research program thus emphasized comparative dimensions in relation to the major subjects of inquiry.

Our research program involved, in addition to the work of the Commission's research coordinators, analysts and support staff, over 200 specialists from 28 universities in Canada, from the private sector and, in a number of cases, from abroad. Specialists in political science constituted the majority of our researchers, but specialists in law, economics, management, computer sciences, ethics, sociology and communications, among other disciplines, were also involved.

In addition to the preparation of research studies for the Commission, our research program included a series of research seminars, symposiums and workshops. These meetings brought together the Commissioners, researchers, representatives from the political parties, media personnel and others with practical experience in political parties, electoral politics and public affairs. These meetings provided not only a forum for discussion of the various subjects of the Commission's mandate, but also an opportunity for our research to be assessed by those with an intimate knowledge of the world of political practice.

These public reviews of our research were complemented by internal and external assessments of each research report by persons qualified in the area; such assessments were completed prior to our decision to publish any study in the series of research volumes.

The Research Branch of the Commission was divided into several areas, with the individual research projects in each area assigned to the research coordinators as follows:

F. Leslie Seidle	Political Party and Election Finance
Herman Bakvis	Political Parties
Kathy Megyery	Women, Ethno-cultural Groups and Youth
David Small	Redistribution; Electoral Boundaries; Voter Registration
Janet Hiebert	Party Ethics
Michael Cassidy	Democratic Rights; Election Administration
Robert A. Milen	Aboriginal Electoral Participation and Representation
Frederick J. Fletcher	Mass Media and Broadcasting in Elections
David Mac Donald (Assistant Research Coordinator)	Direct Democracy

These coordinators identified appropriate specialists to undertake research, managed the projects and prepared them for publication. They also organized the seminars, symposiums and workshops in their research areas and were responsible for preparing presentations and briefings to help the Commission in its deliberations and decision making. Finally, they participated in drafting the Final Report of the Commission.

On behalf of the Commission, I welcome the opportunity to thank the following for their generous assistance in producing these research studies – a project that required the talents of many individuals.

In performing their duties, the research coordinators made a notable contribution to the work of the Commission. Despite the pressures of tight deadlines, they worked with unfailing good humour and the utmost congeniality. I thank all of them for their consistent support and cooperation.

In particular, I wish to express my gratitude to Leslie Seidle, senior research coordinator, who supervised our research analysts and support staff in Ottawa. His diligence, commitment and professionalism not only set high standards, but also proved contagious. I am grateful to Kathy Megyery, who performed a similar function in Montreal with equal aplomb and skill. Her enthusiasm and dedication inspired us all.

On behalf of the research coordinators and myself, I wish to thank our research analysts: Daniel Arsenault, Eric Bertram, Cécile Boucher, Peter Constantinou, Yves Denoncourt, David Docherty, Luc Dumont, Jane Dunlop, Scott Evans, Véronique Garneau, Keith Heintzman, Paul Holmes, Hugh Mellon, Cheryl D. Mitchell, Donald Padget, Alain Pelletier, Dominique Tremblay and Lisa Young. The Research Branch was strengthened by their ability to carry out research in a wide variety of areas, their intellectual curiosity and their team spirit.

The work of the research coordinators and analysts was greatly facilitated by the professional skills and invaluable cooperation of Research Branch staff members: Paulette LeBlanc, who, as administrative assistant, managed the flow of research projects; Hélène Leroux, secretary to the research coordinators, who produced briefing material for the Commissioners and who, with Lori Nazar, assumed responsibility for monitoring the progress of research projects in the latter stages of our work; Kathleen McBride and her assistant Natalie Brose, who created and maintained the database of briefs and hearings transcripts; and Richard Herold and his assistant Susan Dancause, who were responsible for our research library. Jacinthe Séguin and Cathy Tucker also deserve thanks – in addition to their duties as receptionists, they assisted in a variety of ways to help us meet deadlines.

We were extremely fortunate to obtain the research services of first-class specialists from the academic and private sectors. Their contributions are found in this and the other 22 published research volumes. We thank them for the quality of their work and for their willingness to contribute and to meet our tight deadlines.

Our research program also benefited from the counsel of Jean-Marc Hamel, Special Adviser to the Chairman of the Commission and former

Chief Electoral Officer of Canada, whose knowledge and experience proved invaluable.

In addition, numerous specialists assessed our research studies. Their assessments not only improved the quality of our published studies, but also provided us with much-needed advice on many issues. In particular, we wish to single out professors Donald Blake, Janine Brodie, Alan Cairns, Kenneth Carty, John Courtney, Peter Desbarats, Jane Jenson, Richard Johnston, Vincent Lemieux, Terry Morley and Joseph Wearing, as well as Ms. Beth Symes.

Producing such a large number of studies in less than a year requires a mastery of the skills and logistics of publishing. We were fortunate to be able to count on the Commission's Director of Communications, Richard Rochefort, and Assistant Director, Hélène Papineau. They were ably supported by the Communications staff: Patricia Burden, Louise Dagenais, Caroline Field, Claudine Labelle, France Langlois, Lorraine Maheux, Ruth McVeigh, Chantal Morissette, Sylvie Patry, Jacques Poitras and Claudette Rouleau-O'Toole.

To bring the project to fruition, the Commission also called on specialized contractors. We are deeply grateful for the services of Ann McCoomb (references and fact checking); Marthe Lemery, Pierre Chagnon and the staff of Communications Com'ça (French quality control); Norman Bloom, Pamela Riseborough and associates of B&B Editorial Consulting (English adaptation and quality control); and Mado Reid (French production). Al Albania and his staff at Acart Graphics designed the studies and produced some 2 400 tables and figures.

The Commission's research reports constitute Canada's largest publishing project of 1991. Successful completion of the project required close cooperation between the public and private sectors. In the public sector, we especially acknowledge the excellent service of the Privy Council unit of the Translation Bureau, Department of the Secretary of State of Canada, under the direction of Michel Parent, and our contacts Ruth Steele and Terry Denovan of the Canada Communication Group, Department of Supply and Services.

The Commission's co-publisher for the research studies was Dundurn Press of Toronto, whose exceptional service is gratefully acknowledged. Wilson & Lafleur of Montreal, working with the Centre de Documentation Juridique du Québec, did equally admirable work in preparing the French version of the studies.

Teams of editors, copy editors and proofreaders worked diligently under stringent deadlines with the Commission and the publishers to prepare some 20 000 pages of manuscript for design, typesetting and printing. The work of these individuals, whose names are listed elsewhere in this volume, was greatly appreciated.

Our acknowledgements extend to the contributions of the Commission's Executive Director, Guy Goulard, and the administration and executive support teams: Maurice Lacasse, Denis Lafrance and Steve Tremblay (finance); Thérèse Lacasse and Mary Guy-Shea (personnel); Cécile Desforges (assistant to the Executive Director); Marie Dionne (administration); Anna Bevilacqua (records); and support staff members Michelle Bélanger, Roch Langlois, Michel Lauzon, Jean Mathieu, David McKay and Pierrette McMurtie, as well as Denise Miquelon and Christiane Séguin of the Montreal office.

A special debt of gratitude is owed to Marlène Girard, assistant to the Chairman. Her ability to supervise the logistics of the Commission's work amid the tight schedules of the Chairman and Commissioners contributed greatly to the completion of our task.

I also wish to express my deep gratitude to my own secretary, Liette Simard. Her superb administrative skills and great patience brought much-appreciated order to my penchant for the chaotic workstyle of academe. She also assumed responsibility for the administrative coordination of revisions to the final drafts of volumes 1 and 2 of the Commission's Final Report. I owe much to her efforts and assistance.

Finally, on behalf of the research coordinators and myself, I wish to thank the Chairman, Pierre Lortie, the members of the Commission, Pierre Fortier, Robert Gabor, William Knight and Lucie Pépin, and former members Elwood Cowley and Senator Donald Oliver. We are honoured to have worked with such an eminent and thoughtful group of Canadians, and we have benefited immensely from their knowledge and experience. In particular, we wish to acknowledge the creativity, intellectual rigour and energy our Chairman brought to our task. His unparalleled capacity to challenge, to bring out the best in us, was indeed inspiring.

Peter Aucoin
Director of Research

PREFACE

IN MODERN DEMOCRACIES, election campaigns are contested to a large
degree in the media. From the days of the openly partisan press to the
contemporary multi-media environment, political leaders have relied
upon mass media to mobilize electoral support. While the right to vote
freely and the credibility of the ballot process are central to democracy,
the conduct of campaigns and the flow of information to voters are also
important. If campaigns are perceived to be conducted unfairly, the
entire electoral process may become suspect. Concern for the legitimacy of the system is one of the primary reasons that most democracies have enacted regulations dealing with aspects of electoral
communication. These regulations cover a wide range of media activities, including campaign advertising, election broadcasting and even
some aspects of news and public affairs.

The Commission's research program on mass media and elections
examined the major developments in electoral communication in Canada
and other democratic countries in recent decades, in the context of electoral reform. The research studies were designed to cast light on major
aspects of election media, whether amenable to regulation or not.
Effective regulation requires an understanding of the entire system of
campaign communication.

The results of the research program provided background for the
Commission's report. Whatever their substantive focus, the studies
examined issues such as fairness in electoral competition and public
confidence in the electoral process, issues that are central to electoral
reform. Some studies examined central elements in the campaign communication system, while others assessed its effectiveness in meeting
the information needs of voters and the communication needs of parties. Several projects considered alternative forms of communication

that might contribute to improved information for voters. The studies examined campaign media in the larger sense, including partisan advertising, free broadcast time, candidate communication strategies, new communication technologies and news and public affairs coverage, among other topics.

Research dealing directly with mass media and elections is reported in volumes 18 through 22. Volume 16, on opinion polling, and Volume 17, on the attitudes of Canadians toward the electoral system, also deal with campaign communication, but include material on other subjects as well. Taken together, the seven volumes provide a comprehensive overview of the issues of campaign communication.

The purpose of the seven studies in Volume 19 is to provide a general description and critical analysis of campaign communication in selected industrial democracies. Six of the studies examine countries (nine in all) that are in some important way comparable to Canada. The authors, well-known specialists in each country, were asked to provide an overview of the principles and practices of electoral communication in their own countries and a critical assessment of those principles and practices, including areas of controversy and possible reform. The final study deals with the Canadian system in similar terms.

The authors were asked to address a number of common topics where appropriate: (1) regulations regarding free and paid time; (2) the regulatory environment for campaign communication; (3) means employed by parties and candidates to reach electors; (4) published opinion polls; (5) principles and practices of news and public affairs coverage, including the status of the party press and control of broadcast media; (6) the impact of new technologies on campaign communication; and (7) televised leaders debates and other high-profile campaign events.

Jacques Gerstlé examines the organization and handling of information in the media during France's 1988 presidential campaign. Gerstlé is concerned that the increased use of media and new technology in election campaigns in fact weakens "equality" among candidates. Holli Semetko examines the British election campaign communication process. Semetko compares the Party Election Broadcasts (PEB) with the partisan press, exploring how the two systems meet the needs of the voter and of the parties, including minor parties. Among the most useful elements of the study is a systematic comparison of campaign coverage on British and American television newscasts. Klaus Schoenbach studies the campaign communication system in Germany with special attention to the impact of the growing commercial broadcasting system on campaign broadcasting and likely changes in the future as the system becomes more market-driven. He deals specifically with the quantity of political information available to electors, the role of print media, party advertising and the use of electronic media for local campaigns.

Karen Siune examines campaign communication in three Scandinavian countries: Denmark, Norway and Sweden. She compares coverage of major and minor parties by newspapers and by public broadcasting systems, noting that both politicians and the public expect higher standards of the latter, especially in terms of balance. Siune notes that concepts of balanced coverage vary among the three countries, with Denmark being the only system to provide equal broadcast time to all parties.

John Warhurst describes the system of campaign communication in Australia in terms of the electronic media election coverage, political advertising spending, public opinion polls and the influence of media on voters.

Doris Graber examines the changing mass media coverage trends in the United States by reviewing data from presidential and congressional campaigns. She explores patterns of voter alienation and cynicism in relation to campaigning strategies and news coverage, and discusses options for addressing these problems through the treatment of political campaigns by the press and political parties.

The editor and his York University colleague Robert Everett provide an overview of campaign communication in Canada, highlighting similarities and differences between our system and those discussed in the earlier studies. This study identifies a number of problem areas that should be confronted to avoid possible erosion of public confidence in the electoral system.

The studies were conducted in late 1990 and early 1991. They will be of interest not only to students and scholars examining the mass media and/or election campaigns, but also to media practitioners, party strategists, policy analysts and others concerned about the electoral process. Taken together, these studies provide an important overview of campaign communication in industrial democracies.

Some central issues are common to most systems, including: (1) the escalating costs of modern campaigns, fueled in large part by new communication technologies; (2) the need to deal with the relationship between paid and free time, as commercial broadcasting emerges in systems that were formerly public monopolies; (3) the challenge of defining what is equitable in allocating broadcasting time among candidates and parties (especially with respect to minor parties); (4) devising appropriate rules for televised leaders debates; (5) coming to terms

with the changing role of the news media in the electoral process; and
(6) assessing the implications of new communications technologies and
changes in the mass media. The studies not only raise these issues but
provide information on the response to them in the various systems. This
volume is one of the few sources that provide a basis for examining
such issues comparatively.

The Commission's research program on mass media and elections
drew on the expertise of a wide range of communication scholars and
political scientists in addition to those whose work was published in
these volumes. Their assistance is greatly appreciated. Among those
who participated as peer reviewers and advisers, several deserve special recognition: Peter Desbarats, Dean of the School of Journalism at
the University of Western Ontario; David Taras, University of Calgary;
Holli Semetko, University of Michigan; and Marc Raboy, Laval
University. The research program also benefited from the advice of
individuals from the parties and the media: John Coleman, President,
Canadian Advertising Foundation; Terry Hargreaves, Elly Alboim and
Colin MacLeod of the CBC; Geoffrey Stevens, political columnist; Lynn
McDonald, sociologist and former MP; and others who prefer to remain
anonymous. On behalf of the authors and the Commission, I must also
acknowledge our debt to the practitioners from the media and the parties, who attended our seminars or agreed to be interviewed and provided much valuable assistance and advice.

The administration of the research program depended heavily on
the work of Cheryl Mitchell, who served as my assistant from the inception of the program, and our research assistants at York University:
Catherine Bolan, Claudia Forgas, Marni Goldman, Todd Harris, Sharon
Johnston and Sheila Riordon. We were also assisted most ably by the
Commission staff. Peter Constantinou and Véronique Garneau had
particular responsibilities for research in this area. The staff of the
Department of Political Science, the Faculty of Arts, Calumet College,
and the Faculty of Environmental Studies at York University were very
accommodating.

The authors themselves deserve special acknowledgement for their
willingness to try to meet tight deadlines, complicated by their normal
academic responsibilities, and in particular to respond with cheerful-
ness and despatch to our requests for revisions. The conscientious peer
reviews were of major assistance to the authors and ourselves in preparing these studies for publication.

The unfailing good humour and encouragement of Peter Aucoin,
the Director of Research, made an important contribution to the work.
It was a privilege to work with the Commissioners, whose willingness

to bring their experience to bear on the most esoteric of formulations was an inspiration. Pierre Lortie's overall direction and, in particular, his suggestions for research and incisive comments on various drafts made a vital contribution, which is reflected in these research volumes as well as in the Final Report of the Royal Commission. Working with the other research coordinators was a genuine pleasure. Richard Rochefort and his staff were crucial in bringing these studies to publication.

On a personal note, I wish to thank my wife and frequent collaborator, Martha Fletcher, for encouraging me to undertake this task, which I have found very rewarding, and for her direct advice on many aspects of the work, as well as for bearing more than her share of the burden of domestic management. My son, Frederick, reminded me that work, however important, must be balanced with other aspects of life and that the future of the democratic process is worth working for.

Cheryl Mitchell brought dedication and skill to the work and must have an ample share of the credit for whatever contribution the research program has made. In addition to her own study, Holli Semetko made a major contribution to this volume by assisting in the recruitment of the researchers. For errors in design and execution, however, I remain responsible.

Fred Fletcher
Research Coordinator

MEDIA,
ELECTIONS
AND
DEMOCRACY

1

ELECTION COMMUNICATION IN FRANCE

Jacques Gerstlé

THE ROLE OF THE MEDIA IN ELECTION CAMPAIGNS

IN FRANCE, as in other Western countries, the media are playing an increasingly important role in the political process, especially during those crucial periods covered by election campaigns. There are many reasons for this increase in the power of the media and of their role in political discourse. New technological developments in the creation, handling, management and transmission of information have appeared and are available to varying degrees to those in the political arena. The behaviour and practices of both the governors and the governed show that they are becoming more and more dependent on the media for support for their communication strategies and as sources of political information. The theories behind the shift in the role of the media are based on a recognition of the power of the media to shape social concepts of political reality.

Not all media, however, are equally effective. Determining effectiveness is in fact extremely difficult, requiring precise empirical criteria that depend in turn on prior theoretical choices.

What is effective election communication? Is it communication that wins the most votes? Communication that maximizes votes and optimizes campaign support in the short term? Communication that creates and maintains a political image? Or does effective communication resolve problems facing the community and enhance public discussion and decision making? Clearly, the period when the evaluation takes place and who participates in the evaluation (i.e., political practitioners or ordinary citizens) will both have significant consequences. These criteria aside, there are obvious differences among the media. In France, as elsewhere, empirical studies have shown repeatedly that television is the most popular medium for political communication in general and election communication in particular. One of the more recent studies is the enlightening comparative analysis of the American and French public during the 1988 presidential elections (Semetko and Borquez 1991). The gap between television and the other media is growing. The other sources of information, in decreasing order of audience confidence, are radio, daily newspapers, weekly newspapers and magazines. Various studies conducted during the presidential election in 1988 show that television is the preferred medium for elections.

This study considers the principle of equality in election campaigns and how it is put into practice by the media (i.e., the organization of the official campaign and the handling of information). It also examines the specific problem of publishing opinion poll results. Finally, it considers the credibility of the media and the response of their audiences. By way of conclusion, several approaches to assessing election coverage are proposed, and recommendations to improve electoral communication advanced.

THE PRINCIPLE OF EQUALITY, REGULATION
AND THE MODERNIZATION OF ELECTION CAMPAIGNS

Certain general principles govern the election campaign process: freedom, nonpartisan election administration and, increasingly, equality among parties and candidates. These principles, and the regulations based on them, are occasionally threatened by modern communication techniques and political practices. Examples range from classic political propaganda and audiovisual techniques to the distinction between the pre-campaign period and the official campaign, and between "official" propaganda and "parallel" propaganda (Derieux 1991).

In France, the principle governing the regulation of official propaganda in election campaigns is founded on the concept of equality among the candidates. The law of 6 November 1962, which regulates the election of the president of the republic by universal suffrage, states that "all candidates shall receive from the state the same facilities for the presidential election campaign." The increasing role of the electronic media has led to regulations providing equal access to these resources. The decree of 14 March 1964 extended this principle to the electronic media.

Over the years, a law limiting the growth of election spending has evolved, but the law has also adapted to the change in the French media landscape arising from the movement toward privatization of the air waves. In 1981, for example, the three public television networks were the only ones available. By 1988, there were two public networks (A2 and FR3) and four private networks (TF1, Canal Plus, La Cinq and M6).

Three new laws dealing with election campaigns have been adopted: the law of 11 March 1988, requiring financial disclosure by those in politics; the law of 15 January 1990, limiting election expenses and requiring disclosure of political spending; and the law of 10 May 1990, regulating election campaigns of presidential and legislative candidates. To some extent, the first law recognizes the existence of parallel forms of nonofficial propaganda. In drafting the law, legislators sought to keep the development of these activities and their potential financial effects from perverting the democratic principle. Debbasch (1989) summarized the trend perceptible in March 1988: "The principle of equality is now one of the major principles governing the activity of the electronic media during a presidential campaign."

The electoral code establishes the duration of the official campaign for each election. The code also prescribes the period during which the candidates may use various types of campaign propaganda: election meetings, election pamphlets (referred to as "declarations of faith") and signs. In practice, however, these traditional methods of communication are used both officially and in parallel. When used officially, the principle of equality is strictly observed, since public funding is involved. (For more information concerning the new rules on political and election financing, see Aïdan and Billebaut-Faillant (1990) and Terneyre (1990).) On the other hand, it is becoming much more difficult to keep parallel propaganda within the limits demanded by the principle of equality. Candidates often flout the rules of the electoral code: for example, by permitting pamphlets or election newspapers and "rogue" signs in locations not provided for in the regulations.

Advertising purchases, mass mailings and telemarketing can all be used to circumvent the principle of equality. In general, as a specialist in election law observes, "The inappropriateness of the provisions of the electoral code explains both the reluctance of judges to punish violators and the contempt of candidates for the provisions" (Masclet 1989).

Apart from the general regulation of election advertising, one must consider specific regulations developed by the independent administrative authority that regulates the electronic media. The law of 29 July 1982 established the Haute autorité de la communication audiovisuel (HACA). It was subsequently replaced by the Commission nationale de la communication et des libertés (CNCL), created by the law of 30 September 1986; this commission was then replaced by the Conseil supérieur de l'audiovisuel (CSA) on 30 January 1989. The HACA dealt with the 1984 European elections and the legislative elections of 1986. Since 12 November 1987, the CNCL has organized, regulated and supervised campaigns for the presidential election, elections for regional councils and for the congress of the territory of New Caledonia, legislative elections, canton elections and a referendum. In 1988, for the first time in France, an independent administrative communication authority organized and monitored the radio and television campaign for the presidential election and for a referendum.

Problems related to overlapping jurisdictions among existing institutions, as in the case of the Commission nationale de contrôle de la campagne présidentielle (CNCCP), also arose. The mission of the CNCCP was to intervene, "where required, with the competent authorities so that all measures to ensure equality among the candidates are taken" (France, decree of 14 March 1964). Under the decree of 6 January 1988, the CNCL replaced the CNCCP for all functions related to election communication and information on radio and television. The CNCCP, however, retained ultimate responsibility for protecting the principle of equality in the treatment of candidates; it also retained its power to regulate printed propaganda. At the top of the hierarchy of agencies that protect equality is the Conseil constitutionnel, which is empowered by Article 58 of the Constitution to "ensure regularity in the election of the president of the Republic."

Each of these regulatory bodies has been responsible, at one time or another, for establishing the rules concerning official broadcasts (production, programming and broadcasting) on the public-sector networks. In the 1981 presidential election, for example, the CNCCP monitored compliance with the principle of equality during the campaign.

Regulatory responsibility relates first to the organization of the official campaign, particularly the programs aired by national broadcasters. Second, the regulatory body must monitor how information programming is handled by these companies and by authorized or licensed electronic media services.

REGULATION OF THE RADIO AND TELEVISION CAMPAIGN

The presentation of official propaganda in the electronic mass media raises some interesting issues. According to the electoral code, national broadcasters must broadcast official radio and television programs for at least the national elections (i.e., presidential and legislative). Private television services, on the other hand, need not offer air time to candidates. For presidential elections, each candidate is allotted equal time, with the order of programs determined by lot.

The decree of 14 March 1964 gives each candidate two hours of television and two hours of radio time. This allotment may be reduced if there are many candidates, as was the case in 1981, when the CNCCP restricted each of the ten first-round candidates to 70 minutes of air time. In 1988, the nine first-round candidates each had 105 minutes of television time spread over six television broadcasts on the public networks (A2 and FR3) and 70 minutes of radio time on the public stations (Radio-France, RFI and RFO). The schedules for assigning air time had to comply with a number of restrictions. For each phase of the election, candidates had to have identical time allotments. The candidates' order of appearance, drawn by lot, changed each day to reduce the chance that voters would attach any significance to the order of appearance. Programs were broadcast several times throughout the day to ensure a larger potential audience. Program lengths varied from five to 15 minutes.

In the second round, the two remaining candidates had two hours of broadcast time for radio and television. By agreement, they each accepted a total of 40 minutes spread over four programs: five minutes for the first and last, and 15 minutes for the other two. Again, programs were rebroadcast to enlarge the potential audience. In addition, a televised debate was held on 28 April, broadcast live by TF1 (a private network) and A2 (a public network) and on tape by FR3, La Cinq and M6. The debate was scheduled for 110 minutes but lasted 140.

This type of televised communication has become a ritual (Legavre 1991); there was a debate in each of the last three presidential campaigns. Valéry Giscard d'Estaing and François Mitterrand faced each other in 1974 (Cotteret et al. 1976), and then again in 1981 (Gerstlé 1981). Finally, in 1988, Mitterrand, the outgoing president, faced Jacques Chirac, who had been prime minister for two years. Because this debate took place before the start of round two of the official campaign, the CNCL was not required to monitor it. Had the debate been organized after the official start, each candidate would have been allowed only half the time devoted to it. Approximately 30 million viewers watched the debate.

By the decree of 10 March 1988, the CNCL established the rules for the production, programming and broadcast of official programs for the 1988 presidential campaign. Because the shows on the private networks provided competition for the election programs, an attempt was made to modernize the official broadcasts by making the format more flexible. The CNCL allowed more time, for example, for video and audio segments.

By the time of the 1984 European elections and the 1986 legislative elections, the HACA was allowing video clips, paid for by candidates or parties, to make up 30 percent of each official television presentation. While accepting this new flexibility, however, the CNCL also imposed strict controls. The regulations prohibited these segments from being used to ridicule other candidates; to show images of celebrities without their prior written consent or that of their representatives; to show representations of official locations in the backdrop; to play national anthems; or to show the French flag or a combination of its three colours.

Candidates were also allowed to film an official broadcast outdoors. In the interests of equality, production facilities were made available to the candidates, but candidates were responsible for the cost of inserting the video clips in the programs. Candidates had a choice of three kinds of presentations: statements where the candidates appeared alone in front of a camera; interviews or replies to questions, which permitted dialogue with an interviewer; and debates with a maximum of four people in addition to the candidate. (For a more detailed study of the content and form of televised broadcasts of the 1988 presidential election, see Johnston (1991).)

For the legislative elections, the law of 29 December 1966 established the right of political parties to air time during general elections. Three hours of radio and television broadcast time were divided equally between the majority and opposition parties. The leaders of the parties then divided the allotted time by mutual agreement. The law also granted air time (seven minutes before the first round and five minutes before the second) to groups not represented in the outgoing National Assembly but fielding at least 75 candidates. The principle of equality in this case, therefore, was applied relative to the number of candidates nominated.

The legislative elections held on 5 and 12 June 1988 gave rise to radio and television campaigns of national scope. Apart from the possibility of up to 40 percent of each presentation being made up of video clips, the CNCL allowed the political parties to mix formats within a single presentation (statements, interviews). The air time available to the various parties was divided as follows:

- In the series covering the Rassemblement pour la République (RPR) and the Union pour la démocratie française (UDF), each group in the campaign received 45 minutes for the first round and 22.5 minutes for the second round.
- In the series covering the Parti socialiste (PS), the Parti communiste français (PCF) and the Front national (FN), each group received 69 minutes, 11 minutes and 10 minutes in the first round, and 34 minutes, 6 minutes and 5 minutes in the second round, respectively. Under the electoral code, this division was

established by the members of the Office of the National Assembly, taking into account the relative size of each group. It was then up to the CNCL to establish the number, length and order of the presentations. (See the CNCL decision of 20 May 1988.) The Parti Ouvrier Européen, which was not represented in the National Assembly, had 7 minutes allotted before the first round and 5 minutes before the second.

The referendum on the future of New Caledonia was held on 6 November 1988. The criteria determining the allocation of the two hours of free air time were different from those used in the presidential and legislative elections. For this event the amount of speaking time was linked to the number of parliamentary deputies and senators each party had. The PS, with 338 parliamentary representatives, was given 48 minutes and 40 seconds; the RPR, with 213 representatives, was given 29 minutes; the UDF had 20 minutes; the Centre des démocraties sociaux (CDS) was allotted 10 minutes; and with 40 representatives, the PCF received five minutes. The Front national had no parliamentary group, but since it had received 5 percent of the vote in the 1988 legislative election, it was also given five minutes of air time, as were the main political families in New Caledonia.

The opposition used the principle of proportionality in exercising their right to reply to remarks on the referendum made by the prime minister on the public broadcast service. (He had made the remarks in the context of a government announcement.) The RPR and the UDF parties were given the same amount of time as the prime minister: 4.5 minutes.

Since 1977, two hours of radio and television broadcast time have been provided for the European elections. This is divided among the groups represented in the National Assembly and the Senate. Small parties with no parliamentary representation have 30 minutes, to be divided equally among them.

HANDLING INFORMATION IN MEDIA COVERAGE OF THE CAMPAIGN

The profound transformation of the French media landscape, particularly since the emergence of privately owned electronic media, has given television viewers much more choice. In the past, viewers could hardly avoid the rebroadcasts of the election programs on the three public networks, which had a television monopoly. Today, the competing private television stations (which are not required to rebroadcast election programming) have enticed some of the audience away from election programs. This reinforces the impact of information broadcasts, such as television news, which are considered nonpartisan.

The CNCL, established in 1986 and replaced by the Conseil supérieur de l'audiovisuel in 1989, devised a whole set of regulations on election broadcasting. Its mission was to ensure compliance with the principles of pluralism, balance and equality in each phase of the election campaign. The decree of 14 March 1964, dealing with presidential elections, had already restated the principle of equality among the candidates in terms of access to information programming; it dealt particularly with production, commentaries on candidates, and the depiction of candidates. Both public and private networks had to comply with the rule of pluralism.

The last presidential campaign provides an enlightening example of equitable enforcement of the pluralism rule. The law of 30 September 1986 states:

> Through its recommendations, the CNCL shall ensure respect for the pluralistic expression of thought and opinion in programs on the national broadcasting networks and particularly in political information broadcasts.

In its recommendations, the CNCL distinguished two phases of the pre-campaign period and the campaign itself. In the first phase of the pre-campaign period, from 1 January to 22 February 1988, the rule of three-thirds, confirmed by the CNCL, applied. For all the networks, the common rule is that in normal periods, one-third of political messages are allocated to the government, one-third to the parliamentary opposition and one-third to the parliamentary majority. Messages from or about the president of the republic are separate. There are difficulties, however, in applying this rule. For example, there is the sometimes delicate process of identifying the shifting boundaries between the majority and the opposition, and this leads to problems in allocating time within the three categories to each political group.

The second phase of the pre-campaign period, from 22 February to 8 April, saw pluralism and balance reflected in the distinction between news reporting connected to the election campaign (which was governed by fairness among candidates) and news reporting unconnected to the campaign (which continued to be governed by the three-thirds rule). These terms, adopted by the CNCL, are confusing, and raise questions about the value of ambiguous terminology. They assume what is in fact very difficult to discern: how people develop their concepts of political reality and the role of the media in this process. It is doubtful whether citizens actually make this distinction as they acquire information.

The CNCL adopted this terminology in its recommendation of 3 February 1988, but it applied only to the national broadcasters (A2, FR3, Radio-France, RFI, RFO). The CNCL also sent the recommendation to the private-sector television companies (TF1, La Cinq, M6) to avoid discrimination and to ensure equal treatment in both public and private broadcasting. Letters were also sent to the cable networks to advise them of the recommendation and to smaller private radio companies and the television company Canal Plus to "invite" them to comply with it. The recommendation outlined the three-thirds rule, which was to apply "strictly to all presentations in all programming," including news reporting not connected to the campaign. For news connected to the campaign, the CNCL recommended that there be "treatment that is balanced in both tone and time ... among candidates, whether declared or presumed, and all those supporting such candidates." It used the following expressions to describe this requirement: "equitable access to air time," "presentation that does not favour any candidate," and "concern for objectivity, impartiality and balance." The principle, therefore, is not strict equality but rather equitable treatment of candidates.

Finally, the election campaign proper, from 8 April to 6 May, was governed by the theoretical objectives of equality and the practical concern for objectivity, impartiality and balance. The CNCL's second recommendation was directed to all electronic broadcasting services: national broadcasters and private organizations. In television, this meant the public networks (A2 and FR3); the private networks (TF1, La Cinq and M6); and the local television stations, cable networks and Canal Plus (a licensee of the public broadcasting service). For radio, it meant the public stations (Radio-France, RFI and RFO) and the smaller or other private radio stations. This second recommendation concerned all information programs, excluding official campaign programs broadcast solely by the national programming companies. But what is the scope of this recommendation? What is meant by "the principle of equality among candidates must be observed"?

The word "equality" was not used alone; rather, it was the "principle of equality." This phrase refers to decisions of the Conseil constitutionnel and the Conseil d'état stating that "the principle of equality before the law" permits "different solutions to be applied to different situations." This in turn suggests there are categories of candidates.

The principle of equality would thus permit candidates with comparable influence to be treated comparably. The CNCL, therefore, did not require strict equality in the treatment of candidates. For news reporting not connected to the election campaign, the three-thirds rule still applied, with its distinction between official functions and campaign activities.

For news reporting connected to the presidential election, the campaign and position statements had to be "presented with constant concern for objectivity, impartiality and balance."

Strict equality in the treatment of the campaign, however, was not required. An assessment of the varying significance of the candidates' presentations was introduced:

> Candidates' public activities must be followed in accordance with the standards for information ethics, taking into account the number and significance of such candidates' presentations, with the same attention to all, whether or not they received the support of one of the political families represented by a group in the National Assembly.

On the other hand, strict equality is required in cases where information services prepare profiles of the various candidates. In France there is no professional group with the authority to regulate journalists, and the body regulating electronic broadcasting has no direct power over journalists. It does, however, ensure that certain obligations, including responsible reporting, are fulfilled by the various programming bodies.

The same principle of equality was applied in subsequent elections. During the Senate elections of 24 September 1989, the Conseil supérieur de l'audiovisuel wrote to all national broadcasters asking them to ensure "balanced treatment in both tone and time among the various candidates and lists" in their information programs (*La Lettre du CSA* 1989).

PROHIBITION ON ELECTION ADVERTISING

Particular attention must be given to advertising, which is treated in a special way in France. On the one hand, political professionals are using advertising more and more as a means of communication; on the other hand, legislators are trying assiduously to stem this tide in an effort to limit election expenses.

The law of 30 September 1986 on freedom of communication provided that advertising programs of a political nature could be broadcast only outside election campaigns. Since 1988, and particularly since the political-financial scandals leading up to the presidential election, the need for greater disclosure in French politics became evident. Behind this move were sometimes ulterior motives on the part of the participants involved in the "cohabitation" period (1986–88). (This era was exceptional in French politics because of the institutional "cohabitation" of a president and a prime minister from opposing political majorities.)

On 11 March 1988, in the middle of the presidential election campaign, new legislation on political financial disclosure was adopted. This law extended the prohibition on political advertising for four more years, in anticipation of a law on party financing. Eventually the law of 15 January 1990 was passed, permanently prohibiting political advertising programs on radio and television. The law also prohibited all election signs other than those permitted in the official campaign. All election signs were banned during the three months preceding the first day of the month of an election, up to election day.

After this law was enacted, the ban was extended to all commercial advertising in the press or any electronic medium. During those three months, telemarketing or telephone advertising that makes a toll-free number available to the public is also prohibited. Finally, during the six months preceding an election, public institutions associated with one candidate or another cannot publicize their accomplishments or management of a community in the area of that community. This means, for example, that public resources such as city facilities may not be used for electioneering by an outgoing municipal team. On the whole, these restrictions on any immediate opportunity for political advertising in France show that legislators are trying to ensure morality in political activities.

As seen in 1986, opening up political communication to advertising was followed by a more rigid attitude and a return to the restrictive approach demonstrated earlier by the Commission nationale de contrôle de la campagne présidentielle (Racine 1989). Moreover, the public was not in favour of political advertising on television (Gerstlé 1992).

PUBLICATION OF POLLS

The extraordinary development of political polling in France has prompted legislators to regulate its use during election periods. The law of 19 July 1977 dealt with "any opinion poll relating directly or indirectly to a referendum, a presidential election or one of the elections regulated by the electoral code, as well as the election of representatives to the Assembly of the European Communities." The law required that polls guarantee technical reliability and disclosure. The Commission des sondages (commission on polling) was established to ensure compliance with ethical standards and was given powers to investigate and require corrective action. Most important, however, the law provided that "during the week preceding each vote, and during the vote, publishing, broadcasting or commenting on any poll, by any means whatsoever, is prohibited." This prohibition applies to all media during presidential and European elections, as well as referendums and elections governed by the electoral code.

Polls could still be conducted if the results were not made public. However, the prohibition did not extend to election "estimations" organized by polling institutes and the media, the results of which may be broadcast after the close of polling stations and before the official announcement of the results of the election.

During the 1988 presidential election campaign, there were many polls – 40 percent more than in the previous presidential election in 1981. According to Gazier and de Leusse (1989), between January and May 1988 the Commission registered and monitored 153 polls. In 1981, 111 were monitored, and of these only 17 were registered. According to Duhamel (1988), in February 1988 alone, 77 political surveys were conducted. In March there were 94, averaging three per day, twice as many as normally observed. These figures represent the polls conducted, not just those published.

In comparison, there were 112 polls during the 1989 municipal elections. As Gazier and Abraham (1989) noted, this figure is below the true figure, because a lot of surveys were unknown to the Commission. Some were not published because they were intended solely for the information of candidates, parties or public authorities. The Commission was unaware of others that were carried out by inexperienced institutes or were published by local media serving a small area. In the 1988 presidential election, most of the polls dealt with the voters' intentions, not with issues that had a high priority with the candidates or the public. We may be able to determine how the polls influenced voters by examining how they were published.

As an illustration, let us consider the attention given by television news programs to polls during the 1988 presidential election (Gerstlé et al. 1991). In 106 days, the news program aired at 8:00 PM on TF1 alone quoted 70 polls: in January, it quoted 10 polls; in February, 18; in March, 23. The 19 quoted during April were restricted to the first 17 days, since publishing results was prohibited during the week preceding a round of voting. These figures show the steady increase in the use of polls to supplement television news. It is also interesting to compare them with the polls taken by the three American networks during the last two months of the 1988 campaign. The prime-time news programs on CBS, NBC and ABC referred to only 25 polls, whereas TF1 alone mentioned 42 in March and April. If we were to add to these the references made on television news programs on the other networks (A2, FR3, La Cinq, M6 and Canal Plus), we would find an even wider gap between the American and French news coverage of polls. This confirms the popularity of political polling in France and also demonstrates its ability to transform the public arena through the weight of its media visibility.

CREDIBILITY OF THE MEDIA AND AUDIENCE BEHAVIOUR

To complete the profile of election communication, we present a brief summary of the characteristic behaviour of the French people regarding the media.

The first parameter to consider is credibility. Television is the dominant medium of information. This was apparent when we asked the following question: "In terms of political information, which of the following sources of information do you trust the most?" (Missika 1989). In October 1988 the results in descending order were television (46 percent), radio (18 percent), daily newspapers (16 percent), and weekly newspapers and magazines (10 percent). A comparison with the results of 12 years earlier shows that television's gain in credibility (+7 percent) was accompanied by a loss in credibility for radio (-5 percent) and daily newspapers (-2 percent) and a gain for weekly newspapers and magazines (+3 percent).

In October 1990, there was a widespread drop in media credibility, perhaps owing to the manner in which international events had been covered that year. Despite this drop, television retained its supremacy over the other media in the area of political information (Missika 1991).

Similarly pre-election polls do not currently have a good image: as of September 1989, 57 percent of the French people considered them as having a negative influence on politicians and the public (*Le journal des élections* 1989).

In 1988, A2 had a larger audience for its broadcasts about the presidential campaign than FR3 did. The A2 audience was larger at 1:30 PM (6–10 audience points) than at either 7:00 PM (3.5–7 points) or 9:00 AM (1–2 points). The same phenomenon appeared in the legislative elections one month later.

If we look at the audience ratings 10 years earlier, we note a downward trend in viewing televised election coverage. The audience total (TF1, A2, FR3) amounted to an average of 38.8 percent at 8:35 PM. The figure was already slipping in 1978, compared with earlier campaign audiences. The 1973 legislative elections, for example, had an average of 51 percent. The 1974 presidential election had 46 percent on the first round and 55 percent on the second (Casile 1978).

Political broadcasts that traditionally found favour with French television viewers no longer have major audience scores during election periods. Appearances by Raymond Barre and Jacques Chirac on "L'Heure de Vérité" (the most watched political television program) on 5 and 7 April 1988 were watched in only 14 percent and 16 percent, respectively, of "total homes." The figures for first-rank leaders were on average more than 20 percent.

We should not be surprised, therefore, that the survey organized by *Le journal des élections* in September 1989 revealed the pessimistic and even critical feeling of the French public toward the "mediafication" of politics. Just over half, or 54 percent, believed this trend was a sign of the impoverishment of political debate, and 43 percent saw it as a sign of modernization. Certainly the media invasion of politics in France today is most intense during presidential campaigns.

The survey by Société française d'enquêtes par sondages (SOFRES) from 15 to 17 March 1988 is very revealing in terms of audience behaviour (*Télérama* 1988). According to 62 percent of the people questioned, television is the most useful medium for determining how to vote, far ahead of newspapers (37 percent), radio (30 percent), conversations (20 percent), polls (12 percent), political meetings (6 percent), signs (4 percent) and pamphlets (4 percent). (Multiple responses were accepted.) However, the motive mentioned most often for paying attention to election coverage was to get information (83 percent) and not to decide how to vote (3 percent).

Viewers answered the survey questions about their reasons for watching political broadcasts on television in the following ways:

- To get information on politicians' platforms (40 percent).
- To learn the arguments of the lesser known politicians (25 percent).
- The ideas of the invited politician reflect the respondent's own (22 percent).
- The respondent is interested in politics and follows political broadcasts on television regularly (21 percent).
- The respondent finds political broadcasts genuinely entertaining (16 percent).
- The respondent never watches political broadcasts on television (14 percent).

When choosing from among the competing programs, only 36 percent watch the official broadcasts, based on self-reporting by the respondents. The majority, 55 percent, however, stated that they would watch other programs instead of the official campaign.

When asked what political broadcasts they preferred, the respondents gave the following replies:

- interviews with politicians by several journalists (42 percent);
- debates between two politicians (40 percent);
- interviews with politicians with questions posed directly by a sample of the television audience (26 percent);

- interviews with politicians interspersed with news reporting (16 percent);
- interviews with politicians by one journalist (11 percent); and
- debates involving journalists and political scientists without politicians present (10 percent).

This hierarchy of preferences was confirmed by a Louis Harris survey taken from 10 to 12 March 1988. Here the question was, "In your view, which type of television broadcast provides you with the best information on the election campaign?" The following responses were given:

- programs that bring together one or more journalists with a politician (50 percent);
- face-to-face encounters between politicians (38 percent);
- political broadcasts with the public present (23 percent); and
- official campaign broadcasts (5 percent).

Semetko and Borquez (1991) analysed the actual behaviour of the French public during the 1988 campaign and compared it with that of the American public. Although the Americans had a higher rate of exposure to information, the French demonstrated more sustained attention to the news:

- 69.5 percent had seen the televised debate between François Mitterrand and Jacques Chirac (the two candidates);
- 53 percent had not seen any official television broadcasts by Chirac;
- 50 percent had not seen any official television broadcasts by Mitterrand;
- 23 percent expressed a very strong interest in the campaign;
- 5.5 percent had watched many Mitterrand broadcasts; and
- 5.3 percent had watched many Chirac broadcasts.

Do these data confirm what was found in earlier studies (Cayrol 1985)? The 1974 and 1981 presidential campaigns had generated greater interest, with only 9 percent of voters stating that they did not follow the campaign every day or almost every day. There had also been a decrease in those who used the media to help them decide how to vote. The proportions who found the media useful in this respect were as follows:

- for television – 63 percent in 1974, 68 percent in 1981, and 62 percent in 1988;
- for radio – 10 percent in 1974, 33 percent in 1981 and 30 percent in 1988; and
- for the press – 13 percent in 1974, 45 percent in 1981 and 37 percent in 1988.

The hierarchy of preferences has therefore remained stable and shows that people favour television. Overall, the drop in interest in the campaign could be explained by political factors and communication variables. The 1988 campaign involved much less conflict in ideological terms than those of 1974 and 1981. On the other hand, the appearance of the private networks allowed voters to avoid official election communication if they wished.

EVALUATION AND OUTLOOK

The change in the French media landscape has been accompanied by a loss of interest in the election programming of the official campaign. Various solutions may be considered to increase the audience, e.g., repeat broadcasts at various points in the program schedule. The experience of the presidential campaign showed that broadcasting at different times (9 AM, 1 PM, 5 PM, 7 PM, 10 PM) and varying the combinations on the different networks would increase one's opportunities to tune in. As well, as in 1986, making the format more flexible (mixing types, inserting video clips, filming outside, and so on) could help to generate audience interest.

In its 1989 annual report (1990), the Conseil supérieur de l'audiovisuel (CSA) looked at the four elections that had taken place since the council was established: municipal, territorial, European and senatorial. The experience of the European elections (June 1989) prompted the CSA to recommend "radical reform of the official radio and television campaign, which has been met with massive disaffection" (*La Lettre du CSA* 1990).

New legislative provisions on political-activity financing, which limit election expenses, might prompt candidates to make better use of the free air time offered under the electoral code. They will also probably put some effort into modernizing the campaign broadcasts to make them more attractive, perhaps by using outside filming and video clips like those that attracted such attention during the 1988 campaign.

The use of program formats like those discussed in the SOFRES survey (discussed earlier in this study) could alternate with the traditional formats of electoral discourse, such as the televised monologue. Will this be enough to bring the number of viewers of election communication back to the levels seen when only the three public networks were available? This is unlikely. At the very most, there will be some positive audience shift if, all political circumstances being equal, there is some flexibility incorporated into the regulations to facilitate the transmission of messages to an audience that is already drowning in information or is apathetic.

It is definitely premature to assess the impact of the new legislative framework on election campaigns, since it has not yet been tested in practice. Candidates will probably try to adopt new practices to get around these legal limits and prohibitions, which have become rigid, for example, in the fields of electronic advertising.

Given the diversity of sources of information, the way in which information is handled during election periods is still problematic. As early as 1981, the Commission nationale de contrôle de la campagne présidentielle, which was then in charge of electronic election communication, stated in its report on the presidential campaign "that it was largely illusory to hope to ensure the equality intended by the legislator in 1962." However, it also noted there was "inequality in air time among the candidates in the first round."

The system for monitoring information during the presidential campaign, updated in 1988, is unsatisfactory on a number of grounds. Distinguishing between news reporting connected to the campaign and news reporting not connected to the campaign was particularly difficult, given the political situation and the candidacies of the incumbent president and prime minister. The outgoing president, a presumed candidate, officially declared his candidacy only one month before the first round of voting. The prime minister, a very early presumed candidate, declared officially on 15 January 1988, more than three months before the first vote. How then was information relating to these two participants to be covered?

Were they candidates, or were they performing their institutional duties at that time? It is clear that the ambiguity of such a situation can be used by the participants to influence the media. It seems impossible to ascertain whether the television viewer puts an item on François Mitterrand in the context of the election or in the context of the exercise of power. It is also doubtful that we can find out if the viewer makes this distinction during a campaign, when any government action is seen by the public in terms of the election. The Commission nationale de la communication et des libertés (CNCL) presented television networks and radio stations with an impossible problem when it made this recommendation:

> National programming companies shall distinguish between comments
> by the individuals, depending on whether they are acting as candidates
> or as supporters of a candidate on the one hand, or speaking in the
> course of their official functions on the other hand.

Another reason for dissatisfaction relates to compliance with and
monitoring of the principle of equality in the allotment of broadcast
time. In its report on the 1988 legislative election campaign, the
Commission nationale de la communication et des libertés (1988b)
noted the need to ensure balance between the candidates in terms not
only of time but also of tone. It added:

> This last requirement dealing with the presentation of candidates and
> comments on their actions is by far the most complex and the most
> difficult to assess. While a degree of diversity among journalists may
> contribute to greater balance, nonetheless this requirement will best
> be met as a result of the ethical rigour brought to bear by each jour-
> nalist and writer.

In fact, the only systematic monitoring done is of the balanced-time rule.

The second recommendation described how the CNCL proceeded
in monitoring this balance. It systematically observed programs,
preparing lists of each type of program, showing the air time given to
a candidate and the candidate's supporters. Each week these lists were
made public. Another document tabulated the activities of others in
the political arena who are subject to the three-thirds rule, as well as
the president of the Republic. The time criterion is quite inconsequen-
tial: it is inadequate for assessing compliance with the equality principle, although it does highlight extreme disparities in the equitable
treatment of candidates. For example, analysis of the content of the
8:00 PM television news broadcast by TF1 between January and April 1988
showed the extent to which journalists ranked candidates according
to their institutional positions and their chances of winning. They
presented some presidential candidates as having more credibility than
others, thereby establishing an ongoing process of building and maintaining legitimacy. The distinction between "minor candidates" and
"genuine candidates" was clear. Similarly, within these categories, there
were symbolic mechanisms by which the candidates and their
supporters differentiated, qualified and disqualified themselves. The
media construction of political and electoral reality proceeds from
symbolic meanings and operations far more complex and sophisticated
than the purely quantitative principle of equality assumes (Gerstlé et

al. 1991). Moreover, it seems that the inadequacy of past approaches is easily established in theory but less so in practice. Thus the Conseil supérieur de l'audiovisuel recommended in its 1989 annual report that a new indicator for monitoring pluralism be found as a substitute for the three-thirds rule, albeit without specifying the form it should take.

ABBREVIATIONS

J.O. Journal officiel (France)

REFERENCES

In this study, quoted material that originated in French has been translated into English.

Aïdan, Gilles, and Frédérique Billebaut-Faillant. 1990. "Le Financement de la vie politique: commentaire des lois de 1990." *Revue française de droit constitutionnel* 3:501–16.

Casile, Nicole. 1978. "Les téléspectateurs et les éléctions de mars 1978." *Les cahiers de la communication* 1:18–29.

Cayrol, Roland. 1985. "Le rôle des campagnes électorales." In *L'Éxplication du vote*, ed. D. Gaxie. Paris: Presses de la Fondation nationale des sciences politiques.

Commission nationale de contrôle de la campagne présidentielle. 1981. "Rapport au Président de la République." In *Textes et Documents relatifs à l'élection présidentielle des 26 avril et 10 mai 1981*. Paris: La documentation française.

Commission nationale de la communication et des libertés. 1988a. *Élection du Président de la République: Rapport sur la campagne à la radio et à la télévision (22 février–8 mai 1988)*. Paris: CNCL.

———. 1988b. *Élections législatives (5 et 12 juin 1988): Rapport sur la campagne à la radio et à la télévision*. Paris: CNCL.

Conseil supérieur de l'audiovisuel. 1990. *Rapport annuel 1989*. Paris: La documentation française.

Cotteret, J-M., C. Emeri, J. Gerstlé and R. Moreau. 1976. *Giscard d'Estaing – Mitterrand: 54774 mots pour convaincre*. Paris: PUF.

Debbasch, Charles. 1989. "Le principe d'égalité dans les médias audiovisuels et la campagne présidentielle." In *Campagnes électorales: Principe d'égalité et transparence financière*, ed. Association française des constitutionnalistes, 73–82. Paris: Économica.

Derieux, Emmanuel. 1991. *Le droit de la communication*. Paris: LGDJ.

Duhamel, Olivier. 1988. "Sondages et médias dans la campagne présidentielle de 1988." Report to the Conseil national de la recherche scientifique for *Sondages et opinion publique* (17 May).

France. *Constitution (Loi du 4 octobre 1958)*, J.O., 5 octobre 1958, p. 9151, article 58.

————. *Décret du 14 mars 1964*, J.O., 17 mars 1964, p. 2491.

————. *Décret du 6 janvier 1988*, J.O., 7 janvier 1988, p. 274.

————. *Loi du 6 novembre 1962*, J.O., 7 novembre 1962, p. 10762.

————. *Loi du 29 décembre 1966*, J.O., 30 décembre 1966, p. 11684.

————. *Loi du 19 juillet 1977*, J.O., 20 juillet 1977, p. 3837.

————. *Loi du 29 juillet 1982*, J.O., 30 juillet 1982, p. 2431.

————. *Loi du 30 septembre 1986*, J.O., 1 octobre 1986, p. 11755.

————. *Loi du 11 mars 1988*, J.O., 12 mars 1988, p. 3290.

————. *Loi du 15 janvier 1990*, J.O., 16 janvier 1990, p. 639.

————. *Loi du 10 mai 1990*, J.O., 11 mai 1990, p. 5615.

Gazier, François, and Ronny Abraham. 1989. *La Commission des sondages face aux élections municipales*, ed. Commission des sondages. Paris: Conseil d'état.

Gazier, François, and Jean-Frédéric de Leusse. 1989. "La Commission des sondages face à l'élection présidentielle de 1988." *Pouvoirs* 48:145–57.

Gerstlé, Jacques. 1981. "Éristique électorale: le débat télévisé de mai 1981." In *Démocratie cathodique: la télévision et l'élection présidentielle de 1981*, ed. J-M. Cotteret et al. Paris: Les cahiers de la communication, Dunod.

————. 1992. *La communication politique*. Que Sais-Je? No. 2652. Paris: PUF.

Gerstlé, Jacques, Dennis K. Davis and Olivier Duhamel. 1991. "Television News and the Construction of Political Reality in France and the United States." In *Mediated Politics in Two Cultures: Presidential Campaigning in the United States and France*, ed. L.L. Kaid, J. Gerstlé and R.K. Sanders. New York: Praeger.

Johnston, Anne. 1991. "Political Broadcasts: An Analysis of Form, Content and Style in Presidential Communication." In *Mediated Politics in Two Cultures: Presidential Campaigning in the United States and France*, ed. L.L. Kaid, J. Gerstlé and R.K. Sanders. New York: Praeger.

Le journal des élections. 1989. "La démocratie consumériste." No. 19.

Legavre, Jean-Baptiste. 1991. "Face to Face: The 1988 French Debate."
In *Mediated Politics in Two Cultures: Presidential Campaigning in the
United States and France*, ed. L.L. Kaid, J. Gerstlé and R.K. Sanders.
New York: Praeger.

La Lettre du CSA. 1989. 1 October. Paris.

———. 1990. 7 April. Paris.

Masclet, Jean-Claude. 1989. *Droit électoral*. Paris: PUF.

Maus, Didier. 1988. *Textes et documents relatifs à l'élection présidentielle des
24 avril et 8 mai 1988*, notes et études documentaires. Paris:
La documentation française.

Missika, Jean-Louis. 1989. "Les Français et leurs médias: la confiance
limitée." *Médiapouvoirs* 113:39–50.

———. 1991. "Les Français et leurs médias: le désenchantement."
Médiapouvoirs 121:97–114.

Racine, Pierre-François. 1989. "Les aspects juridiques des deux
recommandations de la CNCL aux chaînes de télévision sur la campagne
présidentielle et de la décision sur la campagne présidentielle."
In *Campagnes électorales: principe d'égalité et transparence financière*,
ed. Association française des constitutionnalistes, 83–95.
Paris: Économica.

Semetko, Holli, and Julio Borquez. 1991. "Audiences for Election
Communication: Media Use and Campaign Evaluations." In *Mediated
Politics in Two Cultures: Presidential Campaigning in the United States and
France*, ed. L.L. Kaid, J. Gerstlé and R.K. Sanders. New York: Praeger.

Télérama. 1988. 6 April, No. 1995.

Terneyre, Philippe. 1990. "Le financement des élections et des partis:
la loi du 15 janvier 1990." *Regards sur l'actualité* 159 (March): 27–41.

2

Broadcasting and Election Communication in Britain

Holli A. Semetko

O<small>BSERVERS OF GENERAL</small> election campaigns in Britain generally agree that television has played an increasing role in the electoral process over the past two decades, both as a primary battleground for politicians and as a primary source of information for voters.[1] As a source of campaign information, mass media have long been more important to Britons than direct contact via canvassing or attendance at political rallies (Blumler and McQuail 1968). Today, there is more election coverage on British television than in earlier times. Moreover, broadcast and print media are nowadays the predominant sources of election campaign information for citizens in virtually all Western democracies, and Britain is no exception (Miller et al. 1990).

In terms of the sheer amount of coverage given to the campaign in television news and the press, however, Britain is unique among Western democracies. A comparative study of the role of the media in recent British and American general election campaigns, based on content analysis of television and press coverage in both Britain and the U.S., suggests that legal and institutional rules guiding election broadcasting are one important reason for the cross-national differences (Semetko et al. 1991). Current research on the German 1990 national election campaign confirms the uniqueness of Britain's campaign-information environment.[2]

This study outlines the key characteristics of the British system, the traditions and regulations surrounding the role of broadcasting in British general election campaigns, and research findings about the content and potential influence of election campaign broadcasting. The study addresses the question of fairness in terms of equitable treatment of the parties, and in conclusion discusses the effectiveness with which the broadcasting system meets voters' needs. A postscript discusses the potential implications of current changes in Britain's broadcasting system in response to new legislation passed at the end of 1990.

KEY CHARACTERISTICS OF BRITISH GENERAL ELECTION CAMPAIGNS

While certain features of British general elections have been standard for many years, the party system underwent changes during the 1970s and 1980s, and voter identification with the two main parties weakened. Unlike the press, British broadcasting has traditionally been obliged to provide impartial coverage of campaigns.

Standard Features of Campaigns

Although there is no fixed date for general elections in Britain, a general election must be held within the five-year life of the current Parliament. The party in power has the authority to call an election and may therefore choose an opportune moment. Margaret Thatcher, for example, held a general election in June 1983 and capitalized on the positive sentiment caused by Britain's victory in the Falklands war (Rasmussen 1983; Norpoth 1987). The announcement of a general election is rarely a complete surprise. There are a number of clues to help opposition parties' campaign managers predict the date of the election and begin to plan their activities in advance. General elections are traditionally held in spring or fall – the months of May, June, September or October. Moreover, since elections always take place on Thursdays, and the prime minister's international summit schedule is usually known months in advance, political journalists can and do speculate about possible dates. A number of factors influence the prime minister's decision to call an election, particularly economic performance and support for the government in published opinion polls, local elections and parliamentary by-elections (Kavanagh 1989). The loss of a vote of confidence in Parliament may also cause a general election.

Campaign expenditure in Britain at the constituency level is very low in comparison with that in the U.S. The statutory limit in 1987 was £3 370 plus 3.8 pence per elector for candidates in county constituencies and 2.9 pence per elector for candidates in borough seats. In most constituencies, this meant that campaign spending ranged between £5 000 and £6 000 (Pinto-Duschinsky 1989, 26). Conservative candidates spend on average somewhat more than their Labour and Liberal–Social Democratic Party Alliance counterparts. According to

Butler and Kavanagh (1988, 201), in the 1987 general election campaign Conservative candidates spent on average £4 400 (a total of £2.8 million), compared with £3 900 (a total of £2.5 million) spent by Labour candidates and £3 400 (a total of £2.15 million) spent by Alliance candidates.

At the national level, however, the amounts spent by the central campaign organizations are far from equal. The ratio of Conservative : Labour : Alliance central campaign expenditure in 1987 was approximately 12:6:3, compared with 12:7:6 in 1983 and 12:7:1 in 1979 (Pinto-Duschinsky 1989, 25). In 1987, Conservative Party central campaign expenditure was estimated at £9 028 000 compared with Labour's £4 194 000 (ibid., 19–20).

Central campaign expenditure includes grants to constituencies, press and poster advertising, production costs of television and radio political broadcasts, internal opinion polling, publications, leaders' tours and meetings, and general staff and administration. Constituency campaign expenditure includes local leaflets and posters, local agents, travel for the candidate and local press advertising. However, three subsidies in kind mean considerable savings for candidates and parties. Candidates do not have to pay for postage, nor do they have to pay for the cost of hiring a hall for an election rally. Moreover, free broadcast time is made available to the political parties to air their platforms and promote candidates. (The allocation of party broadcast time is discussed in detail in a later section of this study.)

General election campaigns are short (three and one-half to four weeks) and intense, with a number of predictable events. Once an election is called, the parties rush to publish their manifestos or platforms, launching their campaigns. A routine campaign day in Britain has three standard features: morning press conferences, afternoon "walkabouts" and evening speeches. Three weeks before polling day, all the parties traditionally begin holding press conferences each morning at party headquarters in London. Journalists travel by special bus from one party press conference to the next. By 10:30 AM, the press conferences have ended, and the politicians begin campaigning in the constituencies. During afternoon "walkabouts" leading politicians meet voters in constituencies, on the street or on visits to shops, hospitals, schools and factories, and sometimes give impromptu speeches. Finally, on most evenings of the campaign, the parties hold rallies where the travelling party leaders and other key party spokespersons make speeches.

While there are no televised debates among the party leaders during a general election campaign in Britain as there are in Canada and the United States, there are forums in which party leaders traditionally appear. Both BBC and ITV main evening news programs, for example, conduct extended interviews with each of the party leaders, and broadcast these in the news programs during the latter part of the campaign. Moreover, in 1987 as in previous campaigns, Sir Robin Day interviewed each of the party leaders for one hour on the BBC's flag-ship current affairs program "Panorama." Party leaders also appear as guests on other current affairs programs, where electors (via call-in, or in the studio) have an opportunity to put their questions directly.

The institutional features and traditional practices of British campaigns – relatively low campaign expenditure, important subsidies in kind, daily morning press conferences, afternoon walkabouts and evening speeches – have remained intact for the past two decades. Meanwhile, however, a number of significant developments in political party campaigning have taken place. Sophisticated campaigning techniques have become an important component of British election-eering over the past decade. Professional publicity managers or image consultants – particularly advertising agencies and opinion pollsters – are now an important feature of British campaign management. The parties are learning how to use the news media to relay positive images in election campaigns. The effects of these developments are many, ranging from Mrs. Thatcher's use of the teleprompter for speeches at Conservative party rallies to the parties' introduction of computerized canvassing at the constituency level. More politicians from all parties use "photo-opportunities" today than ever before. Mrs.Thatcher stand-ing before an enormous replica of the Union Jack was one of the mem-orable "photo-ops" of 1987. Occasionally, "photo-ops" are used to make a point about party policy, as in 1987 when Labour leader Neil Kinnock spoke about the environment while standing amid the green, rolling Welsh hills. While the parties have been developing increasingly sophis-ticated approaches to campaigning, the British party system and broad-casting system have also been undergoing change.

The Changing Party Landscape and Voter "Dealignment"

For much of the post-war era, Britain has been described as having in effect a two-party system. The Conservative and Labour parties com-peted against one another for the absolute majority of seats in Parliament; one party would almost always succeed in winning a majority of seats and govern alone, and voters and party leaders could reasonably expect that power would continue to alternate between the two parties. At election time, voter turnout was high, and voters' party loyalties were strong, with most of the vote divided evenly between the Labour and Conservative parties. In the 1966 general election, for example, the Conservative and Labour parties captured over 90 percent of the vote.

In this era, votes were cast primarily along class lines, the left-right division between the two main parties was reflected in a similar division between their supporters on most matters of policy, differences in party support in the regions were limited, and movements of the vote were nationally uniform.

By the 1970s, however, this situation had begun to change. The increased support for nationalist parties led some to argue that Britain had at least a "two and a half" if not a multi-party system (Drucker 1979). The strong relationship between class and voting was called into question (Miller 1978; Franklin 1985; Crewe 1983; Sarlvik and Crewe 1983; Heath et al. 1985; Himmelweit et al. 1981; Rose and McAllister 1986). Sarlvik and Crewe (1983) describe the period since the early 1970s as a "decade of dealignment." This period has been characterized by: decreasing voter support for the Conservative and Labour parties; an increase in support for the Liberals at certain general elections and for the nationalist parties in their regions; a lesser association between social class and voting preferences; increasing electoral volatility; a greater tendency toward abstention; more pronounced regional differences in party support; and, geographically diverse movements of the vote.

Over the course of the 1980s, Britain's party system expanded and then contracted. In 1981, after a period of intense internal conflict in the Labour Party, the Social Democratic Party (SDP) was established with the aim of "breaking the mould" of the party system, and within three months entered into an electoral alliance with the Liberal Party. At one time in its first year, the SDP alone captured more than 35 percent in public opinion polls, and in late 1981, the Alliance parties together captured an unprecedented level of about 50 percent in the polls. At this time, political observers spoke of a "three-party system" (Denver 1983). In the 1983 general election, the Liberal–SDP Alliance came close to taking second place from Labour, but by the 1987 general election, Labour had regained support at the expense of the Alliance.

Britain's single-member, simple-plurality electoral system, however, remains a formidable obstacle to the development of minor parties and particularly to parties like the Liberals and the SDP, whose popular support is not concentrated geographically but rather distributed fairly evenly across the country. The effect of the system is a disproportionate relation between the number of votes won by a party and the number of seats the party captures in Parliament. The importance of the electoral system in hindering the SDP's prospect of "breaking the mould" of British politics cannot be minimized.

The SDP and the Liberals, whose support was and is spread fairly evenly across the country and among classes, were persistently penalized in recent elections by the "first-past-the-post" system. In the February 1974 general election, for example, the Liberals captured 19.3 percent of the vote but won only 14 seats, or 2.2 percent of the seats. In October 1974, the vote was 18.3 percent for the Liberals, which translated into 13 seats. The general election of 1979 saw a smaller share of the vote for the Liberals – 13.8 percent – but a similar effect: the Liberals won 11 seats. In 1983, the Liberal–SDP Alliance won 25.4 percent of the vote and Labour won 27.6 percent; this translated into 23 seats for the Alliance and 209 for Labour, far from enough to present a challenge to the Conservatives, who won 397 seats with only 42.4 percent of the vote. In 1987, with 22.6 percent of the vote compared with Labour's 30.8 percent, the Alliance held only 22 seats while Labour held 229. The Conservatives held 376 seats with 42.3 percent of the vote.

Since the 1987 general election, there have been a number of changes at the centre of British politics. In 1988, the majority of the SDP voted to merge with the Liberal party and formed the Social and Liberal Democratic Party (SLD). The SLD was sometimes dubbed the "SaLaD" party by journalists who joked that "green, leafy and wet" aptly described its centre-left politics. At the same time, a minority of the SDP also decided to continue as a centre-right party, under the leadership of Dr. David Owen. Support for the centre parties dropped to single digits as the two fought one another in by-elections. By 1990, the SLD had changed its name to the Liberal Democrats, and in that year, Dr. David Owen, leader of the SDP, reluctantly announced that the SDP would no longer exist as a national political party. In early 1991, support for the Liberal Democrats began to increase, and the party captured a parliamentary seat from the Conservatives in a by-election in Lancashire. Britain now appears to be the two and one-half party system it was in the 1970s with two major parties, a Liberal centrist half and support for nationalist parties in the Celtic regions.

Although the party system appears to have returned to its previous state, voters have not returned to the old parties. The weakening of party identification with the two main parties in the post-war era corresponded with an increase in vote switching between one general election and the next, and in by-elections. Fluctuations in opinion polls have also become greater. The entrance of the SDP into the political arena in 1981 fuelled this further. Between the May 1979 and June 1983 general elections, for example, each of the main parties – the Conservatives, Labour and the Liberal–SDP Alliance – was ahead by 20 percent in the opinion polls.

In the more fluid electoral circumstances outlined above, communication factors in the period leading up to and during a general election campaign may have a potentially greater influence on voter preferences than credited in the past (cf. Blumler and Gurevitch 1982; Dunleavy and Husbands 1985; Whiteley 1986; Norpoth forthcoming). To put it simply: "One possibility is that the emergence of television as the main mass medium of politics has made the short campaign period – and the issues, people and events it brings into prominence – a more powerful determinant of the vote" (Crewe 1983, 190).

Britain's Broadcasting System

The most significant division within Britain's political communication system is between the partisan press and impartial broadcasting. The British press is strongly partisan, although this is more evident in tabloids – such as the *Sun* and the *Daily Mirror* – than in the broadsheets or "quality" newspapers – such as the *Independent*, the *Times*, the *Financial Times*, the *Daily Telegraph* and the *Guardian* (cf. Seymour-Ure 1974). In the 1983 general election, of Britain's 17 national newspapers, only two (the *Daily Mirror* and its Sunday equivalent the *Sunday Mirror*) firmly endorsed Labour, and even the *Daily Mirror* expressed concern about some aspects of Labour's manifesto; no national newspaper endorsed the Alliance as its first preference (Harrop 1984, 175). The Conservatives continued to hold the majority of editorial endorsements in the national press in the 1987 general election, despite the launch of the *Independent* and *Today* in 1986 (Harrop 1988, 163).

British broadcasting, however, is obliged to remain impartial in its coverage of politics. The broadcasting authorities also make free time available to political parties to air their advertisements. The Committee on Party Political Broadcasting (CPPB), which determines the allocation of party broadcast time, is another important feature of the system. (The workings of this Committee are described in a subsequent section.)

British broadcasting is based on a public service model, with a duty to "inform, educate and entertain." Two committees of inquiry into the role of broadcasting – Sykes (United Kingdom, Parliament 1923) and Crawford (United Kingdom, Parliament 1926) – laid the foundations for public service broadcasting in Britain. The British Broadcasting Corporation (BBC) was created by royal charter, and the Ullswater committee (United Kingdom, Parliament 1934) set out the formal independence of the BBC from the government in the daily management of its affairs, but the BBC's special relationship with and obligations to Parliament have presented difficult problems for the corporation over the years. (See, for example, May and Rowan 1982; Burns 1977; Briggs 1979; Schlesinger 1974; Tracey 1978.)

The BBC is financed by a licence fee paid annually by all television owners while the Independent Broadcasting Authority (IBA) oversees the 15 Independent Television (ITV) companies which are financed solely by advertising. Increases in the licence fee must be approved by Parliament. The IBA, created in the mid-1950s, is confronted with some of the same problems with Parliament in fulfilling the statutory obligations set out in the Acts of 1964 and 1973. The BBC is required to broadcast a daily impartial account of the proceedings of Parliament, and both organizations are obligated to be impartial in the reporting of political affairs, although the IBA's obligation to impartiality is set out in statute, while the BBC's is self-imposed (cf. United Kingdom, Parliament 1977).

Broadcasting in Britain is relatively centralized, although the launch of Independent Television (ITV) in the 1950s created key centres of production outside London, particularly in Lancashire and the Midlands, and later in Yorkshire. During the late 1960s and mid-1970s, BBC radio and Independent Local Radio (ILR) together operated 40 local radio stations. By 1985, the total had increased to 79 (48 ILR stations and 31 BBC stations), covering close to 90 percent of the country. Although ITV is a federation of 15 regional television companies, and the BBC has regional production centres and newsrooms, there are no equivalents to the American locally owned television network affiliates. Most of the television programming is networked across the country, and all main news programs on the four channels are networked, with a local bulletin sometimes coming afterwards.

In 1990, Britain had four primary television channels – BBC1, the main BBC channel, and BBC2; ITV, the Independent Television channel now called Channel 3; and Channel 4, another independent channel. The latter channel came on the air in 1982, and although the majority of its programs are taken from independent producers and foreign sources, it shares ITN news services with ITV. BBC1 and ITV's Channel 3 attract the largest audiences and carry the country's flagship news and current affairs programs.

Over the course of the 1980s, the Thatcher government applied its philosophy of free market competition to the domain of broadcasting. New media such as cable and satellite broadcasting were introduced, but these did not gain a significant foothold in the market (Dutton et al. 1987). Although satellite dish sales are now increasing, with 1.5 million households equipped in 1991, the vast majority of Britons continue to receive only four television channels. The number of channels is likely to increase, however, once economic conditions improve. The long-term implications of the *Broadcasting Act*, passed in December

1990, for British broadcasting and election campaign broadcasting are not entirely clear. The possible consequences for campaign broadcasting are discussed in a postscript at the end of this study.

POLITICAL BROADCASTING OBLIGATIONS AND REGULATION

British broadcasting is obligated to be impartial in its coverage of politics. The following describes the obligations of public service broadcasting and how they are put in practice by the BBC (public service) and the Independent Television (commercial) channels to provide the parties with air time for communication of issues and policies, allocated according to an agreed-upon formula and within legislated restrictions. Mechanisms for expressing complaints about access and coverage exist and have been exercised. Televised coverage of the House of Commons has focused on the two major parties, causing the smaller parties serious concern.

Broadcasters' Obligations: Access, Balance and Impartiality

Political broadcasting in Britain is covered by the obligations of public service broadcasting. It is subject not only to the guidelines set out in various statutory Acts and the BBC's aides-mémoires, but also to evolving interpretations of those guidelines in cases that have been brought before the courts, as well as the traditional arrangements between the broadcasting authorities and the political parties for the allocation of broadcast time. Since neither the BBC nor the IBA makes broadcast advertising time available for purchase by the political parties, it is important that the way in which decisions are made about the allocation of free broadcasting time to the parties be fair. This is particularly important because the broadcasters use the ratio of party election broadcast time as a guide in the news coverage of the parties during election campaigns. In 1987, for example, the party election broadcast ratio was 5:5:5 (Conservatives: Labour: Liberal–SDP Alliance), and this translated into equal time in news coverage for each of the parties.

The BBC's political broadcasting obligations were set out in 1947 and 1969 in aides-mémoires, the main details of which were agreed on by the Conservative and Labour parties and the BBC. The 1947 document was modified in 1948 to include the "14-day rule," which prohibited the BBC from broadcasting any news or discussions of any issue coming before Parliament for debate within a fortnight's time. The 14-day rule was suspended indefinitely in 1957. The guiding principles pertaining to political broadcasts were set out formally for the first time in the 1947 document, and except for the guidelines pertaining to ministerial broadcasts these were still the same 40 years later. There are two significant aspects to the 1947 document that concern how broadcasters should respond to changes in the party system, for example the creation of a new political party or changes in support for an established party. First, the BBC actually considered the possibility of individuals breaking away from the established political parties. Section 6 (ii) of the 1947 aide-mémoire states that the "BBC reserve the right, after consultation with the party leaders, to invite to the microphone a member of either House of outstanding national eminence who may have become detached from any party." Second, the aide-mémoire enjoins the BBC to make the final decision over matters relating to political broadcasting in those circumstances in which agreement cannot be reached among the parties.

Political broadcasts, in which the parties have free, direct and unmediated access to the airwaves, were described in the 1947 aide-mémoire as being of three types: ministerial broadcasts by the government of the day for which a right of reply could be given to the Opposition, subject to the agreement of the government or the permission of the BBC; "party political broadcasts" aired during the year in noncampaign periods; and "party election broadcasts" aired during general election campaigns. The 1947 aide-mémoire put the BBC in a difficult position if the government of the day refused to agree to the Opposition's request for a reply to a ministerial broadcast the Opposition believed was of a controversial nature. On such occasions it was left to the BBC to decide whether to permit the Opposition a right of reply.

The 1969 aide-mémoire was concerned solely with ministerial broadcasts, and sought to relieve the BBC of difficult decisions about whether to offer a right of reply to the Opposition. The document divided ministerial broadcasts into two types. The first would seek to explain legislation or encourage the public's awareness and cooperation on a matter over which there is a broad consensus of political opinion; for such broadcasts there would be no right of reply. The second type was controversial ministerial broadcasts for which a right of reply would be given to a leading member of the Opposition, after which a third stage would bring together, in the forum of a round-table discussion, representatives of the government party, the Opposition parties, a Liberal and a member of any other party with comparable electoral support. Prime Minister Harold Wilson's broadcast on the withdrawal of the government's legislation on trade unions, aired on 19 June 1969, was the first occasion on which the BBC used this new three-stage formula. The reply from Edward Heath, Leader of the Opposition, was broadcast on the following night, and the three-way discussion was held on 23 June.

The Independent Television Authority (ITA), which became the Independent Broadcasting Authority (IBA) in 1973, did not carry political broadcasts and had not taken part in the discussions surrounding the 1947 and 1969 aides-mémoires. ITV was free to broadcast only those ministerials it deemed important. Of the 12 ministerial broadcasts with Opposition replies carried on the BBC in the first 10 years of ITV's existence (1955–65), ITV carried only three, and these were over the 1956 invasion of Suez, the 1957 Commonwealth Prime Ministers' Conference and Rhodesia. In 1970, the ITA committed ITV to taking all future ministerial broadcasts of a controversial nature (the second type), although it would not necessarily transmit them simultaneously with the BBC. ITV incorporated a similar version of the stage-three discussion, often using the same party spokespersons as the BBC.

The 1969 aide-mémoire was significant for two reasons. First, it signalled a new style of party access to television. More than one prime minister in the 1970s used a ministerial broadcast to launch a general election campaign, despite the BBC's view that campaigns should be launched by "party election broadcasts." Second, it formalized the Liberal (or third-party) response to ministerials, in the form of a "stage-three" round-table discussion with representatives of the two "major" parties. The Liberals had not been involved in the discussions with the BBC in the drafting of the 1969 aide-mémoire, and were concerned about appearing to be dominated by the two "major" parties in the round-table discussion. At the same time, the Conservative and Labour parties were concerned that the stage-three round table appeared to give the Liberals the final word on the subject. Despite objections from the parties, and from ITV which from 1972 mounted its own program with party spokespersons, agreement was not reached to drop the stage-three arrangements, and they remained in use. The round-table forum for dealing with the third-party response to ministerial broadcasts was potentially open to change when the SDP came into existence in 1981 and subsequently joined forces with the Liberals in an electoral alliance.

Party Political and Party Election Broadcasts
The political parties first accepted the BBC's offer of free television time and broadcast facilities to produce party political broadcasts (PPBs) and party election broadcasts (PEBs) in 1953. The content of these broadcasts is determined by the parties alone, and the broadcasts are not under the editorial control of the broadcasters. Prior to 1959, PEBs were the only form of televised general election communication since, as a matter of broadcasters' policy, television news did not cover election campaigns. The broadcasting authorities decided to cover the general

election campaign in news bulletins for the first time in 1959, and have done so since then. The parties have continued to accept the offer of free broadcast time, although they have come to place more importance on the other free outlet, television news.

The allocation of party broadcast time has been the result of consensual agreement between the political parties and the broadcasting authorities. The understanding has been that the latter would make broadcast time available free of charge, and the parties would agree on how to allocate that time. Since free political party access to broadcast time was not required by law, the broadcasting authorities could in theory refuse to grant such privileged access at any time. Since PPBs and PEBs have become an enshrined tradition in British politics, however, any attempt to stop their free transmission would probably be resisted strongly by the political parties and perhaps also by the broadcasters, some of whom believe that there is a strong case for direct, unmediated access for politicians during election campaigns.

Over the years, an ad hoc committee evolved to facilitate the share-out of PPB and PEB time. The Committee on Party Political Broadcasting (CPPB) is made up of BBC and IBA representatives and the leaders of the parties represented in Parliament. It decides upon the parties' ratio of PPBs and PEBs, and has traditionally reached decisions on this ratio by consensus, with the aid of guidelines that take account of the vote for the parties in the previous general election.

The CPPB originated after 1945 as an ad hoc arrangement between the BBC and the Labour and Conservative parties. ITV came on the air in 1955 and joined the CPPB shortly thereafter. It was not until the 1960s that the Liberals were admitted to the Committee and the 1970s that the Scottish Nationalist Party (SNP) and Plaid Cymru, the Welsh nationalist party, became members. (Arrangements for the allocation of party broadcasting in Northern Ireland are handled by the broadcasting authorities there.) The Committee is chaired by the Lord President of the Council or by the government Chief Whip if the Lord President is absent. The secretary to the CPPB traditionally has been the secretary to the Chief Whip's office. The CPPB convenes when all members are agreed that a meeting is necessary. In the past, the CPPB met at least once annually to consider PPBs and once again shortly before a general election campaign to agree on the allocation of PEBs. The CPPB last met after the 1983 general election, and since then has conducted its business without meeting.

The CPPB is a prime example of "institutional continuity" in the relationship between the broadcasting authorities and the politicians (Smith 1979). The 1947 aide-mémoire states in reference to ministerial broadcasts "where, however, the Opposition think that a Government broadcast is controversial it will be open to them to take the matter up through the *usual channels* with a view to a reply" [emphasis added]. The CPPB is one of the "usual channels" through which the parties express their concerns to the broadcasting authorities. The Committee, which meets under the ground rules of consensual agreement and confidentiality, has been described as "the club" by some of its members. The broadcasting authorities view it as a working mechanism by which direct political access to television and radio can be achieved without compromising the broadcasters' own editorial independence.

The basis for allocating PPB time has changed over the past 40 years. From 1945 until the early 1960s, the percentage of votes polled in the previous general election served as the basis for the allocation of PPBs aired in noncampaign periods between general elections. The results of the 1945 election meant that Labour was allocated six PPBs on the basis of nearly 12 million votes, the Conservatives were allocated five PPBs for 10 million votes, and the Liberals received one PPB for 2.5 million votes. At that time, PPBs were broadcast only on radio and ranged from 15 to 25 minutes each. The Liberals complained about this allocation but had to do so from outside the CPPB. Until 1960, when the Liberals became formal members of the CPPB, they attended only the pre-general election meetings to discuss the allocation of PEBs.

The acceptance of the Liberals into the CPPB opened the way for greater discussion about different proposals for allocating broadcast time. In 1962, for example, after the Liberals' victory in the Orpington by-election, the party proposed that by-election results be considered in the allocation formula. The Liberal leader, Jo Grimond, proposed that one-third of the PPB allocation be based on the general election results and two-thirds on the basis of subsequent by-elections. The change to which the Labour and Conservative parties eventually agreed went only part of the way toward satisfying Grimond: it was agreed that after two years of a parliament, two-thirds of the PPB allocation would be based on the general election and one-third on subsequent by-elections. In 1963, when this change became effective, the Liberals' PPB allocation was raised from one broadcast of 15 minutes to one of 25, and all parties were given the option of dividing one 25-minute PPB into two (one of 10 and one of 15 minutes). The Conservative and Labour parties were each granted four PPBs (one of 25 minutes, one of 20 minutes and two of 15 minutes). With the launching of BBC2 in 1964, PPBs were broadcast simultaneously on all three existing channels (BBC1, BBC2 and ITV), and simultaneous transmission of PPBs continued until 1980.

The two nationalist parties, the SNP and Plaid Cymru, had greater difficulty than the Liberals in gaining admittance to the Committee. The report of the Pilkington Committee on broadcasting (United

Kingdom, Parliament 1962) urged the broadcasting authorities to permit these two parties to transmit PPBs in their regions. In 1965, before either nationalist party had won a seat in Parliament, each was granted one five-minute PPB on TV and radio in its own region. In the February 1974 general election, the nationalist parties and the Liberals entered Parliament in force, together taking nearly 22 percent of the popular vote. The Liberals won 14 seats, the SNP seven and Plaid Cymru won two. In the subsequent October 1974 general election, the Liberals lost one seat, but the SNP gained four, bringing its MPs to 11, and the Welsh nationalists gained one seat to number three MPs. The SNP became a member of the CPPB in May 1974 after its significant gains in the February election, and until Plaid Cymru joined in April 1975, the SNP represented the views of both the nationalist parties.

In 1974, the CPPB agreed to a different basis of allocation of PPB time that continues to apply today: 10 minutes of broadcast time are granted for every two million votes cast in the previous general election, subject to the provision that the government and the official Opposition have an equal number of broadcasts. Somewhat different arrangements apply to the nationalist parties; the SNP is allocated 10 minutes in Scotland for every 200 000 votes it receives, and Plaid Cymru is granted 10 minutes in Wales for every 100 000 votes it receives.

The ratio and the criteria for allocating party broadcast (PEB) time in general election campaigns have been rather more static. For the parties not represented in Parliament, there has been a long-standing practice of giving a five-minute PEB if they contest 50 or more seats. For the parties in Parliament, the principal measure for allocating PEB time has been the proportion of the votes cast in the previous general election, but the parties' performance in by-elections and local elections is also relevant. From the 1964 to the 1979 general elections, the allocation of PEBs for the three main parties was 5:5:3 (Conservative: Labour: Liberal), as shown in table 2.1; the sole exception was the October 1974 general election when the Liberals were allocated four broadcasts on the basis of their strong performance in the February 1974 general election. The 1983 campaign was the first for which the broadcasters decided on the PEB ratio because the main parties could not reach a consensus. The PEB ratio changed again in 1983 to 5:5:4 (with 4 for the Alliance), and became 5:5:5 in 1987. The distribution of PEB time among the various political parties was similar for television and radio, as shown in table 2.2.

The parties are not permitted to break up the five 10-minute segments into more but shorter segments. They may choose to air a shorter broadcast, say 5 or 7 minutes instead of 10, but there is a maximum of five broadcasts. Therefore, there is no British equivalent of the

30-second TV spot so often seen in the United States.[3] Like U.S. political ads, however, PEBs sometimes do contain negative content and there are no regulations or controls over content. Nevertheless, the 10-minute length often means that some part of the broadcast is devoted to discussion of party policy, and many PEBs end with "talking heads" of politicians explaining party policy. At least one of the five Conservative and Labour PEBs is usually devoted to developing the party leader's image.

Table 2.1
Allocation of party television broadcast time in Britain,1959–87
(minutes)

	Party political (non-election) broadcasts			Party (general) election broadcasts		
Year	Conservative	Labour	Liberal/SDP	Conservative	Labour	Liberal/SDP
1959	N/A	N/A	N/A	95	95	25
1961a	80	80	15			
1962a	80	80	15			
1963a	75	75	25			
1964a	75	75	25			
1964b	40	40	15	75	75	45
1965	60	60	20			
1966	60	60	20	75	75	45
1967	60	60	20			
1968	60	60	20			
1969	60	60	20			
1970	60	60	20	50	50	30
1971	60	60	20			
1972	60	60	20			
1973	60	60	20			
1974c	60	60	30	(Feb.) 50	50	30
				(Oct.) 50	50	40
1975	60	60	30			
1976	60	60	30			
1977	60	60	30			
1978	60	60	30			

Table 2.1 (cont'd)
(minutes)

	Party political (non-election) broadcasts			Party (general) election broadcasts		
Year	Conservative	Labour	Liberal/SDP	Conservative	Labour	Liberal/SDP
1979	60	60	30	50	50	30
1980	60	60	20			
1981	60	60	20			
1982	60	60	20			
1983	60	60	20			
	(Liberal–SDP Alliance)		10	50	50	40[d]
1987	60	60	30	50	50	50[d]

Source: Semetko (1987, 166).

[a]From July the preceding year to June in the current year.
[b]From July to December.
[c]The Scottish and Welsh nationalists were allocated PEBs in their regions for the first time.
[d]Allocated to the Liberal–SDPAlliance, not to the separate parties. The Alliance was also allocated an extra PPB for 1983, which was broadcast on 26 April and was produced solely by the SDP.

N/A = not applicable.

In 1987, for example, the Conservatives reduced one 10-minute broadcast to five minutes about Margaret Thatcher as a world stateswoman. Labour's first PEB was used to portray Neil Kinnock, the new leader, as a strong family man who is admired, trusted and respected by his political colleagues. The seven-minute Kinnock PEB was so popular that Labour decided to broadcast it again, as the fourth of its five PEBs.

A BBC document published in 1987 refers to the allocation of PEB time, and notes that "the allocation of time between the parties is decided by the Committee on Party Political Broadcasting. If the Committee fails to reach an agreement (as happened in 1983) the broadcasters impose a decision. There is no precise mathematical formula for the allocation of time for Party Election Broadcasts. Clearly it would be unfair only to take into account votes cast at the last General Election if substantial political changes have since taken place" (BBC 1987, 30). By not specifying a precise formula for the allocation of PEB time, the broadcasting authorities remain flexible, and have the option of taking new political developments into account.

As noted above, the PEB ratio is of particular importance in election campaigns since, by tradition, broadcasters rely on it as a guideline for maintaining balance in election news. According to the BBC (1987, 31),

Table 2.2
Breakdown of party election broadcast allocations on television and radio, 1950–87

	Television		Radio	
	No.	Minutes	No.	Minutes
1950 and 1951				
Conservative	—	—	5	2 of 30, 3 of 20
Labour	—	—	5	2 of 30, 3 of 20
Liberal	—	—	3	1 of 20, 2 of 10
1955				
Conservative	3	1 of 30, 2 of 15	4	4 of 20
Labour	3	1 of 30, 2 of 15	4	4 of 20
Liberal	1	1 of 15	1	1 of 20
1959				
Conservative	5	4 of 20, 1 of 15	8	4 of 15, 4 of 5
Labour	5	4 of 20, 1 of 15	8	4 of 15, 4 of 5
Liberal	2	1 of 15, 1 of 10	2	1 of 15, 1 of 5
1964				
Conservative	5	5 of 15	7	4 of 10, 3 of 5
Labour	5	5 of 15	7	4 of 10, 3 of 5
Liberal	3	3 of 15	4	2 of 10, 2 of 5
1966				
Conservative	5	2 of 15, 3 of 10	7	4 of 10, 3 of 5
Labour	5	2 of 15, 3 of 10	7	4 of 10, 3 of 5
Liberal	3	1 of 15, 2 of 10	4	2 of 10, 2 of 5
SNP[a]	1	1 of 5	1	1 of 5
Plaid Cymru[b]	1	1 of 5	1	1 of 5
1970				
Conservative	5	5 of 10	7	4 of 10, 3 of 5
Labour	5	5 of 10	7	4 of 10, 3 of 5
Liberal	3	3 of 10	4	2 of 10, 2 of 5
SNP	1	1 of 5	1	1 of 5
Plaid Cymru	1	1 of 5	1	1 of 5
1974 (Feb.)				
Conservative	5	5 of 10	7	4 of 10, 3 of 5
Labour	5	5 of 10	7	4 of 10, 3 of 5
Liberal	3	3 of 10	4	2 of 10, 2 of 5
SNP	1	1 of 10	1	1 of 10
Plaid Cymru	1	1 of 10	1	1 of 10
1974 (Oct.)				
Conservative	5	5 of 10	7	4 of 10, 3 of 5
Labour	5	5 of 10	7	4 of 10, 3 of 5
Liberal	4	4 of 10	5	3 of 10, 2 of 5
SNP	2	2 of 10	2	2 of 10
Plaid Cymru	1	1 of 10	1	1 of 10

Table 2.2 (cont'd)

	Television		Radio	
	No.	Minutes	No.	Minutes
1979				
Conservative	5	5 of 10	7	4 of 10, 3 of 5
Labour	5	5 of 10	7	4 of 10, 3 of 5
Liberal	3	3 of 10	5	3 of 10, 2 of 5
SNP	3	3 of 10	3	3 of 5
Plaid Cymru	1	1 of 10	1	1 of 5
1983				
Conservative	5	5 of 10	7	4 of 10, 3 of 5
Labour	5	5 of 10	7	4 of 10, 3 of 5
Liberal–SDP Alliance	4	4 of 10	6	4 of 10, 2 of 5
SNP	2	2 of 10	2	2 of 5
Plaid Cymru	1	1 of 10	1	1 of 5
1987				
Conservative	5	5 of 10	7	4 of 10, 3 of 5
Labour	5	5 of 10	7	4 of 10, 3 of 5
Liberal–SDP Alliance	5	5 of 10	7	4 of 10, 3 of 5
SNP	2	2 of 10	2	2 of 5
Plaid Cymru	1	1 of 10	1	1 of 5

Source: Semetko (1987, 168–69).

[a]Scottish Nationalist Party (SNP) PEBs were broadcast in Scotland only.
[b]Plaid Cymru's PEBs were broadcast in Wales only.

"during an election campaign, the BBC accepts an obligation to achieve balance over the period of the campaign in the use of recorded actuality of political speeches and in film, videotape, and studio contributions from politicians. The basis for balance between the major parties is [the] formula derived from allocation of PEBs."

By using the PEB ratio as a guideline for maintaining balance among the main parties in election news and current affairs programs, broadcasting presents "a wider perspective on the election for the voters" than the press (Harrop 1984, 186). The PEB ratio of 5:5:4 (Conservative: Labour: Alliance) in 1983 was also evident in BBC and ITV news broadcasting, in terms of news time devoted to each of the parties, whereas the ratio of party coverage in the printed press was only 5:5:2 (ibid.). Press coverage in an election campaign is determined largely by journalists' news values, unlike broadcasting, which is guided by the PEB ratio. This suggests that the Alliance received more time on TV news and current affairs programs than it would have done if news values alone determined coverage. In comparison with the press, then, British broadcasting presents a broader picture of the political spectrum during an election.

Political parties have thus come to place a great deal of importance on the amount of time allocated for PEBs, more because of their influence on the allocation of news and current affairs time than because of their potential to persuade. There is some evidence, however, that a third party – notably the Liberals, and more recently the Liberal–SDP Alliance – benefits disproportionately from its PEBs. A study of the 1964 campaign, for example, suggests that Liberal support had been strengthened by exposure to Liberal PEBs (Blumler and McQuail 1968). Liberal–SDP Alliance PEBs had a similar effect on their viewers in 1983 (McAllister 1985). A BBC/Gallup survey taken on the eve of the election in June 1983 found that those who claimed to have been influenced by any PEBs were more likely to vote Alliance (45 percent) than Conservative (35 percent) or Labour (20 percent) (Crewe 1986). Another study of viewers' responses to PPBs found that those who watched more PPBs learned more about politics; Wober and Svennevig (1981,1) concluded that PPBs, "for all their evident defects [of low popularity] ... have some positive function in the process of political communication."

The *Representation of the People Act 1983:* Section 93

The *Representation of the People Act 1983* (RPA) governs some aspects of political broadcasting during election campaigns. In particular, the Act deals with the "taking part" of candidates in programs during the election campaign. From the start of the "pending period" until the close of nominations, candidates may not take part in broadcasts about their constituency or electoral area.[4] During the campaign itself, after nominations have closed, broadcasts about a particular constituency or electoral area should not take place without the consent of the candidates. According to the BBC (1987, 32), "'taking part' has been legally defined as 'active and conscious participation' by a candidate. It does not therefore include such coverage as film of a candidate conducting ordinary electoral activity." In addition, the BBC has its own editorial requirements that restrict election broadcasting. Although this is not required by law, the BBC expects editors to maintain political balance, as measured by a count of the party affiliations of guests, within their respective programs over a period of time. Outside of election campaigns, a refusal by a member of Parliament to participate in a program is not reason enough to deny another party the chance to participate. During election campaigns, however, current affairs programs are expected to offer all main party candidates in a constituency a chance to take part, and the refusal of one candidate to participate could jeopardize the airing of a program. On polling day itself, all broadcast news coverage avoids any reference to the issues of the campaign until the polls have closed.

There are no restrictions, however, on the amount of opinion poll coverage aired during the election campaign; coverage in the press and on television is substantial. Polls have been a regular feature of campaigns since 1959, but coverage of polls during campaigns is becoming more evident. In 1983, for example, polling approached the point of "saturation," with 49 national polls published or broadcast between the announcement of the election (9 May) and polling day (9 June), an average of three every two days (Crewe 1986, 234). In 1987, polling in the marginal constituencies became very important in the news because of the issue of tactical voting (Norris 1989). Although the increased number of polls in general election campaigns has caused some to question their value and potential impact on the vote, there is no expectation of any ban on reporting polls in future elections.

Complaining to the Broadcasters

During general election campaigns, the political parties maintain a keen watch over news and current affairs coverage, and they frequently complain to the broadcasters about perceived bias in the news. Complaining has become a tactic by which the parties attempt to influence election news. Complaints may be made in writing, for example, to the BBC's Board of Governors or its Director General or officials at the IBA, or more informally, through conversations and contacts on a routine basis. The BBC has a high-level official who deals with the parties' complaints about political broadcasting on the BBC. In addition to making complaints about unfair coverage, a party may also organize viewers to call in and complain about political bias in a program or news item. This tactic is more common during a general election campaign.

Political parties and other groups may also complain about coverage through the mechanism of the Broadcasting Complaints Commission (BCC). A case brought by the SDP in 1984 illustrates, however, that the Commission is not a particularly useful avenue for redress concerning allegations of systematic bias.[5]

In June 1984, on the basis of the SDP's monitoring of main evening news on BBC and ITV between February and April, the SDP submitted a complaint to the BCC about a lack of political balance in television news coverage. In his letter to Baroness Pike, Chair of the BCC, Dr. David Owen, leader of the SDP, cited the 1983 general election result and the breakdowns of support for the parties in the subsequent six by-elections as pointing to an increase in support from what the Liberals on their own had achieved in the post-war period. He wrote: "It is our contention that this change in voting patterns has not been matched by an equivalent change in the way British politics is reported and dis-

cussed by the BBC and the IBA." Dr. Owen indicated his party's acceptance that the activities of the government of the day should receive
more prominence than the comments of the opposition parties, and
that if one opposition party had acted specifically then that activity
should receive more prominence than government or other party statements about it; in dealing with comment from party spokespersons,
however, the Liberal–SDP Alliance expected to be treated fairly and in
a non-discriminatory way. Dr. Owen suggested that a balance need
not occur in each program, but that "over a sustained period of time
there must be fairness and manifest impartiality."

Dr. Owen made three specific complaints. First, he noted that over
the 10-week period studied, the amount of time given to the Labour
Party was "out of all proportion to what can be justified as being fair and
impartial." In the Alliance's view, the status of Labour as the Official
Opposition in Parliament did not justify such an imbalance. Second, the
imbalance was particularly marked in certain news items in which "only
the Labour Party opposition is asked to comment on Government decisions or policy to the exclusion of the SDP–Liberal Alliance." A third
complaint concerned the broadcasting authorities' reluctance to accept
anyone other than the SDP or the Liberal leader to express the viewpoint
of the Alliance in news and current affairs programs. Dr. Owen commented that the term "shadow minister," which was often used to refer
to Labour Party spokespersons, had no constitutional authority and
reinforced the impression that Labour was the only alternative government. He also alleged inconsistent treatment by broadcasters of the
Alliance in current affairs programs. He praised "Question Time" as
the only program in which there appeared to be a genuine attempt to
achieve a balanced representation of views, in contrast to "Panorama,"
"TV-Eye," "Newsnight" and Radio 4's "The Today Programme."

Dr. Owen cited the main evening news coverage of the Commons
on 19 June 1984 as a particularly marked example of imbalance, since
it made no mention of his or David Steel's statements in the House on
a day of severe disorder in picket lines set up by striking miners. The
Alliance, Dr. Owen argued, was advocating a distinct policy position
on the issue of secondary picketing in calling for the use of civil law
but this received very little coverage in television news that day. He
also alleged that a current affairs program refused to accept an Alliance
spokesperson other than himself to appear with the Home Secretary
and his Labour counterpart that evening, when the SDP leader had a
previous engagement.

In July 1984, the BCC indicated that it was unable to investigate a
complaint of the kind made by the SDP. Baroness Pike replied that the

BCC could only investigate specific complaints about a particular program (or series) and could not investigate a complaint about general
coverage or broadcasters' editorial policy. Even if the SDP's complaint
fell within the BCC's terms of reference, Baroness Pike suggested that
the BCC would exercise its power of discretion and refuse to investigate the complaint. The BCC argued that it was not prepared to reach
what would be a political judgement. The SDP then decided to take
legal action and challenge the BCC's decision in the High Court, assuming that if the party did not win then it would at least draw public
attention to the party's grievance. The SDP urged the High Court to
rule that its complaint was within the BCC's jurisdiction and to order
the BCC to investigate.

In January 1985, the Court issued its ruling that under the terms
of the *Broadcasting Act*, the BCC had been wrong to claim that it had no
jurisdiction to review the SDP's complaint, but the political nature of
the complaint left no clear guidance about the course of action the BCC
should take. The Court therefore upheld the BCC's right to use its discretion in exercising its power not to investigate the complaint. The SDP
had to pay only its own costs in bringing the case, and these were minimal. In the view of the party leadership, the case made the broadcasters look more carefully at how decisions about news coverage of
politics were being made (*Owen v. Broadcasting Complaints Commission
(BCC)* 1985).

In the subsequent months, the SDP sought opportunities to argue
its case in the public domain. Dr. Owen chose the columns of the *Sunday
Times* on 28 April 1985 to say "Why it's time to call foul on the BBC"
and Anne Sofer, a member of the SDP's National Committee, described
the BBC as "a beacon of bias" in her article in the *Times* on 29 April.

The SDP then decided to commission a study of television news
from researchers at Oxford Polytechnic with the aim of using the
results to support its claim of unfair treatment. The study of two
months of TV news coverage showed that the Alliance received significantly less news time than the two main parties. David Owen and
David Steel, the Liberal leader, then decided to challenge the BBC
directly in the High Court. They chose to concentrate on the BBC because
it was the "more important and the public broadcasting corporation."
In a protracted correspondence with the BBC, the SDP sought to dis-
cover what criteria the Corporation used to decide whether or not it
was being fair in news coverage and comment and also to learn the
results of the BBC's own detailed monitoring. According to Dr. Owen,
the BBC had "steadfastly refused to give us either its criteria, monitoring results, or to explain how it tries to ensure fair balance ... it also

failed to respond to our complaints of gross imbalance." The High Court case sought to make the BBC disclose fully all relevant information on its own monitoring of political coverage and to challenge the BBC on the grounds of fairness; the Alliance drew on a substantial body of monitoring evidence to support its claim that it was not given fair coverage in comparison with the two main parties. The case also had another point, to challenge the BBC's defence that the Corporation was not liable to judicial review.

The Alliance leaders and the BBC eventually agreed to an out-of-court settlement. The BBC agreed to provide full details of its monitoring and the criteria it uses in assessing news coverage given undertakings that the Alliance leader would not disclose this information. In settling out of court, the parties acted in self-interest; they believed they had won on the first point because the leaders had received all the information on the BBC'S monitoring and editorial criteria, which had been requested repeatedly. The Alliance was advised by its counsel that it could win on the question of challenging the BBC through the courts, but that it would most likely lose on the question of fairness, given that the BBC had disclosed all relevant information about editorial criteria. The cost of taking the case further, with only the possibility of winning on the point about judicial review, would have been upwards of £100 000. The out-of-court settlement did not address the question of fairness, and the Alliance obtained the power to seek fresh leave to bring proceedings in the future in relation to its subsequent treatment by the BBC. On 14 July 1986, the Alliance leaders issued a press statement calling for the BBC's Board of Governors to disclose fully all of the information on editorial criteria and internal monitoring that was made available to the Alliance in the out-of-court settlement, which probably would have come out in court had the proceedings continued. In June 1987, the BBC published a document entitled "Fairness and Impartiality in Political Broadcasting" that included the material made available to the Alliance in the affidavits. The document contained no surprising revelations.

The SDP case suggests that the Broadcasting Complaints Commission is not a useful mechanism for political parties' complaints about coverage since the BCC is reluctant to deal with complaints of political bias, particularly of a systematic kind. Nevertheless, the third party's efforts between 1984 and 1986 to challenge the broadcasters probably contributed to the broadcasters' decision to increase the amount of PEB time for the Alliance in the 1987 general election, despite the protests of the Conservative and Labour parties. The PEB ratio had been 5:5:4 (Conservative: Labour: Alliance) in 1983, and in 1987 it was 5:5:5.

Televising Parliament

Over the course of the 1980s, television cameras were permitted first in the House of Lords and, after a successful experimental period, in the House of Commons (cf. Franklin 1986, 1989, in press). Prior to this, television news and current affairs programs carried only still photographs of Parliament with sound excerpts.

Research on television coverage of the House of Commons reveals a consistent emphasis on the Conservative and Labour parties in news programs, with little attention to spokespersons for the eight other parties represented in Parliament (Blumler et al. 1990). Coverage of House proceedings is thus distinctly bipartisan, focusing almost entirely on Conservative and Labour spokespersons and virtually excluding those from smaller parties. In addition, the study found undue emphasis on the party of the government (ibid.). Moreover, the higher up the ladder of political seniority, the greater the disparity between government and opposition coverage. For example, television carried 3 1/2 times as many appearances and "actualities" (extended sound bites) of Prime Minister Margaret Thatcher as of Labour leader Neil Kinnock. At cabinet level, the disparity was 2 1/2 times in favour of the government, whereas backbench level government and opposition spokespersons received more or less equal treatment. In sum, the research reveals a preoccupation with the "stars," the leaders of the two major parties, to the virtual exclusion of minor parties, as well as an undue emphasis on the government. If this pattern of coverage remains, the government is likely to have a distinct advantage in the run-up to the next general election, with government spokespersons having more time to put their arguments before the electorate.

The emphasis on the major parties stems in part from both the overall division of debate time and individual decisions of the Speaker, and obviously causes the minor parties great concern. The Liberal Democrats are especially concerned about the impact this pattern of coverage may have on the centre party's image in the run-up to the next general election (Kennedy and Culey, in press). The 1991–92 general election will be the first contested since cameras were permitted in the House of Commons.

CAMPAIGN MEDIA CONTENT AND INFLUENCE

British television devotes substantial news and current affairs coverage to general election campaigns. Election coverage may have a variety of effects on voters' perceptions of the parties and on the voting decision itself.

Television Coverage of General Election Campaigns

British election coverage is highly concentrated because of the campaign's short duration. The sheer amount of attention given to the campaign often provokes complaints from viewers.

Leeds University's audio-visual service recorded all election news and current affairs output on all four channels in 1983, which over the three and one-half week campaign amounted to 304 programs or 208 hours of broadcast time (Blumler and Semetko 1987, 424). In 1987, there was at least as much news and current affairs coverage. In addition to the breakfast, lunch time, early evening and prime time news programs, there were daily current affairs programs such as "Newsnight," and "Nationwide" and weekly programs such as "Panorama," "Weekend World," "World in Action," "TV-Eye" and "A Week in Politics." In addition, there were election specials such as: the "Election Call" live phone-in programs, which began on radio in 1974, and were transmitted every morning in 1983; the "Granada 500" series in which audiences put questions to a panel of politicians; a BBC series called "On the Spot" in which viewers asked questions of individual politicians; and a number of ad hoc editions of other regular programs for specialist audiences such as "Black on Black" and "First Tuesday." Moreover, BBC and ITV companies also produced some regional election television programming. Finally, there were the party election broadcasts. In 1987 this meant five each for the Conservatives, Labour and the Alliance, in addition to one for the Green Party (which had changed its name from the Ecology Party since 1983). The National Front and British National Party did not put up enough candidates for a PEB in 1987.

News coverage is focused heavily on the campaign. The BBC actually extended its main evening news bulletin by about 20 minutes in 1983 and 1987 to accommodate news about the campaign. And although Independent Television News (ITN) could not extend its 22-minute (commercial) news program by more than two to three minutes, ITN devoted the majority of bulletins to news about the campaign. Broadcasters treat elections with "due seriousness," and view their role as a social responsibility (Blumler et al. 1989, 157).

An analysis of main evening news coverage of the 1983 British general election and the 1984 U.S. presidential election campaign, comparing BBC and ITV coverage in Britain with ABC, CBS and NBC coverage in the United States, reveals distinct differences in approaches. According to Semetko et al. (1991, 142), British television news about the campaign is "more ample, more varied, more substantive," more concerned with the statements and activities of politicians and "more respectful." By contrast, U.S. election news on television is "more terse and concentrated," more "horse-racist" i.e., concerned with standing in the opinion polls and who is ahead, more inclined to "pass judgment and to be occasionally disrespectful in passing judgment." In covering politicians on the campaign trail, for example, U.S. reporters were more likely to take a line in a story and "reinforce" or "deflate" the message of the candidate. British reporters instead provided more straight or descriptive remarks about politicians' activities on the campaign trail.

There is also considerably more coverage of substantive issues in a British campaign than in a U.S. campaign. For example, an average of 20 percent of subjects in U.S. network evening news stories about the campaign concerned substantive issues such as defence, the economy, social welfare, foreign policy, energy and the environment, compared with over 35 percent on the BBC and 32 percent on ITV. This stems not only from a greater emphasis on non-substantive and emotional themes by U.S. candidates, but also from a greater interest among the U.S. networks in opinion polls and the candidates' personal qualities. For example, 20 percent of subjects in CBS campaign stories concerned the "horse race" or polls, compared with 16 percent on NBC and 12 percent on ABC and 30 percent of CBS subjects concerned presidential candidates' qualities, compared with 25 percent on NBC and 28 percent on ABC. In Britain, an average of 12 percent of subjects in BBC and ITV campaign stories concerned the polls or the horse race, and less than 5 percent concerned the party leaders' qualities.

Another fundamental difference between the two countries was in the handling of politicians' statements in election news. "Sound bites," or "actualities," are film segments in which politicians are seen on the screen and heard speaking. Over 33 percent of main evening campaign news in Britain was taken up by politicians' sound bites, compared with an average of only 11 percent of news across all three U.S. networks. And there is no difference between BBC and ITV on this point. In the U.S., there is an emphasis on the simplistic and snappy, whereas in Britain there is room for politicians to make more extended or complex points. Together, these findings point to a greater discretionary role of U.S. journalists in shaping the campaign agenda than in Britain, where politicians face less difficulty in getting their agendas and comments into the news.

The one great exception concerns the visuals. Content analysis of the television pictures of politicians on the campaign trail shows that U.S. and British politicians are on a more equal footing in their ability to get good pictures into the news. In both countries, parties and candidates were highly successful in initiating positive visuals. In both countries, therefore, parties and candidates are clearly able to determine much of the pictorial part of the coverage. In the U.S. and Britain, about 70 percent of visuals were positive and nearly 78 percent of visuals were initiated by the parties or candidates (i.e., conducting planned campaign engagements). Journalists in both countries therefore appear to exert little discretion over the visual domain of election news.

In the U.S., however, reporters sometimes try to counter the impact of the positive visuals with critical voice-over commentary about "pseudo-events." A report by NBC's Chris Wallace, for example, began this way: "A campaign that even Hollywood would envy, tonight our White House correspondent takes us backstage on a Reagan tour. The point of all this, to make the President look good on television. The audience would largely be extras on a stage. The well rehearsed rally was the usual show stopper" (Semetko et al. 1991, 131–32).

Although such remarks are rare, they are more prevalent in the U.S. coverage than in Britain. Disdainful commentary by reporters surfaced in 11 percent of U.S. news stories but in only 5 percent of those in Britain. And when British reporters made disdainful remarks, they were less direct. BBC's Nick Witchell, for example, in covering what was clearly one of Mrs. Thatcher's campaign photo-opportunities, was ostensibly descriptive: "The Prime Minister climbed aboard a tractor, showed an extraordinary interest in silage making, and had her photograph taken several thousand times" (Semetko et al. 1991, 132).

A comparison of party and media issue agendas also reveals that British politicians have a greater opportunity than their U.S. counterparts to influence the campaign news agenda. Party issue priorities were much closer to media priorities in Britain than in the U.S. In other words, in Britain the subject priorities of the parties "are more closely aligned with the subject priorities of television news" (Semetko et al. 1991, 141).[6] In short, "this lends further support to the idea that in comparison with British reporters, U.S. reporters are exercising greater discretion in taking up and reporting the subjects put forward by candidates. In Britain, on the other hand, it appears that political parties have greater potential to shape the campaign agenda" (ibid.).

If fairness is assessed in terms of the access provided to political parties, British broadcasting rates very highly. Compared with the British press, broadcasting provides a wider spectrum on the election campaign by presenting a broader picture of the party system. Moreover, in comparison with U.S. election news broadcasting, British broadcasting is far more oriented toward taking up and reporting the parties' views and positions on issues.

Research on British election news coverage in 1987 shows that British politicians continued to retain substantial news coverage in comparison with their U.S. counterparts (Semetko 1989a). Sound bites from all politicians in 1987 accounted for approximately one-third of election news coverage. This was true for both the public service (BBC) and the commercial (ITV) news programs. Moreover, the parties retained and even strengthened their advantage in providing positive visuals for television news.

Nevertheless, the third party (Liberal–SDP Alliance in 1983 and 1987, and the Liberal Democrats today) remained concerned about the position of its coverage in the election news bulletins. In 1983, despite the fact that the Alliance finished within two percentage points of Labour in terms of the popular vote, news about the third party often came much later in the news bulletins, with the lead stories focusing on the Conservative–Labour battle (Semetko 1989b). In 1987, broadcasters carried more stories focusing on all three parties, and stories about the Alliance occasionally appeared at the top of the bulletin, but the two-party battle (Conservative v. Labour) nevertheless predominated in news coverage.

The Influence of Election Broadcasting

Despite the amount of news coverage given to British elections, there is no clear consensus among British political and social scientists on the degree to which campaign communication makes a difference to public perceptions of parties, leaders, and issues, and eventually, to the voting decision. In part, this is due to the fact that in recent years very little research has been designed to measure directly the influence of the media in British election campaigns.

In general, two different perspectives currently exist on the relative importance of the British campaign for influencing the voting decision. One view places great importance on short-term factors, particularly campaign communication, suggesting that people vote on the basis of issues (Crewe 1982, 1983, 1986). The other perspective places more importance on long-term attachments to political parties – and social class in particular – as an influence on the voting decision, suggesting that the campaign may not be as important (Heath et al. 1985, 1987).

Both of these perspectives are partially correct. Whereas some voters hold long-term attachments to political parties and vote for the same party in every election, others look to the campaign for guidance in making their voting decision. The Conservatives' decision to change leaders makes the next general election an extremely interesting testing ground for research on media influence.[7] The leaders of all three key parties are relatively new figures, and the sense of public attachment to them may not be particularly strong. The Conservative leader will rely heavily on the media to project his own image and a new image for his party. Thus the potential for media to influence opinions about the leaders and parties in the forthcoming British general election is probably greater than in any previous campaign in the past decade.

Election communication may have a variety of effects. In addition to influencing the decision about which party to vote for, election communication may also influence the decision to vote at all. One study of first-time voters in the 1970 British general election found that election communication variables – such as exposure to election coverage on television and in the press, and political discussion – are important factors affecting turnout (Blumler and McLeod 1974, 295).

Evidence from the first studies of broadcasting and election campaigning in Britain shows that viewers also learn something about the issues and the parties from election broadcasting. There is a positive and significant correlation between the number of television programs viewed and political knowledge (Trenaman and McQuail 1961; Blumler and McQuail 1968). A more recent pre-election survey of voters in the 1983 campaign showed that 48 percent believed they knew "a fair amount" about the parties' policies, while 9 percent said they knew "a great deal." Moreover, 21 percent of electors said television helped them decide which party to vote for, and 39 percent of vote-switchers and 36 percent of first-time voters said they were helped by television (Harrison 1984, 174). This also suggests that election broadcasting plays an important educative role.

Other studies suggest that the third party – the Liberals in the 1960s and 1970s and the Liberal–SDP Alliance in the 1980s – benefits electorally from the extra exposure it receives on television during an election campaign. Blumler and McQuail (1968) found a positive and significant relationship between the use of television and improving attitudes toward the Liberal party in the 1964 campaign. McAllister (1985) suggests that in the 1979 and 1983 elections, television exposure accounted for 3 percent of the campaign-period votes gained by the Liberals and the Alliance.

A study of the 1987 general election campaign focused on how voters' opinions about the parties and the voting decision changed over the course of the campaign (Miller et al. 1990). Using a rather complex multi-wave panel design, in which the same respondents were interviewed at different stages of the campaign, the study found evidence of significant individual-level electoral volatility. In the short, three- to four-week campaign period, two-fifths of the electorate changed their voting intentions. "Tactical considerations outweighed any impact of changing attitudes on economic optimism, issue priorities, or leader images in those last few weeks" (ibid., vii). This suggests that media coverage of polls may play a more important role in the voting decision than previously. So although Mrs. Thatcher and the Conservatives were ahead of Labour and the Alliance at the start of the 1987 campaign, and the Conservative victory appeared to be a foregone conclusion, there was indeed a lot of vote switching by individuals that was masked by the stability of the published opinion polls at the aggregate level.

Toward the final weeks of the campaign, television news stories focused increasingly on the two-party (Labour v. Conservative) battle, while opinion polls showed that the public had dismissed the Alliance as a real contender. The Alliance nevertheless continued to obtain an equal proportion of news time. Using a day-by-day analysis of opinion change based on random sub-samples of the electorate, the Miller et al. study shows that television's focus on the two-party battle "occurred AFTER the voters had dismissed the Alliance as a real contender and not before" (Miller et al. 1990). In other words, television coverage of the party battle followed public opinion about the electoral chances of the Alliance and did not lead it.

CONCLUSIONS

Against a backdrop of increasing electoral volatility and new developments in British broadcasting and campaigning techniques, the institutional features and traditional practices of British election campaigns have remained much the same over the past two decades. Campaign spending remains low in Britain in comparison with the United States largely because the broadcasting authorities make free time available to the political parties to air their broadcasts during campaigns. This free broadcast time is a great leveller, guaranteeing that a wealthy party will not have greater access than other parties to audiences for broadcast advertising. The parties' ratio of PEB time and the willingness of the broadcasting authorities to take account of new developments in the political arena also suggest that during election campaigns the system is open to party inputs. In addition, the decision by both public service and commercial television channels to use the ratio of PEB time as a guide for maintaining balance in election campaign news and current affairs programs guarantees that broadcast audiences are presented with a wide perspective on the political arena and the election. The main division in Britain's political communication system – between Britain's partisan press and impartial broadcasting system – is most evident in the presentation of the parties during election campaigns. That said, however, it is still the case that the political parties are not entirely satisfied with their coverage in election news, and often complain to the broadcasters. Moreover, because most political news stems from the parties represented in Parliament, extra-parliamentary forces rarely surface in election broadcasting.

Equal time for the main parties in election broadcast news coverage does not mean that news values are unimportant, and the parties readily complain to the broadcasters about what they occasionally perceive to be unfair treatment in election news. Television reporters and editors are expected to apply news values in selecting election news stories. As a result, in 1983, for example, a great many of the television news stories on the main channels concerned the two-party battle between Labour and the Conservatives. News about the Alliance was often covered separately from the two-party battle (Semetko 1989b). Nevertheless, the near equal ratio (5:5:4) of news time for the Conservatives, Labour and Alliance parties in the 1983 election meant that the third party received much more news coverage than it would have had in a normal non-election period. With the 1987 election, the ratio became 5:5:5. The equal time ratio does not mean that a stopwatch rules, nor does it mean that news should become bland or uninteresting. But it does mean that broadcasters work under certain constraints, and that ordinary news values are sometimes abandoned to ensure the requirements of balance are met.[8]

Net perceptions of bias by audiences for television news during the 1987 campaign were very small, although they pointed toward a slight pro-Conservative, anti-Labour and anti-Alliance bias (Miller et al. 1990, 277). Perceptions of press bias are much greater, however, revealing that electors themselves clearly distrust the newspapers they read regularly (ibid.). In general, then, voters trust broadcasting for impartial information about the parties and the issues.

Election television therefore comes out well when measured against the criterion of serving the needs of British voters. The public service broadcasting ethos that has guided British broadcasting since its inception is largely responsible for this. The unanswered question, however, is whether future developments in British broadcasting will result in a decline of the public service ethos and hence a decline in the quality and quantity of election broadcasting. The government has asked the BBC to consider alternatives to the licence fee as a form of financing, by replacing the licence fee with limited advertising, subscription or sponsorship (Blumler et al. 1986). The government has expressed doubt about the long-term viability of the licence fee, and this will become a major issue for discussion in the mid-1990s. The implications of recent legislation are discussed in a postscript.

The current openness of British election broadcasting to covering a range of political parties and a range of issues is matched, however, by the closed nature of the first-past-the-post electoral system. Britain remains the only democracy in western Europe without some form of proportional representation in national elections. The result is that some parties, particularly the Liberals or the Alliance in the past, are barely represented in the parliamentary debating chamber. Because news about politics comes largely from the activities of the parties in Parliament, the small and third parties so apparent in election news virtually disappear from routine news coverage in non-election periods (Semetko 1989b; Blumler 1984).

The significance of Britain's biased electoral system is not lost on the voters. In the 1987 campaign, voters were asked to assess Britain's electoral system, and "not just the losers criticized the rules" (Miller et al. 1990, 286). Alliance voters were the most critical, but almost one-third of Conservative voters agreed that the "voting system produced an unfair result in terms of seats for each party in Parliament" (ibid.).

POSTSCRIPT: THE FUTURE OF BRITISH BROADCASTING

In the future, Britain will have a more competitive broadcasting environment with a larger number of channels. This may have ramifications for amount and content of election broadcasting in the long term, but should not have an impact in the short term. Specifically, it should not affect the coverage of the 1992 British general election campaign – at least as far as the BBC is concerned.[9]

A more competitive broadcasting environment was one of Mrs. Thatcher's major goals after her re-election in 1983. Mrs. Thatcher appointed the Committee on the Future of Broadcasting, chaired by Sir Alan Peacock, to consider the issue. The report of the Peacock Committee (United Kingdom, Parliament 1986) encouraged a more open and competitive broadcasting system. It recommended that the licence fee not remain the BBC's sole source of funds, and that the BBC derive some part of its revenue from subscription television (perhaps on BBC2) or limited advertising on BBC radio. A government white paper followed, entitled "Broadcasting in the '90s: Competition, Choice and Quality" (United Kingdom, Parliament 1988). The white paper outlined plans for reforming British broadcasting in which the BBC was encouraged to move toward replacing the licence fee eventually with finance through subscription payments and sponsorship (cf. Negrine 1990).

Parliament passed the new *Broadcasting Act* in December 1990. Like the white paper, the Act recommends a more competitive broadcasting environment with more radio and television channels. It mandates the creation of an independent national radio service to compete with the BBC. Prior to this, independent radio had been local only.

In the domain of election broadcasting, the Act continues to prohibit paid political advertising, so there is no change on this point of policy. It sets forth obligations of impartiality in the coverage of political affairs that are likely to mean the same kinds of ground rules for any new channels covering political news in election campaigns.[10]

The Act does not apply directly to the activities of the BBC. The BBC's royal charter is due for renewal in 1996, and in the next few years there should be a major discussion about the future of the licence fee. In the meantime, advertising as a source of revenue for the BBC has been ruled out. Subscription is used in a limited way but at present only for late-night broadcasting. Sponsorship is a form of financing for BBC programming that may be more prominent in the near future.[11]

The major question, however, one that cannot be answered at present, concerns the long-term implications of the more competitive broadcasting environment for election news and current affairs coverage. Will the public service model, which has been the predominant model for BBC and ITV election broadcasting, continue to prevail? Or will the new competitive environment, coupled with changes in the BBC's form of financing, mean a reduction in the amount of resources allocated to election news and current affairs programs? Will the election campaign feature as prominently on the new channels, where ratings and competition for advertising are primary goals? And will the content of election news remain heavily focused on the issues? If the competitive broadcasting environment in the United States is a reliable indicator, British election broadcasting in the year 2000 could be very different from what it is today.

ABBREVIATIONS

c.	chapter
Cm., Cmd., Cmnd.	Command papers (UK)
s(s).	section(s)

NOTES

This study was completed in May 1991.

I am very grateful for the comments of the Commission's anonymous reviewers as well as a number of colleagues who read an earlier version of this study, including: Jay G. Blumler, Margaret Douglas, Bob Franklin, Ralph Negrine, T.J. Nossiter and Jorgen Rasmussen.

1. See the Nuffield College series of studies on British general election campaigns, published by Macmillan. In the past two decades, these have been edited by David Butler and Dennis Kavanagh.

2. In terms of both the sheer amount of campaign news and the amount of issue content in campaign news, British broadcast news programs are far ahead of those in the U.S. and Germany. The comparison with Germany is based on this writer's work in progress on "the influence of parties and the media in the 1990 German national election campaign," which is supported in part by the German Marshall Fund of the United States.

3. According to Margaret Douglas, BBC chief political adviser: "We try to ensure that broadcasts are about 4'40" for a 5 minute slot or 9'40" for a 10 minute slot. We are more concerned that the 5 minute slot does not fall significantly short in time because we want to ensure the broadcasts do not look like advertisements." Correspondence with this writer, 14 May 1991.

4. However, according to Jorgen Rasmussen, "any candidate can participate in a public affairs program as a representative of his or her party to discuss something like education without any of the other candidates in that constituency having to be invited." Correspondence with the author, 22 May 1991.

5. This section draws extensively on chapter 5 of Semetko (1987).

6. The Spearman's Rhos rank-order correlation coefficients between party and television news agendas in Britain range from .38 to .83 (a perfect correlation would be 1.0), whereas those in the U.S. range from .14 to .37.

7. See Holli A. Semetko, "The Role and Influence of the Media in the 1991 British General Election Campaign," an unpublished grant proposal that outlines such a research project. The project involves collaboration with T.J. Nossiter of the London School of Economics and Political Science and Anthony Heath, Roger Jowell and John Curtice, directors of the British General Election Study.

8. One BBC news staffer, for example, commented that "news values *are* the basis for reporting the election in television. But – and this is our compromise – if we are using recorded extracts of speeches by politicians in television news bulletins, then we say we must achieve a fair balance between the political parties" (Blumler 1990, 16).

9. Telephone interview with Margaret Douglas, BBC chief political adviser, BBC Broadcasting House, 20 March 1991.

10. Ibid.

11. Ibid.

REFERENCES

Blumler, Jay G. 1984. "The Sound of Parliament." *Parliamentary Affairs* 37 (3): 250–66.

––––––. 1990. "Television and Politics: The British Public Service Model." Paper presented at the Aspen Institute Conference on Television Coverage and Campaigns: Models and Options for the U.S.-USSR Commission on Television Policy.

Blumler, Jay G., Malcolm Brynin and T.J. Nossiter. 1986. "Broadcasting Finance and Programme Quality: An International Review." *European Journal of Communication* 1 (3): 343–64.

Blumler, Jay G., Bob Franklin, David Mercer and Brian Tutt. 1990. "Monitoring the Public Experiment in Televising the Commons: The Final Report." In *First Report of the Select Committee on Televising of Proceedings Session 1989–90.* Cm. 265-1.

Blumler, Jay G., and Michael Gurevitch. 1982. "The Political Effects of Mass Communication." In *Culture, Society and the Media,* ed. Michael Gurevitch, Tony Bennett, James Curran and Janet Woollacott. London: Methuen.

Blumler, Jay G., Michael Gurevitch and T.J. Nossiter. 1989. "The Earnest vs. the Determined: Election Newsmaking at the BBC." In *Political Communications: The General Election Campaign of 1987,* ed. Ivor Crewe and Martin Harrop. Cambridge: Cambridge University Press.

Blumler, Jay G., and Jack M. McLeod. 1974. "Communication and Voter Turnout in Britain." In *Sociological Theory and Survey Research: Institutional Change and Social Policy in Great Britain,* ed. T. Leggatt. Beverly Hills: Sage Publications.

Blumler, Jay G., and Denis McQuail. 1968. *Television in Politics: Its Uses and Influence.* London: Faber and Faber.

Blumler, Jay G., and Holli A. Semetko. 1987. "Communication and Legislative Campaigns in a Unitary Parliamentary Democracy: The Case of Britain." *Legislative Studies Quarterly* 12 (3): 415–43.

Briggs, Asa. 1979. *Governing the BBC.* London: BBC Publications.

British Broadcasting Corporation. 1987. *Fairness and Impartiality in Political Broadcasting.* London: BBC Publications.

Burns, Tom. 1977. *The BBC: Public Institution and Private World.* London: Macmillan.

Butler, David, and Dennis Kavanagh. 1988. *The British General Election of 1987.* London: Macmillan.

AUGUSTANA UNIVERSITY COLLEGE
LIBRARY

Crewe, Ivor. 1982. "Is Britain's Two-Party System Really about to Crumble?" *Electoral Studies* 1 (3): 275–313.

———. 1983. "The Electorate: Partisan Dealignment Ten Years On." *West European Politics* 6 (4): 183–215.

———. 1986. "Saturation Polling, the Media and the 1983 Election." In *Political Communications: The General Election Campaign of 1983*, ed. Ivor Crewe and Martin Harrop. Cambridge: Cambridge University Press.

Denver, David. 1983. "The SDP–Liberal Alliance: The End of the Two-Party System?" *West European Politics* 6 (4): 75–102.

Drucker, Henry M., ed. 1979. *Multi-Party Britain*. London: Macmillan.

Dunleavy, Patrick, and Christopher T. Husbands. 1985. *British Democracy at the Crossroads: Voting and Party Competition in the 1980s*. London: Allen and Unwin.

Dutton, William, Jay G. Blumler and Kenneth L. Kraemer. 1987. *Wired Cities: Shaping the Future of Communications*. Boston: G.K. Hall.

Franklin, Bob. 1986. "A Leap in the Dark: MPs Objections to Televising Parliament." *Parliamentary Affairs* 39 (2): 284–97.

———. 1989. "Televising Legislatures: The British and American Experience." *Parliamentary Affairs*. 42 (4): 485–503.

———, ed. In press. *Televising Democracies*. London: Routledge.

Franklin, Mark N. 1985. *The Decline of Class Voting in Britain: Changes in the Basis of Electoral Choice, 1964–1983*. Oxford: Clarendon Press.

Harrison, Martin. 1984. "Broadcasting." In David Butler and Dennis Kavanagh, *The British General Election of 1983*. London: Macmillan.

Harrop, Martin. 1984. "The Press." In David Butler and Dennis Kavanagh, *The British General Election of 1983*. London: Macmillan.

———. 1988. "The Press." In David Butler and Dennis Kavanagh, *The British General Election of 1987*. London: Macmillan.

Heath, Anthony, Roger Jowell and John Curtice. 1985. *How Britain Votes*. London: Pergamon.

———. 1987. "Trendless Fluctuation: A Reply to Crewe." *Political Studies* 35 (2): 256–77.

Himmelweit, Hilde T., Patrick Humphreys, Marianne Jaeger and Michael Katz. 1981. *How Voters Decide: A Longitudinal Study of Political Attitudes and Voting Extending Over 15 Years*. London: Academic Press.

Kavanagh, Dennis. 1989. "The Timing of Elections: The British Case." In *Political Communications: The General Election Campaign of 1987*, ed. Ivor Crewe and Martin Harrop. Cambridge: Cambridge University Press.

Kennedy, Charles, and C. Culey. In press. "Televising the Commons: A View from the Third Party." In *Televising Democracies*, ed. Bob Franklin. London: Routledge.

McAllister, Ian. 1985. "Campaign Activities and Electoral Outcomes in Britain 1979 and 1983." *Public Opinion Quarterly* 49 (4): 489–503.

May, Annabelle, and Kathryn Rowan. 1982. *Inside Information: British Government and the Media*. London: Constable.

Miller, William L. 1978. "Social Class and Party Choice in England: A New Analysis." *British Journal of Political Science* 8 (3): 257–84.

Miller, William L., Harold D. Clarke, Martin Harrop, Lawrence Leduc and Paul F. Whiteley. 1990. *How Voters Change: The 1987 British Election Campaign in Perspective*. Oxford: Clarendon Press.

Negrine, Ralph. 1990. *Politics and the Mass Media in Britain*. London: Routledge.

Norpoth, Helmut. 1987. "Guns and Butter and Government Popularity in Britain." *American Political Science Review* 81:949–59.

———. Forthcoming. *Confidence Regained: Economics, Mrs. Thatcher and the British Voter*. Ann Arbor: University of Michigan Press.

Norris, Pippa. 1989. "The Emergence of Polls of Marginals in the 1987 Election: Their Role and Record." In *Political Communications: The General Election Campaign of 1987*, ed. Ivor Crewe and Martin Harrop. Cambridge: Cambridge University Press.

Owen v. Broadcasting Complaints Commission (BCC), [1985] 2 All E.R. 522.

Pinto-Duschinsky, Michael. 1989. "Financing the British General Election of 1987." In *Political Communications: The General Election Campaign of 1987*, ed. Ivor Crewe and Martin Harrop. Cambridge: Cambridge University Press.

Rasmussen, Jorgen. 1983. "How Remarkable Was 1983? An American Perspective on the British General Election." *Parliamentary Affairs* 36 (4): 371–88.

Rose, Richard, and Ian McAllister. 1986. *Voters Begin to Choose: From Closed-Class to Open Elections in Britain*. Beverly Hills: Sage Publications.

Sarlvik, Bo, and Ivor Crewe. 1983. *Decade of Dealignment: The Conservative Victory of 1979 and Electoral Trends in the 1970s*. Cambridge: Cambridge University Press.

Schlesinger, Philip. 1974. *Putting "Reality" Together*. London: Constable.

Semetko, Holli A. 1987. "Political Communications and Party Development: The British Social Democratic Party." Ph.D. diss., University of London, London School of Economics & Political Science, Department of Politics.

———. 1989a. "Images of Britain's Changing Party System: A Study of Television News Coverage of the 1983 and 1987 General Election Campaigns." Paper presented at the annual meeting of the American Political Science Association. Atlanta.

———. 1989b. "Television News and the 'Third Force' in British Politics: A Case Study of Election Communication." *European Journal of Communication* 4 (4): 453–81.

Semetko, Holli A., Jay G. Blumler, Michael Gurevitch and David H. Weaver. 1991. *The Formation of Campaign Agendas: A Comparative Analysis of Party and Media Roles in Recent American and British Elections.* Hillsdale: Lawrence Erlbaum.

Seymour-Ure, Colin. 1974. *The Political Impact of the Mass Media.* London: Constable.

Smith, Anthony. 1979. *Television and Political Life: A Study of Six European Countries.* London: Macmillan.

Tracey, Michael. 1978. *The Production of Political Television.* London: Routledge and Kegan Paul.

Trenaman, Joseph, and Denis McQuail. 1961. *Television and the Political Image: A Study of the Impact of Television in the 1959 General Election.* London: Methuen.

United Kingdom. *Broadcasting Act 1990,* 1990, c. 42.

———. *Independent Broadcasting Act 1973,* 1973, c. 19.

———. *Representation of the People Act 1983,* 1983, c. 2, s. 93.

———. *Television Act 1964,* 1964, c. 21.

United Kingdom. Parliament. 1923. *Report of the Broadcasting Committee.* Cmd. 1951.

———. 1926. *Report of the Broadcasting Committee.* Cmd. 2599.

———. 1934. *Report of the Broadcasting Committee.* Cmd. 5091.

———. 1962. *Report of the Committee on Broadcasting, 1960.* Cmnd. 1753.

———. 1977. *Report of the Committee on the Future of Broadcasting.* Cmnd. 6753.

———. 1986. *Report of the Committee on the Future of Broadcasting.* Cmnd. 9824.

———. 1988. *Broadcasting in the '90s: Competition, Choice and Quality. The Government's Plans for Broadcasting Legislation.* Cm. 517.

Whiteley, Paul. 1986. "The Accuracy and Influence of the Polls in the 1983 General Election." In *Political Communications: The General Election Campaign of 1983,* ed. Ivor Crewe and Martin Harrop. Cambridge: Cambridge University Press.

Wober, Mallory, and B. Svennevig. 1981. *Viewers' Responses to Party Election Broadcasts.* London: Independent Broadcasting Authority.

3

MASS MEDIA AND ELECTION CAMPAIGNS IN GERMANY

Klaus Schoenbach

Due to the introduction of commercial radio and television in 1983 and to German unification in 1990, Germany's media system has changed considerably. These changes have also transformed the opportunities for parties, politicians and the electorate to use press, radio and television in election campaigns.

The focus of this study will be on the relationships in Germany between politics and the media, particularly television. For this purpose, peculiarities of the German voting and media systems will be outlined first. The way in which the audience both evaluates and uses media campaign information will be another major concern. The study concludes by summing up what we know about media effects on voters' political knowledge, attitudes and behaviour.

THE GERMAN ELECTION SYSTEM AND ITS VOTERS

Germans can vote in legislative elections at up to five levels, differing from state to state[1] (Woyke and Steffens 1984). The frequency of elections varies from four to five years. In national (Bundestag) elections, most statewide (Landtag) and the European elections, a voting system of "personalized proportionality" applies. Voters must choose both a local candidate and a party list for the state.[2] The number of votes for the rank-ordered party list determines the size of the parliamentary party and how many persons from the list obtain seats. Only the composition of the parliamentary parties is to some (usually small) extent determined by which local candidates the voters prefer.[3]

Ticket splitting – that is, voting for a specific party list and for a local candidate of a different party – is still practised only by a minority of voters in Germany, but has become increasingly popular. Some industrious and popular local candidates (including cabinet members) often get a few percentage points more than their party. But this difference has hardly ever been very dramatic, a fact that may be both a consequence of, and a reason for, the fairly uninspired campaigns of most local candidates. There is one exception to this rule: small parties, whose local candidates are never elected directly, sometimes ask their supporters to vote for their party list, but also to select a local candidate of a larger party with which the party wants to form a coalition. In the federal elections of 1987, for example, this strategy proved successful for the Free Democrats (FDP), who won only about 5 percent of the local-candidate votes but more than 9 percent of those for the party list, and therefore obtained 46 seats out of the then 497 in the Bundestag.[4]

The holders of the top executive positions in the Federal Republic – the chancellor, the state prime ministers, and most of the mayors – are not determined by the people directly but by the prevailing majority in the national, state or community Parliaments. In other words, in order to see specific persons elected, Germans have to vote for the parties or coalition partners supporting them.

Composing lists and selecting candidates is the job of parties alone, at least in principle. On the other hand, state and federal candidates are not selected in "smoke-filled back rooms." The media are full of speculations about whom a party might nominate for what important office. Parties themselves discuss candidates fairly openly. For candidates seeking positions such as the chancellorship, personal standing in the media certainly has some influence on nomination.

None of the above applied to East Germany before 1990. It was a tightly controlled, communist country without free elections. In the process of unification, it has step by step adopted the procedures employed in the former West German state.

Election turnout in Germany is traditionally high: up to 92 percent of the electorate in West Germany have voted in national elections, though in the Bundestag elections of 1987 and 1990 the turnout was considerably lower (84 and 78 percent, respectively). In elections of the "second rank" – those on the European, state or local level – fewer voters usually show up at the voting booth. But even on these occasions, turnout rates rarely drop under 60 percent. In former times almost 100 percent turned out to vote in the German Democratic Republic. There, however, everyone was *forced* to cast a vote.

THE GERMAN MEDIA SYSTEM

Until the end of 1983 there was a strict division between West Germany's private and public media systems. Newspapers and magazines were, and still are, owned and operated by private individuals or companies; all radio and television stations were publicly controlled, nonprofit corporations, with their transmitters operated by the Federal Postal Service. Some of them are commercial services now. In East Germany, all the media were under the tight control of the communist government up to 1989.

The Print Media

In 1949, after a four-year period of restricted licensing by the Western Allies, virtually anyone could establish a newspaper or magazine in West Germany. Freedom of the press was guaranteed by Article Five of the 1949 West German constitution, and only certain libel laws applied. Since then, the print media have been run both privately by individuals or companies and, increasingly, as commercial ventures. More and more, advertising has become the most important source of financial support; in recent years, more than two-thirds of the newspapers' revenues have come from advertising.

Only a few years after the print-media market had been opened again, the concentration of the press started. Currently there are 119 daily newspapers in West Germany, down from 225 in 1954. Almost half (49 percent) of the counties and larger cities (containing 36 percent of the West German population) have only one local newspaper. In only 10 percent of the counties and cities are there more than two local newspapers available (Schuetz 1989).

However, newspapers have diversified by offering "sublocal" editions directed toward single suburbs or areas within counties. These geographically restricted editions either supplement or completely replace the traditional local sections of the city papers. Accordingly, in spite of press concentration, the number of editions of all newspapers differing by at least one page decreased only from 1 500 in 1954 to 1 344 in 1989. Simultaneously, newspaper circulation has grown considerably – from 13 million in 1954 to 20 million in 1989 (Schuetz 1989).[5]

Five daily newspapers in West Germany (*Frankfurter Allgemeine, Die Welt, Handelsblatt, Taz, Bild*) are nationally distributed and widely available. The two former, plus two other more regional organs (*Frankfurter Rundschau, Sueddeutsche Zeitung*), are "prestigious newspapers." *Der Spiegel* is Germany's weekly news magazine, fairly similar to *Time* and *Newsweek*. Three national weekly newspapers (*Die Zeit, Deutsches Allgemeines Sonntagsblatt, Rheinischer Merkur*) are known for their political analyses. One of the illustrated weekly magazines, *Stern* (somewhat similar to *Life*), also contains some political coverage.

Among the owners of newspapers and magazines in West Germany, political parties play only a peripheral role; practically none of the 119 different newspapers in West Germany are under the economic control of a party. That does not mean, however, that print media are completely neutral in political terms. Many of them lean more or less openly or are perceived to lean toward a specific political party or at least a political ideology, such as free enterprise or the social responsibility of the state. The vast majority of the West German newspapers support conservative views – particularly as far as economic issues are concerned.

Since the opening of the wall in 1989, the East German print-media landscape has been changing dramatically. More and more it resembles that in Western Germany: state control has ceased completely, party-owned newspapers have been sold or handed over to West German commercial companies, and new papers of all sorts have been founded. How many newspapers there are at present can only be estimated – probably about 80. New outlets, however, are having difficulties. There is an obvious trend toward concentration of the former regional newspapers.

The Electronic Media

After the Second World War, the Western Allies in their respective zones tried to prevent a revival of the centralized control over national broadcasting that the Nazis had perfected. Accordingly, the new constitution of West Germany, reconfirmed by several constitutional court decisions, gave jurisdiction over radio and television to the states rather than to the federal government. The British public service model most influenced the system that finally emerged when the Western powers withdrew (Head 1985, 151 ff.). Nine broadcasting stations were in operation until 1983 and all were confined to either a specific state, a large area within a state or a combination of states, still depending on how the Western Allies defined their zones in 1945. These stations usually broadcast up to four different radio services or channels each.

Only by means of interstate treaties did the German broadcasting corporations become national in scope. Thus in 1954 the first German television channel (incorporated as Arbeitsgemeinschaft der Rundfunkanstalten Deutschlands, or ARD) started as a joint enterprise of all the state radio services. These services contribute programs to the national network in amounts proportional to their respective financial standing. In 1963 a second television channel (Zweites Deutsches Fernsehen, ZDF) was added – a new corporation, but again one based on a treaty among the West German states. Finally, in 1965, West German stations (some of them independently) began to broadcast on a third channel in five different regions.

Until 1983, therefore, the average West German had a choice of three or four television channels. The first – national – channel (ARD) broadcast contributions from the state services; the second (ZDF) produced programs in its own centralized facilities and transmitted them nationwide; and lastly, one or two regional channels were provided by local state broadcasting stations.

These services were and still are all publicly controlled. The nine state broadcasting organizations and the ZDF vary somewhat from one to the other, but each has a broadcasting council or board of trustees to set general policy, an administrative council to supervise operations, and a director-general to serve as chief executive officer (Head 1985, 168). State laws specify how to achieve representativeness in the broadcasting council. Some of its members come from the state Parliaments and reflect the complexion of political powers there. The majority of council members are appointed by recognized interest groups such as youth organizations, women, workers, employers or churches. Traditionally, and sadly, however, the representatives of interest groups align themselves in many council decisions according to their *party* affiliations or sympathies.

Public radio and television in West Germany are mainly funded by licence fees. Every household running a radio or a television set pays a monthly fee of about Cdn.$14. Only about 20 percent of the revenues of the first national television channel and roughly 40 percent of the second channel (up to the end of 1990 the only public channel for nationwide TV advertising) come from commercials. This proportion is so low because laws have restricted the total amount (20 minutes daily per channel) and the scheduling of advertising (not after 8:00 PM and never on Sundays) to protect newspapers and magazines from losing too many ads to the electronic media.

In early 1984, the first commercial radio and television stations were established, funded by advertising alone and supposed to exist side by side with the old publicly controlled stations. Virtually all the new radio channels are confined to specific local or regional areas within the country. For television, the situation is different: only *national* TV networks were added to the broadcast offering in Germany. Four of them are German-based commercial organizations: RTLplus, SAT.1, Pro7 and Tele 5. Two – 3SAT and 1plus – are derivatives of the public services, for the most part dedicated to information and serious culture. At first the new channels, together with some foreign transmissions, such as MTV or Super Channel, were only distributed via cable. Now more and more households can get the German commercial ones via the airwaves. In early 1991, 66 percent of West German households received the signals from RTLplus, 62 percent from SAT.1, 27 percent from Pro7 and about 30 percent from Tele 5.

As far as supervision goes, the formal differences between the old and new systems are not significant: West German broadcasting laws have been designed to secure pluralism and objectivity by regulating the new stations in the same way as the old ones; therefore, new services are controlled by state broadcasting authorities (Landesrundfunkanstalten) with councils similar in composition to those already in operation. Their power, however, is significantly weaker than in the case of the public service channels, for two reasons. First of all, the Landesrundfunkanstalten are less "close" to the private stations because they have to supervise all the commercial channels within a state (and that can be many). Secondly, as commercial corporations do not depend on licence fees, the party members in the Landesrundfunkanstalten cannot threaten to keep licence fees down. For public stations this power is very important; the state governments have to approve any increase in licence fees approximately every four years, so they and their parties can put public stations under pressure.

German broadcasting is obliged by state laws and constitutional court decisions to be an instrument of information, to help its audience with the formation of opinion, to contribute to education and to offer entertainment. The entertainment portion of the services has certainly increased in the last decade. The new channels depend on advertising, and thus on ratings, much more than the old ones funded mainly by licence fees. Consequently, the constitutional court of the Federal Republic allowed them to be less "complete" in their information and educational offering than the public TV and radio services. By way of responding to their new competition, though, the old services have also raised the share of entertainment in their programming. It now takes up to 60 percent of public television.

In eastern Germany, the same "dual" broadcast system is emerging: the old central TV (two-channel) and radio (four-channel) systems have been restructured according to the organization of the former GDR into new Laender (states). The old West German "nationwide" channels (widespread in the east even before 1989) can now be received officially and – at least in principle – everywhere. And the first licences for commercial radio were issued in 1990.

ELECTION CAMPAIGN CHANNELS

On the state and national levels, German voting procedures have important consequences for the way in which the mass media are used for election campaigns; the successful marketing of persons, for instance, is often not the sole task. In many elections, the images of the candidate for highest office, such as the chancellorship, and that of his or her party have been very different; sometimes the person was highly respected but the party was not, and vice versa. This poses problems for campaign managers. They must not only attract voters who support their candidates, but must also win votes for the party list from those who do not approve of the candidates. The first goal suggests a candidate-centred appeal, the second a party-centred one. Most of the time campaigners make compromises, although in national and state elections, personal characteristics of the top candidates have become increasingly important.

This mild type of candidate centrism, however, is usually not applied to local candidates in national, state and even community races, who are often seen as mere supporters of a leading figure. The German state and national election system lends itself particularly to a campaign structure organized from the top down; the outcome for the party list and thus for the principal candidate is accordingly the most crucial goal.

Parties in Germany use a wide range of communication channels in election campaigns. Of course, television advertising plays an important part; but the lack of local television means that this role still is important only at the state and national levels. During national and state election campaigns, all competing political parties have the right to free air time to broadcast party commercials on public radio and television. No additional ads may be purchased, though. Those commercials are usually scheduled immediately before or after prime-time news shows. Four restrictions have been applied to this privilege in public broadcasting (Grundsaetze 1983):

1. Parties must supply the commercials themselves. Public broadcasting stations are not allowed to assist parties in producing the ads. On the other hand, the channels are entitled to reject commercials, but only if they contain material deemed criminal or unconstitutional, such as texts propagating violence or racial discrimination. As far as I know, this has never happened.
2. Commercials may be broadcast only during the "hot" phase of the election; in general this is three to six weeks before election day. The beginning of this phase is determined by an agreement between parties and broadcasting corporations.
3. The television ads must not exceed two and a half minutes. Consequently, unlike similar transmissions in other European countries such as Britain, Denmark or the Netherlands, party broadcasts are often highly professional commercials of the "Coke is it" type: fast-paced cuts, suggestive music, colours, and

slogan-like wording. Deviations from this pattern occur among smaller parties, mainly due to the lack of financing for professionally produced commercials.

4. Each party running in the election is granted at least one commercial spot. Additional spots are determined by the parties' level of representation in the relevant Parliament. The number of extra spots is very roughly proportional to the number of seats the party holds. For example, in the Bundestag election campaign of 1983, the Christian Democrats (CDU) and the Social Democrats (SPD) were allowed to broadcast nine spots each. Their respective shares of the number of votes in the previous national election had been 34 percent and 43 percent. The Free Democratic Party (11 percent of the 1980 vote) and the Bavarian Christian Social Union (10 percent) got five commercials each, the Green Party had four and all the others parties had two each.[6]

Similar rules apply to public radio.

Since 1987, though there has been some controversy on the subject, parties have been allowed to buy advertising time on commercial TV and radio stations. They still are somewhat reluctant to pay for air time, however, although they are charged only the cost price. For example, only the Christian Democrats (CDU) purchased time for running commercials on RTLplus in 1990. Again, there are constraints on the format of the ads and their distribution. For the 1990 Bundestag campaign on RTLplus and SAT.1 – the most important and interesting stations for paid advertising – the following rules applied:

- The parties with the most seats in the Parliament, SPD and CDU, were allowed to buy air time up to a total of 25 minutes each; the Christian Social Union (CSU) and the Free Democratic Party (FDP), as well as the Green Party, were allotted 12.5 minutes each. All other parties would have received only up to five minutes each.
- The spots were supposed to be produced by the parties and to last for 30 to 90 seconds.
- The time period in which RTLplus and SAT.1 would transmit the commercials was determined to be the month before election day.
- The two stations explicitly refused to be responsible for false statements in the ads and their possible legal consequences.
- Parties had no say on the placement of their ads in the program schedule, except for a choice between weekends and weekdays. RTLplus and SAT.1 promised not to broadcast more than two different spots in a row and to place them only before or after programs (no program interruption by political commercials).

The director-general of the Landesanstalt fuer das Rundfunkwesen (the state broadcasting council) in Schleswig-Holstein suggested that in future almost all the restrictions in effect for the 1990 Bundestag election should be dropped. Parties should be allowed to buy as much air time as they wanted to, if their commercials were broadcast separately from those of other organizations and within a specified time period before election day (Direktor der Unabhaengigen Landesanstalt fuer das Rundfunkwesen Schleswig-Holstein 1990).

Because of German political traditions and the former restrictions on television advertising, political parties extensively use other ways of presenting themselves to the public. One way is to advertise in the print media. There are almost no restrictions there, although some newspapers and magazines occasionally refuse to print specific ads or those for specific parties; for example, extremely leftist or rightist ones, and once in a while even spots for the SPD or Green Party. In 1980, for example, the CDU/CSU spent 20 percent of all their campaign money on print ads, compared with 35 percent for the FDP.[7]

A second and still important way of presenting party messages is to send flyers and brochures directly to potential voters' homes, delivered by mail or by party workers. Sometimes weekly newspapers, written by party activists or affiliates, are also distributed to spread the party's message.

A third and again very significant advertising instrument is the use of posters and billboards. During the "hot" phases of election campaigns, densely populated Germany is covered with posters of candidates and parties. The Free Democrats, for instance, claim to have found that the optimal number is 800 posters per 100 000 citizens (Schroeder 1983, 159), and therefore spent almost half of their 1980 budget (46 percent) on posters and other printed material. Other parties spent 20 to 28 percent.

All parties set up information desks in market-places, shopping malls and pedestrian zones, where material is distributed or politicians are available for discussions. Rallies are of some significance, too. In national elections, the leading politicians try to fill market-places and even soccer stadiums for political rallies. From 5 to 17 percent of the parties' campaign money was used for this purpose in 1980. Finally, smaller parties in particular rely heavily on their members as party workers. The Free Democratic Party, for instance, spent one-third of its budget for the 1980 Bundestag election on motivating its members to persuade other people to vote for the FDP (Schroeder 1983, 158).

Except for local elections, however, personal contact with local candidates, or at least encounters with their local campaigns, is neither common nor very important to voters. Although there is no survey evidence available, everyday experience suggests that most voters do not even know the names of their local candidates or of their representatives in state or national Parliaments.

The parties' presentation of themselves within the regular coverage of the mass media has become increasingly popular. Aside from the advantage that it is inexpensive, regular coverage is a means of disseminating information and propaganda that profits from the credibility media coverage has when compared to advertising.

As in other Western societies, one way for politicians to achieve more frequent coverage is to use journalistic news values or even to design "pseudo-events" which serve journalists' needs (Boorstin 1963; Radunski 1980). These include rallies, statements about important issues, press conferences, journeys to foreign countries and the like. Some media in the Federal Republic even facilitate politicians' attempts to obtain frequent and positive coverage. In national elections, public television stations broadcast a series of debates among the top candidates and other politicians, for which journalists often only supply the cues. Similarly, in state elections, the television channel of the state in question offers this opportunity to the leading candidates of the region. Some newspapers allot political parties a certain amount of space to be filled with information of the parties' choosing (see Bauer 1989). Explicit endorsements by the mass media, however, are somewhat looked down upon in Germany. Even the most politically outspoken newspapers would not directly ask their readers to vote for specific parties or candidates.

Politicians have often used to their own advantage the electronic media's legal obligation to provide their audience with politically balanced coverage. Radio and television have been pressured many times by party managers and candidates, complaining that they or their parties were not covered frequently or positively enough. As both the laws and the respective court decisions are not particularly clear as to what "balance" really means, only practice teaches what TV and radio are supposed to do. Widely accepted now is a balance model that refers to the time devoted to a party and its politicians in the total programming of a station instead of in every single program. Parties often count the seconds of their coverage to make sure that their time-share is not smaller than that of their opponents. Parties have even complained about biased entertainment programs. "Showmasters" were accused of partiality. As a consequence, quiz shows, for example, stopped inviting prominent politicians six weeks before any election.

Another way to encourage frequent and positive coverage is confined to *public* broadcasting and apparently unique to German television and radio: the parties control the hiring of TV and radio managers and journalists. Many top positions in German broadcasting corporations are filled according to a system of party affiliation. In practice, that means that if one important post is occupied by a Christian Democrat or by someone with at least some sympathy for that party, the next comparable vacancy must eventually be filled by a Social Democrat. This system has been increasingly perfected in the publicly controlled stations: by 1972 already 50 percent of all the top managers in German radio and TV stations were party members. By 1981 this proportion had increased slightly to 54 percent, and this trend is expected to continue in the 1990s. Party affiliation has become more and more important, even for reporters and editors in public broadcasting. During the same period of time, party membership in the printed press decreased, from 23 percent in 1972 to 14 percent in 1981 (Hoffmann-Lange and Schoenbach 1979, 59; Kutteroff 1982).

The two other ways of getting positive coverage may look surprising to those unfamiliar with the German system, but party sympathy is, as described above, also a significant structuring element in the broadcasting councils. As a result, West German television journalists may have become more afraid of political pressure and may more frequently give in to it than do their colleagues in other countries. In a 1979 survey, television journalists in the nine countries of the European Community were asked whether they should "have any role to play in defining the issues" of the first direct elections to the European Parliament, or whether that should be up to the parties alone. Of the German respondents, 57 percent denied that they had any share of that task, presumably due to fears of political retribution rather than to any sense of laissez-faire journalism; this proportion was second only to the Belgians' response (Noël-Aranda 1982).

Recently, the amount of TV time devoted to the presentation of politicians via personal appearances seems to have dropped, however, both in the news and in other information programs. Public TV channels now increasingly try to keep politicians from using TV only as a platform. Although the fear of party pressure certainly still exists, public television managers are beginning to be even more afraid of losing ground in their new, competitive situation if they present too many dull and uninformative political programs.

THE CONTENT OF MASS MEDIA IN ELECTION CAMPAIGNS
Our body of knowledge about the mass media's coverage of German election campaigns remains limited. Only a few scattered case studies have tried to shed some light on how issues and personalities are

covered by newspapers, magazines, television and radio in specific elections. Two general points emerge from a review of the literature.

First, at least until recently, viewers of the two German national public television channels could hardly avoid political information during the "hot" phase of a Bundestag election campaign. In 1980, during the last four weeks of the campaign, more than 80 hours of political programs of all sorts were broadcast by the two services, averaging almost three hours of political information a day (Feist and Liepelt 1982, 621). Fourteen percent of television prime-time news was devoted directly to the campaign. In nontabloid daily newspapers an average of 21 percent of the front-page space contained campaign-related reports (Weiss 1982, 268). In tabloids, this proportion is considerably lower (see also Buss et al. 1984).

Second, at first sight, incumbents in West Germany seem to receive more coverage than their opponents. Kaltefleiter and Johann (1971) found that the federal government was covered twice as much in the West German television news (in terms of time devoted to its politicians and actions) as the opposition. The study was conducted in 1970, a year when there was no election. Results may be different during election campaigns, however: Kepplinger's (1982) study of television coverage of the 1976 Bundestag campaign reveals only a slight preponderance of the incumbent Bundestag coalition (for 1980 see Weiss 1982, 269). Its politicians were shown in 1 679 shots on televised political magazine programs, only a little more prominently than those of the Christian Democratic opposition (1 436 shots). German politicians of the coalition and the opposition were depicted similarly in terms of camera angles, except for the two candidates for the chancellorship: Kepplinger (1982) found that the incumbent, Helmut Schmidt, was filmed a little more advantageously than his challenger, Helmut Kohl.

Krueger's (1978) results show a somewhat different picture in the printed press. At least during the Bundestag election campaign of 1976 there was no "chancellor bonus" – that is, Helmut Schmidt was not covered more positively than other candidates in the West German prestige newspapers *Frankfurter Allgemeine, Die Welt, Sueddeutsche Zeitung* and *Frankfurter Rundschau*. In 1980, critical remarks about the incumbent coalition even prevailed in two of the four newspapers as well as in prime-time news (Weiss 1982, 274; Baker and Norpoth 1990), another finding that makes a positively biased evaluation of incumbency doubtful in today's West German media. Schoenbach and Wildenmann (1978) go even further. They state that in the 1976 election, there was no particular correlation between the issues any party tried to propagate and those the prestige newspapers wrote about. The political discussion among electors, however, and the coverage of those newspapers in 1976 did resemble each other to some extent. One might suspect that the content of television and radio rather more closely reflected the party agenda, given the effective ways of party control in these media as described above. In 1987, Mathes and Freisens (1990) found that the incumbent Christian Democrats were successful in getting their issues into the media. A positive *evaluation* of this party did not follow, however.

There is empirical evidence that in German, as in U.S., election campaigns, media coverage often concentrates on the "horse-race" and "hoopla" aspects. The personal characteristics of the leading candidates, the structure and development of the campaign, the parties' chances of winning and so on seem unduly important (see Patterson and McClure 1976, for the United States). Results of a content analysis of reports about the 1986 state election in Lower Saxony show that 34 representatively selected newspapers paid considerable attention to those elements. Also, their coverage was highly event-centred, while political analysis and background reporting did not play a very important role (Schoenbach and Schneider 1987; see also Rust 1984).

EXPOSURE TO THE MEDIA DURING ELECTION CAMPAIGNS

In Germany, 97% of households own at least one television set and at least one radio. However, on an average workday in West Germany, newspapers reach as many members of the adult population (79%) as do television (77%) and radio (77%) (Wild 1990). In 1989, the average West German adult spent 2 hours and 13 minutes of an average workday in front of the television set. In all households with cable TV (roughly 20% of all West German households) this figure was slightly higher: 2 hours and 25 minutes. There, in 1989, 40% of the viewing time was devoted to the new commercial TV channels (Darschin and Frank 1990). The average time spent on listening to the radio is 2 hours and 36 minutes (Wild 1990), and on reading the newspaper about 30 minutes per workday. In eastern Germany, the media reach even more people than in the West: 89% read a newspaper virtually every day in 1990, 91% watched TV and 90% listened to the radio. They also devoted more time to the electronic media: 2 hours and 22 minutes to television, and 3 hours and 6 minutes to radio (Wild 1990).

The numbers of people in West Germany reached by the political coverage of the three mass media differ somewhat from one another: in 1985, 62% of the population 18 years and older got at least some political information from television on an average workday, 54% from newspapers but 73% from radio (Berg and Kiefer 1987).

The extent to which West Germans generally rely on their news media is demonstrated by the following figures: in 1985, 57% would have "greatly" or "very greatly" missed the newspaper had it not been available, 54% the radio and 42% television. The media would have been missed for different reasons, however. The newspaper, for instance, was the local information source for most Germans; its local coverage would have been missed by 37% of the people. Only 2% and 4% of the population respectively would have missed local and area-related reports on television and radio; this was certainly due to the still mainly statewide and national organization of the electronic media in 1985. On the other hand, television's domain was national political coverage: 47% would have missed it greatly for that reason, compared with 38% for radio and 31% for newspapers. Regarding entertainment, 29% of the people would have missed television, 39% their radio and 6% their newspapers (Berg and Kiefer 1987).

Television is still considered to be the most trustworthy source of information in general, but on a fairly low level. In 1985, 27% of Germans agreed that its coverage is true to reality; as many as 25% held this belief about radio coverage and 18% trusted the newspapers. This represents a dramatic loss of trustworthiness by the media in general: the respective figures in 1980 were 41% of the population for TV, 32% for radio and 21% for newspapers (Berg and Kiefer 1987).

Data from the campaign for the first all-German Bundestag election in 1990 show the significant role of television in political campaigns. But they also reveal how important local newspapers and posters were (see table 3.1). These results, by the way, are very similar to those we have found for all the national elections in the last two decades (Schoenbach 1987). "Other TV programs" usually include party leaders' and principal candidates' debates; however, this was not the case in 1990. The "Great Debates" had drawn a large audience in the past. In the federal election of 1972, for example, up to 40% of all TV sets were switched on (Weiss 1976); in 1976, 35% of the electorate watched the top candidates' discussions, at least in part (Baker et al. 1981); in 1980, 68%, and in 1983, 57% of people 18 years and older saw at least a portion of those debates (Baker and Norpoth 1990).

On average, more than a third of those who found at least something about the 1990 election on a medium actually reaching them claimed to have been interested in that information. The relatively few people who either managed to find the fairly limited election coverage in the tabloid *Bild*, or discussed the election with other persons, quite reasonably showed the greatest interest in these election information channels. Party materials, such as posters, TV commercials and

Table 3.1
West German voters' exposure to and interest in campaign media, November 1990
(first all-German Bundestag election, in percentages)

Campaign media	Reached by the medium at all	"Often" finding something about the election in that medium	Reached by the medium and "often" finding something about the election	"Very interested" by what they found about the election
Television news	98	63	63	37
Other TV programs	98	31	31	37
Local newspaper	97	60	61	36
National prestige newspapers	29	13	50	40
Bild (national tabloid)	28	9	34	47
Radio	not asked	26	—	29
Personal conversations	not asked	23	—	55
Posters	not asked	73	—	
Party commercials on TV	98	67	67	14
Advertisements in newspapers or magazines	not asked	49	—	
Leaflets and brochures	not asked	13	—	
N	*(896)*	*(896)*		

Source: ipos, 1990.

so forth, were, however, received without great enthusiasm. These – at first sight fairly encouraging – impressions of voters' attention to the 1990 campaign should be seen in perspective, though. The fairly high penetration of campaign information by no means indicates that Germans are breathlessly following whatever happens in an election campaign. Darkow and Zimmer (1982) demonstrate in their diary survey that for most of the voters, even for those interested in politics, election campaigns are fairly marginal events in their everyday lives.

THE EFFECTS OF THE MASS MEDIA ON ELECTION CAMPAIGNS
Mass communication research in Germany, as virtually everywhere, has abandoned the idea that the only media effect worthy of research is the change of voting preferences. Knowing what is at stake, being able to discuss the campaign issues and having an image of the candidates are some of the media effects studied in recent research. That is

not to say that the media do not influence voting decisions; they may do it in a more subtle, indirect way, as for example in Goldenberg and Traugott's model of electoral success (1984, 154). What are the effects to be found in Germany? The findings are mixed.

In their analysis of four Bundestag elections between 1957 and 1969, Baker and Norpoth (1978) describe strikingly similar patterns. They confirm the classic results of the Lazarsfeld, Berelson and Gaudet (1944) study of the 1940 U.S. presidential election: the use by voters of political information both from the mass media and from personal conversations is highly correlated with voting stability. The strength of partisanship goes a long way toward explaining this relationship; strong partisans are both more likely to be exposed to political information and highly stable in their voting behaviour.

In studies of three national elections in West Germany (1972, 1976, 1980) Elisabeth Noelle-Neumann tried to shed some light on the specific impact of television on voters. In the Bundestag election campaign of 1972, frequent viewers of political information programs on TV obtained an increasingly improved image of Social Democratic politicians (Noelle-Neumann 1980). In 1976, again, those who watched many political programs had different feelings about which party might win the election. More often than other voters, they believed that the incumbent Social-Liberal coalition would win again. Noelle-Neumann suggested that this impression may have furthered the eventual victory of the coalition in 1976 (Noelle-Neumann 1977). Her finding is also confirmed by Feist and Liepelt (1982, 620 ff.), with their data for 1976 and 1980. Noelle-Neumann (1977) assumed that her results were caused by a leftist bias of West German television. In 1980, however, she did not report any particular television effect, due to what she called a "frozen political landscape." The race between the parties had been decided more than a year before the election by the sheer fact that the Christian Democrats had nominated Franz Josef Strauss as their candidate for the chancellorship (Noelle-Neumann 1983). Even among conservative voters, Strauss seemed to have no chance against a more popular politician like Helmut Schmidt.

The picture becomes confusing if one takes another study into account. For the first supranational election in West Germany, that of the European Parliament in 1979, Schoenbach (1983a, 118 ff.) found an effect opposite to that which Noelle-Neumann had discovered for 1976. Media use did not enhance the expectation that the Social Democrats would win. Rather it meant that the Christian Democrats would. Both watching – according to Noelle-Neumann — "leftist" television and reading a left-leaning newspaper were linked to that view.

Feist and Liepelt (1982, 622) have a simple and plausible explanation for their own, Noelle-Neumann's (1977) and Schoenbach's (1983a) results. As a rule, they state, "heavy users" of political information in the mass media know more about political developments. They are informed earlier than other citizens about who is probably going to win an election. They are, for example, confronted more frequently than others with opinion-poll results. In the Bundestag election of 1976, the Social–Liberal coalition, and in the European election of 1979, the Christian Democrats, indeed got the major share of the votes.

Although Noelle-Neumann herself never explicitly demonstrated any impact of television on voting behaviour, her 1976 results in particular were interpreted by some politicians and scholars as proof of the decisive power of television in German election campaigns. Their suspicion led to even closer political control of the public broadcasting organizations.

Other media effects on images and opinions in West German election campaigns may be summarized as follows:

1. Media use evidently leads to greater political knowledge, particularly the use of media with more space and time for thorough information, such as newspapers, magazines and special political programs on television (Schoenbach 1983a, 93 ff., 1983b; Horstmann 1991; Schoenbach and Eichhorn, in press). The types of knowledge investigated so far mostly refer to simple facts, such as the number of seats in Parliament to be elected, the date of the election, recognition of top candidates' names and the like.

2. Schoenbach and Weaver (1985) assume that West German election campaigns cause a "cognitive bonding" effect; voters' attitudes and beliefs become more and more coherent as the campaign progresses. For example, those who regarded European political issues as important during the first European election campaign also were becoming more and more favourable toward European unification and vice versa. This was especially true for those not very interested in the election.

3. Hildebrandt's (1984) analysis of the 1980 Bundestag election reveals that the mass media had "agenda-setting" effects, a finding confirmed by Buss and Ehlers (1982, 251). "Agenda setting" is the notion that mass media have an impact on the topics and issues that voters are concerned about in election campaigns. Hildebrandt's study shows that electorates in counties and cities with more than one newspaper discussed a significantly greater variety of national political issues.

Press and television also changed voters' attention toward

political issues in the European election campaign of 1979. Results were similar to those of U.S. studies (e.g., McCombs 1977) in that long-term effects of the press and of documentaries on television and the short-term impact of television news could be discerned (Schoenbach 1981). For many voters, television news "highlights" issues shortly before election day; parts of the electorate, however, are made familiar with campaign topics, for example by their newspapers, as early as two months ahead of the election. Agenda-setting effects of the press have also been demonstrated for the issues of a municipal election (Schoenbach and Eichhorn, in press). Some evidence of a "priming" effect of issue salience on party sympathy is demonstrated by Kepplinger and Brosius (1990).

4. As already noted, there are clear effects of local newspapers in municipal election campaigns; for example on knowledge about the principal candidates and their perceived prominence, on awareness of issues, but also on party and candidate sympathy. Virtually never, however, was even a great amount of campaign coverage in local newspapers sufficient as a cause of voter behaviour. Almost all newspaper effects needed some sort of specific interest of the readers in local political matters as a "catalyst" (Schoenbach and Baran 1990; Schoenbach and Eichhorn, in press). In other words, a still-popular notion was proven wrong: no one who was not at least somewhat curious about the election campaign was "overwhelmed" by the information surrounding them; they would, in fact, show a gain in knowledge.

5. Surprisingly, German mass media have had no particular influence on the turnout at elections (Schoenbach 1983a, 122ff.; Blumler 1983). Schulz (1981) showed that the voting behaviour of most Germans did not even fluctuate according to their varying attitudes toward what the election was about. Obviously, even today, most Germans regard casting their votes as an undisputed duty, even as a ritual.

There are only a dozen or so empirical studies about media effects on election campaigns in West Germany. Unfortunately, they are scattered over almost two decades and at least three levels of elections. So no single conclusion can be drawn as to which medium has what precise effect on the electorate. It seems that the impact of the mass media, although undoubtedly real, depends heavily on the specific situation of each election. This is not to say, of course, that no patterns of the media's impact on knowledge, attitudes and voting behaviour have been discerned. There clearly needs to be more research.

As far as we can see from the 1990 experience with the first free elections in East Germany, the potential for effects of the media is probably greater than that in the West. Party preferences according to the socio-economic characteristics of the voters have only just begun to emerge, thus making issues and candidates' images, as conveyed by the mass media, more important for the voting decision.

CONCLUSIONS

The German media system has been restructured for more than six years now and the publicly controlled monopoly of the electronic media broken up. We can already both see and expect some major consequences for the role of the mass media in election campaigns.

- There may be more campaign advertising on television and radio. It appears likely that after a slow start, parties will buy more and more commercials as the number of people reached by the new channels increases.
- The electronic media may, moreover, also be used for local campaigns. Today, "localization" is emerging as one of the most important structural changes in the German media system. In southern Germany, more and more local radio stations are operating. Parallel to this process, probably even furthered by it, the concentration of the print media on the localities and neighbourhoods continues.

Regarding consequences for the structure of future German election campaigns we may expect greater specialization of campaign strategies; for instance in distributing different messages to different areas. More local and neighbourhood media mean better chances to reach specific target audiences.

Whether the way in which West German media deal with election campaigns has contributed to issue-oriented election campaigns and to enlightened voting decisions, and whether the media have strengthened democracy as a whole, are questions that are hard to answer. Many critics in Germany fear that the at least partial commercialization of radio and television since 1983 has endangered what they regard as enviably high levels of both political interest and information of the audience.

Certainly there is now a relatively (not necessarily absolutely) smaller quantity of political information on radio and television. The new, more commercially oriented stations transmit more light entertainment, and the old channels, funded mostly by licence fees, are reacting to this competition by offering more movies, shows and music programs. Whether this is a worrisome development, however, as far as the enlightenment and participation of voters is concerned, we do not know. Readership figures show for example, that politically interested people are turning to the élite print media for political information and are relying less on television.

One definitely deplorable feature of the German electronic media system has, however, persisted: party pressure on radio and television. The parties' impact on political TV coverage, in particular, has not necessarily made campaign reporting more exciting or more critical. Admittedly, the parties may have served pluralism in Germany; they may once in a while have kept the electronic media from becoming too partial, but they have also made them overly cautious, even subservient. Fortunately, the parties' power has not been very important in the newly established commercial sector of the electronic media. As a consequence, however, there are signs that the parties are even tightening their grip on the old, public stations.

NOTES

1. In municipal elections, members of the community's council are elected. County council members are chosen simultaneously with local council representatives. On the state level, members of the state Parliament (Landtag) are to be voted for. Every four years there is a national election in which the members of the national Parliament (Bundestag) in Bonn (later on in Berlin) are chosen. In 1979, elections to the European Parliament were added for the first time.

2. Ballots for this purpose contain two columns: on the left, voters find the names of their local candidates running for a seat in Parliament. On the right, next to its local candidate, each party with a statewide list is named.

3. In most cases the local candidates are members of the party list as well. Some parties – for example, the Social Democrats (SPD) – even insist that those who run on a state list must also run as local candidates. Their reasoning is that only candidates willing to campaign in their constituencies also deserve a position on the list, since the list might bring them into Parliament automatically. There are significant regional variations in the importance of list candidacy. For the SPD in Hamburg, for example, the list side is far less important, because the party normally wins most or all of the district contests. But in Bavaria the opposite is true and list placement is crucial.

4. In national and in most state and local elections, a 5 percent threshold applies; that is, only parties that win at least 5 percent of the vote (or succeed in having a certain number of local candidates elected directly – almost never a real alternative) obtain seats in Parliament.

5. "Free papers" or "shoppers" have also become more and more important. As early as 1985, more than 900 of these weekly newspapers, most of them owned by daily newspapers, were published and had a circulation of about 48 million. Free papers in West Germany contain advertising and some entertainment or public service reports. Only a few publish political articles, and these concentrate mainly on community politics.

6. The case of the Green Party was somewhat peculiar. They had not yet been represented in the Bundestag, yet the broadcasting stations agreed they should receive more ads than other small parties because of their importance in the state elections between 1980 and 1983.

7. Next to membership dues and donations, there is another important financial source for election campaigns in Germany: for every vote in a Bundestag or European election, a party receives five German marks from the government to subsidize the expenses of campaigning. Interestingly, campaign spending has dropped somewhat in the last 10 to 15 years. It is particularly noteworthy that second-rank elections, like those for the European Parliament, have been used to refill the parties' coffers.

REFERENCES

Arbeitsgemeinschaft der Rundfunkanstalten Deutschlands. 1990. *ARD-Jahrbuch 90*. Hamburg: Hans-Bredow-Institut.

Baker, Kendall L., and Helmut Norpoth. 1978. "Mass Media and Personal Communication in West Germany: Changing Patterns and Electoral Impact, 1957–1972." Paper presented at annual meeting of the Western Political Science Association, Los Angeles.

———. 1990. "Television Debates and Press Coverage in the 1980 and 1983 West German Elections." In *Germany at the Polls: The Bundestag Elections of the 1980s*, ed. Karl H. Cerny. Durham: Duke University Press.

Baker, Kendall L., Helmut Norpoth and Klaus Schoenbach. 1981. "Fernsehdebatten der Spitzenpolitiker im Bundestagswahlkampf 1972 und 1976." *Publizistik* 26:530–44.

Bauer, Michael. 1989. *Regulierter Journalismus: Spielregeln lokaler Wahlkampfberichterstattung*. Munich and Muelheim: Publicom.

Berg, Klaus, and Marie-Luise Kiefer. 1987. *Massenkommunikation III*. Frankfurt Main: Metzner.

Blumler, Jay G. 1983. "Communication and Turnout." In *Communicating to Voters*, ed. Jay G. Blumler. Beverly Hills: Sage Publications.

Boorstin, Daniel. 1963. *The Image*. New York: Atheneum.

Buss, Michael, and Renate Ehlers. 1982. "Mediennutzung und politische Einstellung im Bundestagswahlkampf 1980." *Media Perspektiven* (4): 237–53.

Buss, Michael, et al. 1984. *Fernsehen und Alltag.* Frankfurt Main: Metzner.

Darkow, Michael, and Karl Zimmer. 1982. "Der Wahlkampf als Alltagsereignis – unbedeutend." *Media Perspektiven* (4): 254–62.

Darschin, Wolfgang, and Bernward Frank. 1990. "Tendenzen im Zuschauerverhalten." *Media Perspektiven* (4): 254–69.

Direktor der Unabhaengigen Landesanstalt fuer das Rundfunkwesen Schleswig-Holstein. 1990. "Die Zulaessigkeit kommerzieller Wahlwerbung der Parteien im privaten Rundfunk." Unpublished manuscript, Bonn.

Feist, Ursula, and Klaus Liepelt. 1982. "Objektiv der Politik oder politische Kamera?" *Media Perspektiven* (10): 619–35.

Goldenberg, Edie N., and Michael W. Traugott. 1984. *Campaigning for Congress.* Washington, DC: Congressional Quarterly Press.

"Grundsaetze der ARD-Rundfunkanstalten sowie des ZDF fuer die Gewaehrung von Sendezeiten an politische Parteien anlaesslich der Bundestagswahl am 6." Maerz 1983. Unpublished manuscript.

Head, Sidney W. 1985. *World Broadcasting Systems.* Belmont: Wadsworth.

Hildebrandt, Joerg. 1984. "Zeitungswettbewerb und Themenvielfalt." Unpublished Master's thesis, University of Munich.

Hoffmann-Lange, Ursula, and Klaus Schoenbach. 1979. "Geschlossene Gesellschaft." In *Angepasste Aussenseiter,* ed. Hans Mathias Kepplinger. Freiburg and Munich: Karl Alber.

Horstmann, Reinhold. 1991. *Medieneinfluesse auf politisches Wissen: Zur Tragfaehigkeit der Wissenskluft-Hypothese.* Wiesbaden: Deutscher Universitaets Verlag.

ipos. 1990. "Ueberblick ueber die Ergebnisse. Wahlpanel 1990. Zweite Welle." Mannheim.

Kaltefleiter, Werner, and Karl P. Johann. 1971. "Chancengleichheit in den Nachrichtensendungen des Deutschen Fernsehens." Unpublished manuscript.

Kepplinger, Hans Mathias. 1982. "Visual Bias in Television Campaign Coverage." *Communication Research* 9:432–46.

Kepplinger, Hans Matthias, and Hans-Bernd Brosius. 1990. "Der Einfluss der Parteibindung und der Fernsehberichterstattung auf die Wahlabsichten der Bevoelkerung." In *Wahlen und Waehler,* ed. Max Kaase and Hans-Dieter Klingemann. Opladen: Westdeutscher Verlag.

Krueger, Udo Michael. 1978. "Publizistisch bedeutsame Tageszeitungen im Bundestagswahlkampf 1976." *Publizistik* 23:32–57.

Kutteroff, Albrecht. 1982. "Problems of Communication and Control in Industrialized Societies: The Media Elites and Their Socio-Political Role in the Federal Republic of Germany." Unpublished manuscript, Mannheim.

Lazarsfeld, Paul F., Bernard Berelson and Hazel Gaudet. 1944. *The People's Choice.* New York: Columbia University Press.

Mathes, Rainer, and Uwe Freisens. 1990. "Kommunikotionsstrategien der Parteien und ihr Erfolg." In *Wahlen und Waehler,* ed. Max Kaase and Hans-Dieter Klingemann. Opladen: Westdeutscher Verlag.

McCombs, Maxwell E. 1977. "Newspapers vs. Television." In *The Emergence of American Political Issues,* ed. Donald L. Shaw and Maxwell E. McCombs. St. Paul: West.

Noël-Aranda, Marie-Claire. 1982. "L'attitude des hommes de TV face à la campagne." In *Television in the European Parliamentary Elections of 1979,* ed. Jay G. Blumler. London: International Institute of Communications.

Noelle-Neumann, Elisabeth. 1977. "Das doppelte Meinungsklima." *Politische Vierteljahresschrift* 18:408–51.

———. 1980. "Wahlentscheidung in der Fernsehdemokratie." Freiburg, Wirzburg: Ploetz.

———. 1983. "Massenmedien und Meinungsklima im Wahlkampf." In *Massenmedien und Wahlen,* ed. Winfried Schulz and Klaus Schoenbach. Munich: Oelschlaeger.

Patterson, Thomas E., and Robert D. McClure. 1976. *The Unseeing Eye.* New York: Putnam.

Radunski, Peter. 1980. *Wahlkaempfe. Moderne Wahlkampffuehrung als politische Kommunikation.* Munich and Vienna: Olzog.

Rust, Holger. 1984. *"Politischer" Journalismus: Landtagswahlkaempfe in regionalen Tageszeitungen.* Tuebingen: Niemeyer.

Schoenbach, Klaus. 1981. "Agenda-Setting im Europawahlkampf 1979." *Media Perspektiven* (7): 537–47.

———. 1983a. *Das unterschaetzte Medium: Politische Wirkungen von Presse und Fernsehen im Vergleich.* Munich: Saur.

———. 1983b. "What and How Voters Learned." In *Communicating to Voters,* ed. Jay G. Blumler. Beverly Hills: Sage Publications.

———. 1987. "The Role of the Mass Media in West German Election Campaigns." *Legislative Studies Quarterly* 12:373–94.

Schoenbach, Klaus, and Stanley J. Baran. 1990. "Mass Media Effects on Political Cognition: How Readers' Images of Journalists Shape Newspaper Impact." In *Mass Communication and Political Information Processing,* ed. Sidney Kraus. Hillsdale: Lawrence Erlbaum Associates.

Schoenbach, Klaus, and Wolfgang Eichhorn. In press. *Zeitungsberichte und Leserinteressen: Medienwirkungen bei Kommunalwahlen und wie sie zustandekommen.*

Schoenbach, Klaus, and Beate Schneider. 1987. "Die Niedersachsenwahl 1986 in den Tageszeitungen der Bundesrepublik Deutschland: Themen, Einfluesse und Konsequenzen." Hanover: Report to the Federal Press and Information Agency.

Schoenbach, Klaus, and David H. Weaver. 1985. "Finding the Unexpected: Cognitive Bonding in a Political Campaign." In *Mass Media and Political Thought,* ed. Sidney Kraus and Richard Perloff. Beverly Hills: Sage Publications.

Schoenbach, Klaus, and Rudolf Wildenmann. 1978. "Election Themes and the Prestige Newspapers." In *Germany at the Polls,* ed. Karl H. Cerny. Washington, DC: American Enterprise Institute for Public Policy Research.

Schroeder, Wolfgang. 1983. "Medien in den Wahlkampfstrategien der F.D.P." In *Massenmedien und Wahlen,* ed. Winfried Schulz and Klaus Schoenbach. Munich: Oelschlaeger.

Schuetz, Walter J. 1989. "Deutsche Tagespresse 1989." *Media Perspektiven* (7): 748–75.

Schulz, Winfried. 1981. "Mobilisierung und Demobilisierung im Europawahlkamf." In *Oeffentliche Meinung und sozialer Wandel,* ed. Horst Baier, Hans Mathias Kepplinger and Kurt Reumann. Opladen: Westdeutscher Verlag.

Weiss, Hans-Juergen. 1976. *Wahlkampf im Fernsehen.* Berlin: Spiess.

———. 1982. "Die Wahlkampfberichterstattung und-kommentierung von Fernsehen und Tagespresse zum Bundestagswahlkampf 1980." *Media Perspektiven* (4): 263–75.

Wild, Christoph. 1990. "Fernseh- und Hoerfunknutzung in der DDR im Fruehjahr 1990." *Media Perspektiven* (9): 558–72.

Woyke, Wichard, and Udo Steffens. 1984. *Stichwort: Wahlen.* Opladen: Leske und Budrich.

4

CAMPAIGN COMMUNICATION IN SCANDINAVIA

Karen Siune

INTRODUCTION

T HE PURPOSE OF this study is to provide a description and critical assessment of campaign communication systems in three Scandinavian countries: Denmark, Norway and Sweden. Although systems in the three countries have many similarities, there are significant differences as well. An examination of the common features and the differences helps to identify some of the central issues in modern campaign communication. These issues and their particular manifestation in the three countries under study here are relevant to any effort at comprehensive electoral reform.

The Scandinavian countries, often just referred to as Scandinavia, are known around the world for a variety of attributes. After their welfare systems, a key attribute is participatory democracy with a high turnout in national elections. Denmark, Norway and Sweden are also known for their highly regulated broadcasting systems, based on public service with a very limited amount of advertising.

This study of campaign communication in Denmark, Norway and Sweden places the emphasis on political parties' access to national broadcasting. In Scandinavia, access to national broadcasting is not something a political party can buy. Equal opportunity for all parties to communicate to the population during a campaign is the normative principle guiding the Scandinavian public service broadcasting institutions. As described in this study, the normative principle has resulted in different practices in the three countries. The Danish system takes the most extreme approach to equal treatment of all parties.

Political Parties' Attitudes to Campaign Communication

As in other industrial democracies, the mass media are perceived as play-ing a central role in the politics of Denmark, Norway and Sweden. The interplay between political parties and the mass media is a very old and ongoing issue for debate in these countries. According to politicians, the mass media are very important in the fight for attention and votes.

Scandinavia has a long-standing tradition of linkages between newspapers and political parties, and for many decades the party press was considered a basic element of Scandinavian democracy. Nowadays, access to television plays a much greater role for politicians. According to interviews with party representatives, politicians are anxious to gain access to television and news programs (their primary target). Politicians are aware of audience resistance to what they perceive as party propaganda. Nevertheless, politicians consider party access to special programs during an election campaign period a necessity for a party, and television the best medium to reach audience members whose interest in politics is low.

Different Types of Elections

The Scandinavian countries have national, municipal and county elec-tions. National elections are held regularly at four-year intervals in Norway and three-year intervals in Sweden. A rule of four years also applies to Denmark, but in practice Danish national elections are held every two to three years. Local media play a much greater role in local elections than in national elections, but are also important in national elections in the campaigns of local candidates and in areas where major social cleavages make local issues important, as is the case in Denmark.

In addition to national, regional and local elections, Denmark, as a member of the European Community, has European elections. Its first direct election to the European Parliament was held in 1979, followed by elections in 1984 and 1989. The results of series of studies of these elections will be referred to below.

In Scandinavia, national parliamentary elections are generally of greater interest to both voters and researchers than elections to the local and county boards. In Denmark, elections to the European Parliament also attract less interest than national elections and, on the basis of turnout, even less than local elections.

The Structure of the Scandinavian Mass Media

In this century, the Scandinavian mass media have developed in three phases relevant to political communication (Siune 1987). In the first phase, partisan newspapers proliferated. In the second, consolidating phase, papers grew in size and decreased in number while professional news criteria began to dominate partisan political communication. Radio and, later, television became the most significant sources of information. In the third phase, the influence of electronic mass media has grown, with satellites, cable, video and local broadcasting breaking the former monopolies.

The constitutions of the Scandinavian countries secure everyone the right to print, but not a right to broadcast, which is strictly regulated by broadcasting acts.[1] A philosophy of public service broadcasting without commercials has been the basis of broadcasting in Norway, Sweden and Denmark, although recent broadcasting acts have allowed the establishment of private local radio and television channels, some of them financed via advertising.

Scandinavia has a long history of private ownership of national and local newspapers with traditional party attachments.[2] These local newspapers have been the primary contact between a party and its supporters. Most of the press and other print media are organized in privately owned stock companies. Some newspapers and publishing houses have a very limited number of stockholders, sometimes private families.

Labour newspapers are owned by trade unions. In Norway, where the local media play the largest role, labour papers are owned by local trade unions and party branches. The labour press is most popular in Norway, with about 20 percent of all newspaper circulation. Its share of total circulation is much lower in Denmark and Sweden.

Traditionally, all political parties had their own newspaper in each region of the country. This system has declined, especially in Denmark, although state support has kept party newspapers alive in the other two countries. The basis for subsidizing the press is the perception that newspapers are of great value to the political system, and the partisan balance of the system is crucial.

Norwegians read a lot of newspapers, each household buying an average of 1.8 papers per day, chiefly by subscription. In contrast, newspaper reading has declined dramatically in Denmark, where newspapers are increasingly sold over the counter, and economic problems have required them to be more market-oriented than party-oriented. Parties are treated according to news criteria, so that the coverage of the party with which the newspaper was associated is hardly distinguishable any more. Although content analyses show significant differences among Danish newspapers, analyses also show that at election time all major parties receive wide coverage in all newspapers. Small parties and new parties do not receive special treatment unless they are perceived as a real challenge to the established parties. If they are a challenge, new parties can obtain wide coverage in the papers. Some of the new parties that have emerged within the last 20 years in Denmark have attracted wide coverage. The most important news criteria appear to be status, power and the ability to challenge the establishment. Colourful party leaders can do a lot to attract coverage, but a colourful personality is not enough. The expectation of influence is necessary as well.

The parties and the voters accept differential treatment of parties by newspapers. They raise no complaints of newspaper bias. However, voters of all parties write commentaries and letters to the editor; and content analyses show that this method of communicating is widely used by all parties, not least by the small parties, which thus try to compensate for their "lack" of news coverage.

NATIONAL BROADCASTING IN SCANDINAVIA: PUBLIC SERVICE

Public service broadcasting institutions are in principle independent public institutions with the purpose of broadcasting news, information and entertainment to the whole population. In Scandinavia, broadcasting belonged for decades to national monopolies, and the responsibility for radio and, later, television was given to Norsk Rikskringkasting (NRK) in Norway, to Danmarks Radio (DR) in Denmark and to Sveriges Radio (SR) in Sweden. The monopoly these institutions held was broken during the 1980s, but many normative expectations are still alive in relation to these "old" broadcasting companies. Among such expectations is balance in politics.

It might be said that public service broadcasting institutions are trapped in a triangle of influences: the political authorities, the audience and the journalists. All three represent challenges to ideas like balance, relevance, quality and independence. Heavy reliance on only one of these bases will easily transform the broadcasting company into a political commissariat, a purely commercial company or a paternalistic institution (Østbye 1991). There are many external pressures, especially in relation to political communication, and the principles for party access to broadcasting can be seen as a form of protection against such pressures.

Rules for Party Access to Broadcasting

Special regulations are set for party access to broadcasting during election campaign time. The rules are set by the broadcasting organizations themselves. Neither the government nor the state as such has direct influence on the rules for party access to broadcasting.

Denmark: Equal Access for All Parties

In Denmark, all parties are treated alike by the former monopoly channel, Danmarks Radio (DR) (1989; 1990). The guiding principle has been equal access for all parties participating in an election. This principle has been strengthened by a statement from the ombudsman and by a Supreme Court decision. Whether a political party is new or old, small or big, represented in the Folketing, the national Parliament, or not, once accepted by the Ministry of Internal Affairs as running in the announced election, the party is allocated free time on Danish national radio and television. Free time means access on an equal footing to special election programs in the format decided by the broadcasting company. To be accepted by the Ministry of Internal Affairs, "a party has to collect signatures amounting to 1/175 of the valid votes cast in the previous election."[3]

Acceptance of new parties challenging the established parties in the national elections is part of Danish democracy. Yet while receptive to the formation of new parties, Danes do not necessarily vote for them. These attitudes are reflected in responses to new parties seeking access to broadcasting. Often, parties able to collect the required number of signatures obtain a much smaller number of votes on election day.

Although no equal access rule applies to the new television channel, TV 2, no parties have complained.[4] On the DR channel, all parties get a public forum in the form of a 10-minute program followed by a half-hour program during which journalists question the party that just presented its platform. At the end of the question segment, a representative from the party, usually the leader, has the opportunity to close the session with a three-minute statement.

The party presentations may be produced by the parties themselves or made in cooperation with the broadcasting company. If the program is produced outside the popular Danmarks Radio, the political party receives a fixed amount of money from the station to produce it.[5] There is no limit to the amount of money a party can spend on the production of the party platform. Over the years, a variety of types of party presentations has developed. Some parties choose to let their leader use all the available time to talk about the party, but such programs built totally around the party leader are no longer the dominant type. Programs in which series of politicians or voters recommend their party have been very common. The most recent development is the presentation of stories built around a young voter telling about the advantages to be gained if the party in question is strengthened. A very subtle program building on a cartoon was used in the most recent election by the major opposition party, the Social Democrats; it was widely praised and generally accepted as an innovative way of presenting a party.

Over the campaign period of approximately three weeks, each party is assigned a series of programs in prime time, beginning at 8:00 PM. The total campaign broadcast time for each party amounts to approximately one hour, including time in panel debates. Dates are allocated according to the size of the party. The largest party receives first choice, and usually selects the last possible day before the election. With respect to scheduling on radio, the parties choose in the opposite order as a counterbalance.

By tradition, a panel debate featuring one representative from each party is broadcast on DR radio as well as on television. Based again on the principle of equal time, this debate is held two days before election day. The program usually takes three hours.

The day before election day is typically exempt from election programs. The idea behind this day – exempt from political propaganda – is that voters should be allowed time to digest the relatively heavy amount of political communication they had been exposed to, and to decide which party to vote for.

When the broadcasting monopoly was broken, the major event of relevance to election communication on the new channel, TV 2, was the introduction of a panel debate on the night before election day. Another break with tradition was limitation of the panel to representatives of parties perceived to be significant. News criteria now generally prevail over established traditions during campaigns, particularly if there are no normative obligations on the broadcaster. (Normative obligations are found in Danmarks Radio with respect to non-election time, when DR gives all parties special coverage of their annual meetings.)

Norway: Criteria for Equitable Media Access

Provision of party access to broadcasting in Norway differs significantly from the approach taken in Denmark. The guidelines for Norsk Rikskringkasting's (NRK's) election programs specify that NRK decides which parties will be allowed to participate in its programs as well as the type of programs to be aired (Norsk Rikskringkasting 1988). This principle is in accordance with a statement from the Norwegian ombudsman. In contrast with the Danish situation, the Norwegian ombudsman concluded that decisions about "who, when and how" belonged exclusively to NRK.

Political-party access to broadcasting has been labelled "minute democracy" in Norway as well as in Denmark. The principle does not, however, apply to all parties running in an election.

To receive "equal treatment" during a national election in Norway, a party must meet three criteria:

1. It must have been represented in the Norwegian Parliament, the Storting, during one of the last two election periods.
2. It must have run candidates in a majority of the districts.
3. It must have a current national organization.

How many representatives each party is allowed on the broadcast election programs is decided by the broadcasting company NRK during a given election. The principle for access is that the same number of participants and the same amount of time are allowed to all parties fulfilling the above criteria. The government as such has its own representative on programs where all political parties are present. This type of program is usually a final panel debate. The government representative will often be the leading minister, speaking on behalf of the government, rather than a party spokesperson. Another exception to the principle that equal time is allotted to all parties fulfilling the criteria is a party in a coalition that forms the government, or a party that is a clear alternative to the government, which is allowed more than one representative in the final debate. The modifications to the criteria for a given election are decided by NRK.

The Norwegian programming format does not provide the parties time to present their own platforms as in Denmark. Instead, candidates respond to questions from journalists or a panel of voters. Parties not qualified for "equal treatment" on Norwegian television, which means parties not fulfilling all three criteria due to lack of representation in the Storting, but acknowledged as running in the election, will be dealt with in shorter programs combining information and questioning.

In Norway, which has major regional differences, regional programs play a much greater role than in Denmark. However, the rules for access are the same as for access to national broadcasting, that is, the criteria mentioned above. A special clause gives all recognized national minorities putting forward candidates for regional representation to the national Parliament access to regional channels. There is no such minority clause in Denmark.

Access to national television and radio in local and county elections in Norway follows the same lines as for national elections. There is, however, a requirement that the party be organized, with candidates in at least one-fourth of the "communes" (municipalities).

Sweden: Equal Access for Parliamentary Parties

In Sweden, only parties represented in the national Parliament, the Riksdag, have equal access to the national radio and television. The program structure is based on questions to party leaders on both national radio and television. The direct broadcast takes place in prime time, and is repeated the following day, subtitled, to ensure general understanding among minority language groups.

Small parties not represented in the Riksdag have only limited access to national broadcasting, and do not participate in the specially arranged issue-oriented debates or in the final debate. Over the years, parties not represented in the Riksdag have complained of their limited access to radio and television, but Swedish broadcasting (now organized into two separate independent units, Sveriges Television and Sveriges Riksradio under Sveriges Radio) has been adamant. Under the broadcasting act,[6] it is this broadcasting organization that decides on the parties' access. The order of appearance is decided by lot.

The principle that only parties represented in the Riksdag have access is well established, but in practice it is flexible. In the 1988 election, two minor parties not represented in the Riksdag were included in the issue-oriented debates because they were seen – by Swedish radio and Swedish television – as having special positions on issues debated at that election. The same happened in the 1991 election when two parties not represented in the Riksdag got access to the types of programs usually restricted to parties already in Parliament. The argument in this instance was that both these parties stood high in opinion polls and therefore should be included in the broadcast debates. One of these parties garnered enough votes to win representation in the new Riksdag (i.e., in Sweden, more than 4 percent).

In news programs on Swedish radio and television during election campaigns, ordinary news criteria prevail.[7] Journalists are not unconcerned with balance, but there are no special rules to ensure fairness in news programs during a campaign. It is considered legitimate to cover parties solely due to the perceived news value of their activities.

Equal Access for All Parties Equals Instability?

Within Scandinavia, the Danish principle of equal access for all parties, including new parties, is considered to be an element that could eventually create political instability. For a time in the 1970s, 10 parties, some of them new, were represented in the national Parliament. The break-up of the Danish party structure in the 1970s is seen as a result of the weakening or disappearance of the party press combined with easy access to television for new parties (Hadenius 1983). The 1991 national election in Sweden resulted in the change from six to seven parties in the Riksdag. Mass media were blamed by several commentators, while others put the blame for the political change on the former governing party, the Social Democrats, and its policies. Television coverage helped the two outside parties get attention but the electorate's attention was drawn to the new populist party "New Democrats" before the election campaign as such had begun.

NEW LOCAL BROADCASTING CHANNELS

The Scandinavian countries experimented with local radio and television in the 1980s. Apart from controversial financial arrangements – funding partly from public and partly from private money – the major issue was the appropriate use of local broadcasting for politics. The decentralization of the electronic mass media raised expectations that politics would become much more relevant to the local citizen with local television as a counterweight to the tendency to centralize via national television.

Today permanent fixtures in Scandinavia, radio and television are now organized according to a new set of regulations. Income from advertising is accepted in Norway and Denmark, but not in Sweden. Local media are now used for political campaigning, and it is not subject to regulation.

The local media play a role in local politics, but their long-standing dream of stimulating local political activity did not come to fruition. In reality, very few channels serve the original goal of decentralizing political life. The majority of the local channels have become much more than an instrument for local political activity, programming locally edited entertainment such as music shows and bingo.

Nevertheless, with the establishment of a large number of local channels, political parties have gained more avenues for access to local audiences. In Denmark, the practice is that parties receive access, sometimes free and sometimes paid for, to air their political messages to a local audience. During the Danish national election campaign in January 1984, 70 percent of the local stations were asked by political parties to air election campaign material, and two-thirds of them agreed. During the European election later in 1984, fewer agreed to do so (Denmark, Ministry of Culture 1985). Most party requests were to air pre-produced tapes, but some sought transmission of press releases, arrangements for cross-party political debates or interviews with candidates. Only 12 of 68 radio stations accepted the parties' prepared tapes, according to a survey by the Ministry of Culture. The main reason for refusing their offer was the desire to remain non-political or neutral.

Due to the problematic financial state of private radio stations today, they are now more willing to sell air time to political parties. As a result, political communication depends on the parties' campaign budgets.

The budgets vary a great deal, thus introducing an imbalance in favour of wealthy parties and candidates.

PAID ADVERTISING IN NEWSPAPERS

Paid advertising in newspapers plays a significant role in election campaigns in all Scandinavian countries. A substantial amount of money is spent on advertising, and the differences in financial capacity among the political parties are vast. The response from voters as shown in election studies, however, suggests that this is not the most efficient way to spend money (although the money could be crucial in a given situation). In general, relatively few voters refer to advertisements as their means of obtaining information. In Denmark, approximately 5 percent of the population refer to advertisements as a source of information.[8]

VOTERS: TIME OF DECISIONS

In the 1985 Norwegian election, 25 percent of the voters had not yet decided how to vote two weeks before election day.[9] When opinion polls indicate a close race between the government and an opposition coalition – as in Norway[10] and in Sweden[11] in the 1985 elections – the number of "undecided" voters stimulates the use of mass media in the final part of the campaign, and leads to a concentration on party leaders.

Danish election surveys during the 1980s have shown that although the majority of voters have decided how to vote before the election campaign period (see table 4.1), a considerable proportion of the electorate decides during the campaign or the last few days before election day.

Table 4.1
Time of decision to vote for a specific party in four Danish national elections
(percentages)

	1981	1984	1987	1988
Before election campaign	72	77	76	69
During election campaign	13	12	10	10
During the last few days	15	11	13	17
Don't know	—	—	1	4
Total	100	100	100	100
N	(842)	(921)	(1 022)	(670)

Source: Danish Data Archive.

VOTERS' USE OF THE MEDIA FOR POLITICAL INFORMATION

Scandinavian voters rely rather heavily on the mass media for election information. The majority of Danes follow political campaigns on television, either for information or out of habit (Sauerberg 1976). Television is their primary source of information, but its dominance varies from election to election (see table 4.2). The old DR channel is viewed considerably more for this purpose than the new TV 2 channel. The use of newspapers has remained relatively constant over the last two decades, whereas the use of radio has declined, but is now relatively stable.

The media's capacity to educate and to give information to voters has been discussed at length. Surveys show that there are differences between subjective perception and objective measures. A significant, but varying, proportion of voters follows the national election campaigns on television to find out which party to vote for. Twenty-three percent did so in 1975, and 35 percent did so in 1973 when Denmark had several new potentially very powerful parties running for election. While this proportion fell to 14 percent in 1987, 16 percent responded that television had been a significant help for them in deciding which party to vote for in 1988. Though a minority, these voters nevertheless represent a sizable number of people open to influence. Among young people, 22 percent indicated that television helped them. Support is especially strong among the youngsters in Denmark for the principles of equal

Table 4.2
Most important source of information in four Danish elections
(percentages)

	1987	1988	1989	1990
Television	37	51	34	46
Newspapers	29	24	27	28
Radio	7	6	13	8
Conversation	8	9	8	5
Other	9	5	4	6
Don't know	9	5	15	7
Total	99*	100	101*	100
N	(811)	(878)	(547)	(1 194)

Source: Danmarks Radio surveys, three national elections (1987, 1988 and 1990) and one European election (1989).

*Percentages do not total 100 due to rounding.

treatment and equal time for all parties. For these young voters, television functions as a necessary window to the parties.[12]

The question has been raised as to how effective the different media are in helping parties convert voters. This is not an easy question to answer. A summary statement might be that television has shown a stronger potential power to convert voters than any other medium. But whether it so functions in a given election depends totally on those using the medium as an information source. A high interest in politics and a high degree of knowledge about political parties often indicated by higher education function to protect the viewer against conversion. Low interest, limited knowledge and a high degree of exposure to television enhance the influence of the medium.

In several instances in Scandinavia, the mass media have changed voter opinion during the campaign period as a result of either specific programs or the performance of a single politician. There is not, however, any firm information about a percentage of voters normally persuaded during an election campaign. Since surveys in Denmark indicate that between 25 percent and 33 percent of voters make up their minds about whom to vote for during the campaign period or its very last days,[13] it is clear that the mass media have a sizable potential to influence voters.

Competition from Commercial Channels

The introduction of an alternative national television channel in Denmark has received much study. The expectation was that when the Danes had a chance to avoid traditional election campaign coverage, fewer would follow campaigns than usual. During the European election in 1989, surveys initiated by Danmarks Radio (DR) found fewer viewers of election programs than in the national election campaigns in 1987 and 1988. This was explained primarily by the limited interest in European elections (Nordahl Svendsen 1989). In 1990, during the most recent national election, DR also found a reduction in the number of viewers of the traditional election programs. The mean share of viewers for the party presentations and question-and-answer session was 13 percent, only half the size of the normal audience for an election campaign in Denmark. This time, the reduction was a result of the competition from TV 2, which was showing a special Christmas program series that attracted a substantial number of voters; when the program stopped, however, they turned to watching election programs (Nordahl Svendsen 1991).

ASSESSMENT OF CAMPAIGN COMMUNICATION IN DENMARK

The equality principle that forms the basis for election communication on national television in Denmark has been evaluated in several elections. (There has been much less evaluation of campaign communication in Norway and Sweden.) In national elections, 85 percent of Danish voters support the principle that all parties, regardless of the number of parties running in an election, have the right to have their own presentation program on television (see table 4.3). The majority sets so high a democratic norm that less than 10 percent of Danes dare to say no. With an alternative national channel, the Danes can always escape political communication, but they support very strongly the principle of equal access, and not only access to programs run by journalists. They support debates as well. National election studies indicate that 43 percent of the voters followed the panel debate in 1988, 45 percent in 1987.[14]

Elderly voters follow most of the presentation programs, which are also closely watched by young voters. In 1988, voters were asked whether they favoured the idea of dropping the programs presenting the parties' platforms, but keeping the "cross-fire" program on which journalists question party representatives. Nearly half of the voters favoured dropping the presentation programs, but a sizable minority of 29 percent wanted them to continue. Young people, in particular, wanted this type of program retained. These programs had been kept at the time of writing.

Table 4.3
Danish voters' attitudes to the principle of equal access to television for all parties running in an election
(percentages)

	1987	1988	1989	1990
In favour	82	85	75	85
Opposed	9	6	9	11
Don't know	8	10	17	4
Total	99*	101*	101*	100
N	(811)	(878)	(547)	(1 194)

Source: Danmarks Radio surveys, three national elections (1987, 1988 and 1990) and one European election (1989).

* Percentages do not total 100 due to rounding.

Table 4.4
Danish voters' attitudes to a proposal to drop party presentation programs but keep the "cross-fire" program
(percentages)

	All	Socialists	Social Democrats	Bourgeois
In favour	45	37	45	51
Opposed	29	45	30	28
Don't know	26	18	25	21
N	(765)	(143)	(194)	(213)

Source: Danmarks Radio survey, 1988 national election.

When voters were questioned about the "minute democracy" based on the principle of equal time for all parties, even during debates, a strong majority (66 percent) were in favour (Danmarks Radio survey, 1988).

PERSPECTIVES ON THE CURRENT CAMPAIGN COMMUNICATION SYSTEMS

In Scandinavia, there are principles for access by political parties to broadcast time during an election campaign period. Access is not equal, however, and it is not allocated according to the same principles in Norway, Sweden and Denmark. Denmark has the most extreme system of equality, with equal time for all parties in special election programs.

Equity is a more appropriate label for the systems which give parties in Norway and Sweden access to broadcasting. The equity principle provides access in a more or less equal way, favouring the already established parties and the government.

Political balance is a principle of all public service broadcasting in Scandinavia. Numerous studies have been made of the actual balance achieved. In general, they have found that the principles formulated in the guidelines are followed.

The practice of putting the issue of balance on the agenda makes journalists very aware of the responsibility spelled out in the broadcasting rules. Balance in the treatment of political parties is carefully watched, and ultimately influences the journalists' perceptions. Journalists must decide about the kind of journalistic function they want to perform, and choose the medium accordingly. The role of a political mediator is different from the role of a political watchdog. There has been a trend in the direction of more critical journalism, most notably in connection with election programs on television, but the ritual role of journalist as transmitter still dominates.

Various election studies indicate that from the voter's point of view, the importance of the mass media is high. Voters use the media as a means of obtaining political information, deeming television the most important. Television's importance as a source of information and help in deciding how to vote is greater for voters with moderate or low interest in politics than for those whose interest is high.

Second most important as a source of information are newspapers, which are mentioned more often by the more highly educated than television is. The Norwegians are slightly more newspaper-oriented than the Danes and the Swedes.

New technologies are not expected to change the format of election campaigning significantly. However, teletext can be used for information. The broadcasting companies in Denmark used teletext widely in the most recent election to report opinion polls and election results from different constituencies. The teletext service, consisting of pages with detailed election results, aired on television and selected by individual viewers, was used widely by citizens during the election campaign. To date, however, no party has bought time to present their party platforms on teletext, although it could be established as a permanent service. Videotape cassettes have been used by individual politicians, as have audio recordings. Audio tapes have been mailed to households, but not to a very wide extent. No studies of their impact have been published.

Television is considered the best medium to target hard-to-reach voters – especially in Norway – and to reduce barriers to political participation. Television also reaches viewers who are not very interested in politics, but if a variety of channels is available as in Canada, it offers these potential voters a means of escape from politics as well. The supply can be regulated as well as the access, but viewer choice cannot.

Table 4.5
Television as a source of information and help in decision making for voters
(percentages)

	Political interest		
	High	Some	Low
Television most important	39	51	59
Election programs on TV helped	11	18	15
N	(175)	(391)	(312)

Source: Danmarks Radio survey, 1988.

Stereotyping of women and minorities has not been a particular problem in election campaigning in Scandinavia. Women candidates typically participate in broadcast programs side by side with their male colleagues. Where minorities exist, they often raise an issue needing coverage, but there is no special model designed to deal with this in Scandinavia. Public service obligations are in principle the best protection against biased coverage of all minorities, unless special channels (i.e., local channels) are made available to minorities.

There is no institutionalized assessment of campaigns, but in practice all parties as well as the media assess campaign activities when the election results are discussed. After every election, the quality of election coverage is up for discussion, and between elections this issue is a frequent topic of discussion. Although parties and politicians, who are keenly interested in having access to the mass media, often blame the media for their lack of success, that too is an element of a democratic society.

Standards for publication of opinion polls have been discussed, but so far no special standard has been agreed upon. The media are very interested given that they all produce and publish opinion polls. Politics remains of interest to both the voters and the mass media in Scandinavia, and the polls are an important element in the Scandinavian democracies (Elklit 1988).

A Comparative Evaluation of the Systems

In Scandinavia, a series of regulations determines party access to national public service–oriented radio and television during election campaigns.

The normative background for all three Scandinavian countries is equitable access for all parties, and the motivation is the desire to strengthen participatory democracy. A high level of information about political parties one can choose among at a given election is considered a prerequisite for the Scandinavian democracies. Serving the voter's needs is the primary goal of campaign communications in public service broadcasting.

The normative principle remaining the same, practice in the three Scandinavian countries nevertheless differs. In Denmark, party access to broadcasting on the old national channels belonging to Danmarks Radio is not dependent on whether a party is new or old, represented in Parliament or not. All parties putting forward candidates and accepted as running in a given election have the same access to the same type of programs and the same amount of time as old parties. Parties forming the government are not treated differently than other parties in the special series of election programs. In contrast, Norwegian and Swedish practice favours established parties with parliamentary representation. In this way, Norway and Sweden reinforce the status quo, making it harder for new parties to gain access to broadcasting and to national Parliaments.

News programs are free to follow ordinary journalistic practice in covering elections in Scandinavia, and this is the most common way for new parties to reach the voters and make the electorate aware of them. If regulations for special election campaign programs did not exist, access would be completely dependent on journalistic news criteria, with a heavy emphasis on power positions, conflict and the individual politician's ability to perform on television.

From the Scandinavian perspective, some kind of regulation of campaign communication on the national broadcasting media is advisable. The Danish model, combining direct presentation of party platforms with a press conference format, and featuring substantially equal access for all parties, is the system that appears to serve the needs of democracy best. Danish voters endorse this view, as shown in the surveys referred to in this study.

The turbulence experienced in the Danish political system in the 1970s might be explained by the easy access given new parties to the mass media. However, experience since then has shown that access to the mass media for new and small parties on equal footing with other parties is definitely not enough for a party to win seats in the national Parliament. Only a very few new parties are successful. Access to the mass media may be seen as a necessary but not sufficient condition for electoral success.

NOTES

1. For descriptions of broadcasting institutions in Scandinavia, see Kleinsteuber et al. (1986).

2. The history of newspapers in Scandinavia is included in national reports in Euromedia Research Group (1991).

3. The Danish Folketing has 175 seats and the threshold is equivalent to one seat, at present approximately 20 000 votes. The minimum required for representation in the Folketing is 2 percent of actual votes.

4. According to information from TV 2, only one party complained to TV 2 in writing, and few politicians called TV 2 to complain, but neither a party political debate nor a parliamentary debate has been raised.

5. For the 1990 election it was approximately Cdn.$11 500 dollars per party. The amount was estimated as the normal cost of a 10-minute television production in a studio, and the money was taken from Danmarks Radio's operating budget.

6. The Swedish broadcasting act contains special provisions empowering the broadcasting organization to decide who has access.

7. Information in correspondence from Sveriges Riksradio and Sveriges Television, March 1991.

8. Data from Danish Data Archive, various election surveys.

9. According to Professor Henry Valen of the Norwegian election research program in a statement on Danish television, DR, 28 August 1985.

10. Article in the newspaper *Politiken*, Copenhagen, 1 September 1985.

11. "TV-Avisen," Denmark, 2 September 1985, referred to a 1 percent difference between government and opposition.

12. Data from Danish Data Archive combined with results of a survey by Danmarks Radio.

13. Data from Danish Data Archive, various election studies.

14. Data from surveys taken from Danmarks Radio.

REFERENCES

Danmarks Radio. 1989. *Regler for udsendelse i radio og TV i forbindelse med valget til Europa-Parlamentet.* Copenhagen.

————. 1990. *Regler for udsendelse i radio og TV i forbindelse med folketingsvalg.* Copenhagen.

Denmark. Ministry of Culture. Committee on Local Radio and Television. 1985. *Report.* Copenhagen.

Elklit, Jørgen. 1988. "Opinionsmålinger og valgresultater." In *To folketingsvalg*, ed. S. Jørgen Elklit and Ole Tonsgaard. Århus, Denmark: Politica.

Euromedia Research Group. 1992. *The Media in Western Europe: The Euromedia Handbook.* London: Sage.

Hadenius, Stig. 1983. "The Rise and Possible Fall of the Swedish Party Press." *Communication Research* 10:287–310.

Kleinsteuber, Hans J., Denis McQuail and Karen Siune, eds. 1986. *Electronic Media and Politics in Western Europe: Euromedia Research Group Handbook of National Systems.* Frankfurt/New York: Campus.

Nordahl Svendsen, Erik. 1989. "EF-Valget 1989 i DR TV." In *Medieforskning i Danmarks Radio 1988/1989*, ed. Nordahl Svendsen. Copenhagen: Danmarks Radio Forskningsrapport nr. 2B/89.

————. 1991. "Lighedsprincip i konkurrence: Folketingsvalget 1990 i Danmarks Radio." Paper from Medieforskningen, Danmarks Radio. Copenhagen.

Norsk Rikskringkasting. 1988. *Retningslinjer for NRK's valgprogrammer.* Oslo.

Sauerberg, Steen. 1976. "Kommunikation til vælgere – og mellem vælgere." In *Vælgere i 70'erne,* ed. Ole Borre et al. Copenhagen: Akademisk Forlag.

Siune, Karen. 1987. "The Political Role of Mass Media in Scandinavia." *Legislative Studies Quarterly* 12:395–414.

Østbye, Helge. 1992. "Norway: Local Orientation and Internationalization." In *The Media in Western Europe.* Euromedia Research Group. London: Sage.

5

CAMPAIGN COMMUNICATION IN AUSTRALIAN ELECTIONS

John Warhurst

THIS STUDY DESCRIBES and discusses the system of campaign communication that operates for elections to the Parliament of the Commonwealth of Australia. The Parliament includes a lower house, the House
of Representatives, with 148 members, and an upper house, the Senate,
with 76 members. Elections are held frequently because the government often does not allow the House of Representatives to complete
its three-year term. The present government, led by Bob Hawke of the
Australian Labor Party, has won four elections – in 1983, 1984, 1987 and
1990.[1] Elections for the two houses need not be held simultaneously.
Usually an election is called for the House of Representatives and half
of the Senate; sometimes for the House of Representatives and the full
Senate. The last occasion in which an election was held for the House
of Representatives alone was in 1972.

Furthermore, this study largely concentrates on the campaign
communication system occurring at the macro-level of national
and state campaigns. Less attention is paid to the style of campaigning
and communication that takes place in the 148 individual electorates
across the country. Such a focus is justified because, increasingly, the
major political actors are focusing their campaigns at the national and
state levels. These campaigns spend the bulk of the campaign funds, they
involve the major political leaders, they determine the images that are
presented and the issues that are raised, and ultimately, they contribute
most to the outcome of the elections.

THE POLITICAL PARTY SYSTEM

Australian elections are dominated by three major political parties: the
Australian Labor Party, the Liberal Party of Australia and the National

Party of Australia (Jaensch 1989). The latter two always form a coalition when in government, and generally do so in opposition. However, they run individual and somewhat competitive election campaigns that are, at best, only loosely coordinated.

In elections for the House of Representatives, the candidates of the three major political parties poll the overwhelming percentage of the votes, only rarely falling below 90 percent. The 1990 elections, in which other candidates polled 17.2 percent of the vote, were very much the exception to the general rule (Mackerras 1990, 205, table A.23). As a consequence, the candidates of other political parties or independent parties are very rarely successful. There have been no successful candidates from minor parties over the past 40 years, and only two successful independents (a genuine independent elected in 1990 and another in 1966, who had previously represented the Australian Labor Party) (ibid., table A.24).

The picture in elections for the Senate is slightly different and somewhat more encouraging for minor parties and independents. Two minor parties, the Democratic Labor Party, between 1955 and 1970, and the Australian Democrats, since 1977, have managed substantial success, and there has been at least one independent candidate elected at each Senate election since 1961 (Mackerras 1990, 206, table A.26). Nonetheless, the major parties still predominate, and over the past 40 years their percentage of the vote has not fallen beneath 80 percent (ibid., 205, table A.25).

In the Australian federal system, the major political parties have traditionally been state-based. The national parties have been federations of independent state parties. The state branches of the major parties are still responsible for the preselection of candidates, party organization and fund-raising, and they have some say in the organizing of election campaigns for the House of Representatives and the Senate. However, the parties have been growing more centralized over the past 20 years or so, and in the case of the Australian Labor Party and the Liberal party especially, campaigns for Commonwealth elections are now largely run on a national basis.

THE ELECTORAL SYSTEM

Australian voting methods have long been complex and have become more so since the Hawke government introduced changes prior to the 1984 elections (Aitkin et al. 1989, 145–63). The members of the House of Representatives are elected from single-member electorates by full preferential voting. Under this system, voters rank the candidates. If no candidate wins an absolute majority of "first preference" votes, then the least popular candidates are in turn excluded and their votes distributed to the other candidates according to the preference of the voter, until one candidate finally has an absolute majority.

The Senate is elected by proportional representation, with twelve senators coming from each of the six states and two from each of the two territories. When six senators are to be elected from each state in an ordinary "half-Senate" election, the quota to be reached for election is 14.3 percent, while the quota is 7.7 percent when all twelve senators are up for election. Prior to the 1984 elections, a major variation was introduced. Political parties are now able to register a ticket that allocates preferences according to the parties' wishes. Voters can now support the ticket by registering a *single* preference.

These methods differ not only from each other but also from those in operation in a number of states. For example, in New South Wales, the largest state, optional preferential voting, in which voters have the choice of allocating preferences if they wish, was introduced for state elections in 1981. There was a relatively high level of informal voting for the House of Representatives elections in 1984 and, to a lesser extent, in following elections because of the juxtaposition of full preference voting in that house with the possibility of registering a single preference in the elections for the Senate.

Voting is compulsory for all elections in Australia. Therefore campaign communication is concerned less with voter turnout and more with the mechanics of voting. It is customary for political parties and for some other groups to distribute how-to-vote cards at polling places on election day. Generally, only the major parties are able to organize enough supporters to arrange for a representative to be in attendance at each polling place in each electorate during voting hours, which are from 8:00 AM till 6:00 PM. Voting always takes place on a Saturday.

ELECTION CAMPAIGN COMMUNICATION

The major communicators in Australian election campaigns are the participants which include the political parties and independent candidates, pressure groups and others who participate indirectly; the communication media, commercial and government, that report and comment on the campaigning; and the government agencies responsible for conducting the elections and monitoring election campaigning.

The Australian Electoral Commission (AEC) is the government statutory authority responsible for the conduct of elections. As part of this task, the AEC undertakes a major program of voter education both between and during election campaigns. Its concerns include motivating unregistered voters, particularly the young, to put themselves on the electoral roll, reducing informal voting, and informing isolated voters and indigenous peoples. The latter function is conducted by the Aboriginal and Islander Electoral Information Service.

The three major political parties are perhaps the most significant actors of those who engage in campaign communication. Their campaigns are centralized and shaped by national considerations. They use the media extensively, particularly television, which reaches a greater percentage of the electorate than either radio or the press. Television is a costly medium, and therefore, it is difficult for other actors to gain access to it.

The media outlets themselves tend to be interested only in the leaders of the major political parties. One aspect of this concentration on leadership has been televised debates during the 1984 and 1990 election campaigns between the prime minister and the leader of the Opposition. The general tendency to concentrate on a few well-known leaders also makes it difficult for anyone but the three major parties to communicate effectively with the electorate.

The major parties have great faith in, and yet fear the power of, the media. There is a general belief that if a party has superior campaign communication skills, it has gone a long way toward success in elections. Therefore, the major parties are unstinting in the resources they devote to campaign communication, especially via the media, and unscrupulous in their approach to communication. Their fear of the media is reflected in the continuance of an electronic blackout: political advertising through the electronic media is forbidden by legislation for 48 hours prior to polling day.

The escalating cost of political advertising on the electronic media threatens to drive the major parties close to bankruptcy and makes it extremely difficult for other parties and groups to campaign through the electronic media. While there has been provision since 1984 for public funding of election campaigns, such funding can only ameliorate and not solve the financial problems of the major parties. The same is true for the limited provisions for free time for political parties campaigning via the electronic media. The criteria for allocating both public funding and free time are based largely on past election performance, so small parties receive little assistance, and new, unproven parties receive none at all.

The campaigns of the major parties are increasingly driven not only by party platforms but also by public opinion research. Public opinion research affects the media campaigns and the direct-mail techniques of communication that are being increasingly utilized by the parties. Public opinion polls are also a major source of campaign news and are much in demand by the media.

There are, in practice, no effective limitations on the content of campaign communication. Existing regulations against misleading political advertising were given such a narrow interpretation by the courts when they were tested in the early 1980s that they were removed from the *Commonwealth Electoral Act* in 1983. An attempt to find a new form of words was short-lived and essentially rejected as unworkable by the major parties. Interestingly, arguments about the ethics of campaign advertising often originate in major party attacks on the minor parties as well as in competition among the major parties. Allegations of impropriety often relate to the advice given by parties to electors about the system of voting and hence the "meaning" of their vote.

The electronic media are divided between the commercial and government sectors. The government broadcaster is the Australian Broadcasting Corporation (ABC), which operates both a television and radio network. Despite having a minority share of the electronic audience, the ABC, rather than the larger commercial networks, is the prime focus of government and community concerns about issues in campaign communication such as balance and access. Of greatest concern is undoubtedly the issue of balance among the major political parties. The question of imbalance between the major parties and the rest seems of little concern.

The ABC's charter calls upon it to be balanced in all political matters, including election coverage. Balance in this context means a balance between the two "sides," and during almost every election campaign, there are allegations of imbalance. As the ABC is considered by its critics to be to the "left" of ideological centre, such allegations usually come from the parties of the "right," the Liberal and National parties. Much less attention is paid to the election coverage of the commercial electronic media.

There has been a great deal of controversy about the news and editorial policies of the press during election campaigns. The privately owned press has traditionally supported the Liberal and National parties editorially, although that has not always been the case with some proprietors in recent years. Most often the critics have come from the "left" and include leaders of the Australian Labor Party (ALP) and, occasionally, journalists. There is no effective regulation of this medium of campaign communication, other than that which is provided by instruments of self-regulation, such as the Press Council, and codes of professional ethics.

The ABC chooses to provide some free time for political parties during campaigns, though it is not duty-bound to do so. It allocates this time using its own rules, a practice consistent with its responsibility of ensuring balance. While the commercial broadcasters do not provide free time, they do broadcast some campaign events free of charge, such as the opening policy speeches of the major political parties.

Regulation of political advertising is carried out by the Australian Broadcasting Tribunal (ABT). The ABT polices the electronic blackout, monitors guidelines for the amount of paid political advertising allowed over any time period, and records all political advertising over the electronic media during election campaigns. While it may respond to complaints, its major value lies in its published post-election reports, which provide full and detailed information on paid political advertising during election campaigns.

There are many aspects of campaign communication in Australia about which there is no consensus among those actively involved in election campaigning. Policies are unsettled, and there have been changes in many areas over the past decade. There is continuing concern about balance and bias in the print and electronic media and continuing debate about various campaign-related matters, such as free time, public funding, the electronic blackout and the type of campaign communication allowed through the media. These concerns have been summed up as involving the Democratic principle and the Quality principle. A recent authoritative discussion of these issues, including the alternative points of view expressed by the major political parties, is contained in *Who Pays the Piper Calls the Tune* (Australia 1989).

It is against this volatile background that the Hawke government foreshadowed, in March 1991, a package of new legislation. This legislation proposed to ban all political advertising on the electronic media, whether during an election campaign or not. The package also included proposals to strengthen provisions for public disclosure of campaign donations to political parties and to raise the level of public funding to parties on the basis of Senate election results to that applicable to House of Representatives elections.

ONCE UPON A TIME ...

A number of elements of campaign communication in Australia are of relatively recent origin. However, it is worth remembering the pattern of Australian campaigning before the advent of radio and television, before large-scale public opinion polling, before the technological developments that allow the sophisticated targeting found in direct-mail campaigns, and so on.

The typical Australian campaign focused on the local electorate. Candidates had to speak in community halls, in workplaces and on street corners, often using a loud hailer. Candidates also had to visit as many houses as possible in the electorate and supplement this with letter-box drops of campaign material, advertising signs and some paid advertising in local newspapers. At the national level, there would be a campaign launch of the party's policies by the parliamentary leader and some visits to individual electorates by party leaders. There was no national campaign as such, partly because of the technological difficulties involved. There were state campaigns (organized by the state branch offices of the parties), which would supplement the local campaigns, mainly through newspaper advertisements and a schedule of visits by prominent party leaders.

Such campaigns are not just of historical value. Some practices, such as street-corner meetings, have virtually disappeared, but the essence of the local campaign has survived. It is in this way that the local party member takes part in the election campaign, communicating his or her party's policies to friends, neighbours, acquaintances and strangers around the local electorate. The modern national campaign has not totally replaced the old-style local campaign. Rather, the former has been superimposed on the latter and has displaced it from the focus of attention. A version of the old-style local campaign still occurs in each electorate during the campaign.

THE ELECTRONIC BLACKOUT

The coming of radio to Australian political campaigns in the 1930s must have made quite an impact. The first *Broadcasting Act* introduced in Parliament by the Australian Labor Party government of John Curtin in 1942 included a provision that there be a total prohibition or "blackout" of electronic broadcasting of electoral matter for 48 hours prior to polling day.[2] The blackout applied only to radio at the time it was introduced, but when television was still on the horizon in 1956, the Liberal government of Sir Robert Menzies extended the prohibition to include television as well (Windshuttle 1984, 319–20; Mills 1986, 177–78; Lloyd 1977, 1979). This approach continues until the present day.

The prohibition was, and is, intended to insulate voters from the power of the electronic media. "The justification for such a tight gag was that voters needed a 'breathing space' or 'cooling off period' between the end of campaigning and the time of casting their vote. The blackout supposedly prevented candidates from releasing a scandalous allegation or scare story which would deceive the voters and secure some unfair advantage" (Mills 1986, 178).

The blackout was never extended to the print media, although it would be constitutionally possible for a government to do so. This reflected a fear that the electronic media are potentially more powerful and more likely to disorient voters, a belief that persists to this day. In 1989, the Joint Standing Committee on Electoral Matters (JSCEM) of the Commonwealth Parliament maintained its support of a modified blackout. "The Committee believes that if the blackout provision did not exist then a party would be able to run negative advertisements up to election day, and the attacked party would have no time to prepare advertisements to reply ... The Committee therefore supports retention of the blackout" (Australia 1989, 109).

The JSCEM was supporting a blackout modified by the Hawke government in 1983 to exclude news broadcasts and commentary. It retained the prohibition on paid advertising. At the time, the Minister for Communications described the blackout as "an infringement of our civil liberties which should not be tolerated by a democratic society" (quoted in Mills 1986, 178).

The blackout has always had its critics. Mills, for example, writing on the modified ban, says,

> This partial move certainly answered the mounting complaints by TV and radio journalists about the restrictions on their activity, but it meets only half the civil-liberties/freedom-of-speech principle Duffy enunciated. The ban on advertising infringes the rights both of listeners and of political Parties, just as the old ban did, and like the old ban it attributed awesome powers of deception to the electronic media. If indeed the old ban embodied 'paternalism' which was out of place in Australia's 'mature electorate,' as Mr. Duffy said, then so too does the current ban. (Mills 1986, 178)

Mills (1986, 177) describes the blackout as "infamous." Lloyd says that there is "no rational justification for this blackout which does not apply to either paid advertisements or news reporting in the printed media" (Lloyd 1977, 196). Only Windshuttle (1984, 319) has some sympathy for the political parties' views because his analysis suggests "there could appear to be some justification in these fears." However he cautions against this view, and concludes that it was "a sorry reflection on the calibre of Australian political debate that the ban lasted as long as it did" (ibid., 320).

The major parties have not been convinced by these arguments. Nor have many others. In 1989, the JSCEM (Australia 1989, 109) reported that "the majority of submission makers supported its retention." Of the three major parties, only the smallest, the National party, argued that the remaining electronic blackout should be abolished.

FREE TIME

Another long-standing Australian campaign tradition is limited free time for election broadcasts. Traditionally, the Australian Broadcasting Corporation (ABC), not the commercial electronic media, allocates free time to the major political parties. The ABC has done so since its inception under rules that have varied over the years (Mills 1986, 171–73).

The ABC has never been directed by government to provide free time, but does so as a result of its own policies. "The Corporation reserves to itself the right to grant or withhold broadcasts at its discretion to political parties, including those not represented in Parliament, on the basis of its estimate of the measure of public support for any party" (quoted in Australia 1989, 30). Section 116 of the *Broadcasting Act*, 1942 provides that "subject only to this section, the Australian Broadcasting Corporation may determine to what extent and in what manner political or controversial matter will be broadcast or televised by the Corporation" (quoted in Australia 1989, 30).

The rules under which the ABC has chosen to allocate this time have evolved over time in accordance with the general principles of balance and representation. The ABC has always given the leaders of the parliamentary political parties equal amounts of free time. Some others have also been given time. As Mills (1986, 171) recounts, free time was even given to the Communist party in 1946, to the dismay of the established political parties.

In 1949, the ABC instituted a threshold to determine access to free time of 5 percent of the vote or one member of Parliament (Mills 1986, 172). This effectively eliminated the Communist party and any other minor party. This situation has prevailed ever since to the detriment of minor parties. On occasion the ABC has attempted to widen the provision of free time. For example, in 1961, after the Kennedy–Nixon debates of 1960 in the U.S. presidential race, the ABC decided that "every candidate within the areas served by television could have three minutes on the screen." The program, called "The Candidates," fell foul of government opposition to the access given to their opponents, including, among minor parties, the Communist party (Inglis 1983, 214).

The present situation is that the allocation of free time is determined by the Election Coverage Committee of the ABC. The responsibilities of this Committee (Australia 1989, 31) are:

- to ensure the equitable use of the total amount of free time on radio and television as allocated by the Board [of the ABC];

- to assess the fairness and balance of news and current-affairs programs in relation to an election campaign;
- to receive and consider complaints from viewers and listeners;
- to enable ABC editors, journalists and producers to carry out their roles in a professional and independent way with a minimum of distraction during a demanding period; and
- to report on its own activities thereby contributing to the public accountability of the ABC and through such reporting to assist in coverage of future federal elections.

Under current ABC rules (Australia 1989, 31), some free time is allocated "to a party which contests at least 10 of the vacant seats for whichever House of Parliament the party nominates candidates." In addition, "the party must command popular support," which means either a party member was elected to the Commonwealth Parliament at the previous election or the party polled 5 percent or more of the valid votes for either federal house or for the lower (or single) house of Parliament in the preceding state election. In the case of independent senators seeking re-election the ABC "exercises a discretion" (ibid., 32).

The ABC varied its criteria to include state elections following its treatment of a new party, the Australian Democrats, in the 1977 national elections (Lloyd 1979, 253–54). The story pointedly illustrates the disadvantages faced by new parties. The Australian Democrats emerged between the 1975 and 1977 elections when the party's first leader, Don Chipp, resigned from the Liberal party. The party had a substantial presence and had polled well at two state elections, in South Australia and Queensland. It could boast "150 branches and 7,000 dues-paying members" (ibid., 253).

The ABC's rules at the time were more restrictive than they are now, and the Commission rejected the Democrats' request for free time on the grounds that the party had neither elected a member of Parliament nor polled 5 percent or more at the preceding election. Yet, as now, the ABC's own policy guidelines spoke of "at its discretion" and it would seem, as the Democrats argued at the time, that it was no defence for the ABC to claim that the refusal of the Democrats' request was automatic under its guidelines (Lloyd 1979, 254, n. 37).

The ABC needs to allocate the free time it does offer in a way that treats the major parties equally. The others are scarcely noticed. As the JSCEM puts it, "the ABC has determined that to ensure evenhandedness between the Government of the day and the official Opposition, both the Government and the Opposition are given equal time. In the case of a coalition in opposition, the combined coalition parties generally receive the same amount of time as the Government. It is then up to the coalition parties to divide the time between them as they see fit. However, the ABC has the discretion to vary this equal time should circumstances change" (Australia 1989, 32).

As table 5.1 shows, in the 1987 election the government and the Opposition received 90 minutes each on both radio and television. The Australian Democrats received less than a quarter of that and the independent senators received five minutes each in their own state.

Traditionally, the free time issued by the ABC has been closely tied to one of the major Australian campaign events – the policy speech of each of the major parties, which signals the beginning of each party's election campaign. As Lloyd (1979, 251) has commented in regard to the political parties, "Each devotes a substantial part of its free time ... to this ritual campaign launching." The policy speeches of the major parties are regarded as such critical events that they are also broadcast free of charge almost universally by major commercial radio and television stations.

Free-time broadcasts, for the ABC especially, have been motivated by strongly educative principles (Mills 1986, 172). Live broadcasts of policy speeches tended to differentiate the free-time usage from paid political advertising. The ABC has attempted to reinforce this differentiation by allocating the free time in longer blocks than the paid time available on the commercial stations. Free time used to be allocated in blocks of not less than five minutes, which was reduced to two minutes prior to the 1984 federal elections (ibid.). The ABC's Election Coverage Committee vets all parties' use of the time because they believe that

Table 5.1
Allocation of free time by the ABC for the 1987 federal election

Political party	Free-time allocation
Australian Labor Party	1 hr. 30 mins. (radio) 1 hr. 30 mins. (television)
Liberal and National parties	1 hr. 30 mins. (radio) 1 hr. 30 mins. (television)
Australian Democrats	20 mins. (radio) 20 mins. (television)
Independent senators (in each senator's state)	5 mins. (radio) 5 mins. (television)

Source: Australia (1989, 33, table 4.1). Commonwealth of Australia copyright reproduced by permission.

party use of this time "should not be aimed simply at influencing electors on an emotional level but rather should enable them to be fully informed on the issues to make a considered decision" (quoted in ibid.). Whether such a distinction, however, can be made between emotion and reason is arguable.

The free-time allocation almost certainly was once more important to the major parties than it is today. Mills (1986, 172) has argued strongly that "the advent of modern campaign styles and of more numerous broadcasters is eroding this educative aim. Free time, with its traditional 'rational voter' assumptions and old-hat format of the leader-addressing-his-supporters, has proven a nuisance to the political Parties. Far from being the only or the principal means of electronic communication between Parties and voters, free-time broadcasts these days provide only a minor subtheme to the Parties' massive advertising on the commercial stations."

Not only has free time been overtaken in quantity by paid advertising but the use to which the time is put is becoming similar at the insistence of the parties. What has happened is that the political parties are now packaging their policy speeches. The campaign launch now may take the form either of a totally synthetic product or of a carefully edited policy speech prepared for a television audience. For example, Lloyd (1990, 99) notes that in the 1990 election campaign the Labor party "opted for a televised address by the Prime Minister to an invited audience, and the Liberals selected a carefully-prepared magazine framework incorporating a mix of political statement, interviews, narration, commentary and allied visual material."

PAID ELECTION ADVERTISING

Election advertising is a controversial issue in Australia. Controversy rages over both the quantity and the quality of paid advertising. As the quantity of paid election campaign advertising is growing, so is concern over the impact of such spending on party finances and the possibility that poverty-stricken parties might be tempted by corruption; that is, they might accept donations in return for favours. Debate about the quality of advertising revolves around the usual allegations that selling political parties like brands of soap is a perversion of the campaign communication desirable in a democracy. One of the critics, Mills (1986, 209), judges the impact of the new technology on election campaigning: "Rather than educating us about politics, it has stooped to conquer us with advertising which is often feverish, garish and uninformative – but effective." The last point is crucial. Advertising through the electronic media is thought to be effective, so the political parties spend more and more on it. The former deputy prime minister, Paul Keating, is reported to have said, after his party's loss in the 1980 elections to what was seen as a very effective Liberal party advertising campaign, "What Labor needs is a couple of vicious and utterly cynical ad men to do to the Liberals what they do to us" (Goot 1983, 200).

Television is the sought-after medium. It has only been part of Australian election campaigns since the late 1950s; since then the impact of television has increased dramatically. The 1972 election, which saw the Australian Labor Party win office for the first time in 23 years with the campaign slogan "It's Time," is regarded as the first "television election" in Australia. Voters have quickly taken to television. "In 1967, [37%] of Australian voters said they followed politics on television, and in 1979, the proportion was 60%. It has been suggested that by the 1980 federal election, the proportion of voters following elections on television was closer to 100%" (Australia 1989, 25). This may be an exaggeration but certainly television became the favoured medium. When young electors were asked in a 1986 survey, "What would you say is your most important source of information about politics?," 41.4 percent said television while 23.9 percent preferred newspapers, which were far ahead of the next most favoured source. The full set of responses is reproduced in table 5.2.

Lloyd's (1990, 101–107) analysis of the 1990 Australian Election Study (AES) shows that 79 percent of all voters watched television news "often or sometimes" compared with 60 percent reading press

Table 5.2
Sources of political information among young electors, 1986

Source	Important	Most important
Newspapers	71.2	23.9
Television	83.6	41.4
Radio	48.4	5.4
Family	33.8	8.1
Friends	32.2	3.9
People at work	23.4	2.8
None	1.8	0.3
Don't know	0.3	0.4

Source: Australian Electoral Commission (1989, 42, table 4.05). Commonwealth of Australia copyright reproduced by permission.

Table 5.3
Election news and party support
(percentages)

All voters	Total	Vote				
		Labor	Liberal	National	Democrat	Other
Watched television news						
Often or sometimes	79	82	82	74	72	64
Rarely or not at all	21	18	18	26	29	36
Total	100	100	100	100	100	100
(N)	(1 990)	(795)	(721)	(108)	(246)	(67)
Read press news						
Often or sometimes	60	62	61	52	61	49
Rarely or not at all	40	39	40	48	39	51
Total	100	100	100	100	100	100
(N)	(1 907)	(756)	(693)	(100)	(240)	(67)
Listened to radio news						
Often or sometimes	52	52	53	49	51	46
Rarely or not at all	49	49	47	50	49	55
Total	100	100	100	100	100	100
(N)	(1 899)	(748)	(692)	(99)	(241)	(68)

Source: Lloyd (1990, 105).

Note: Percentages may not add to 100.0 because of rounding.

news and 52 percent listening to radio news. The full responses are shown in table 5.3.

As far as political advertising is concerned, the AES revealed that "90 percent of the electorate had at least some exposure to political advertising on TV, compared with 72 percent for press advertising and 68 percent for radio advertising" (Lloyd 1990, 101). As table 5.4 shows, while television election advertising is not as widely watched as television election news, it is still relatively the most popular form of advertising: 65 percent watched television advertising "often or sometimes" compared with only 39 percent reading press advertising "often or sometimes" and 35 percent listening to radio advertising "often or sometimes."

The consequence of such audience patterns has been that electronic advertising, especially on television, has been used more frequently by the political parties. Mills (1986, 105) points to a 300 percent increase in television and radio advertising costs between 1974 and 1984 (a period when the consumer price index rose by 180 percent). Between 1983 and 1987, the amount the parties spent on television

Table 5.4
Campaign advertising and party support
(percentages)

	All voters	Vote				
		Labor	Liberal	National	Democrat	Other
Watched television advertising						
Often or sometimes	65	69	66	64	53	53
Rarely or not at all	35	31	34	36	47	47
Total	100	100	100	100	100	100
(N)	(1 996)	(795)	(725)	(108)	(247)	(68)
Read press advertising						
Often or sometimes	39	39	41	45	33	32
Rarely or not at all	62	60	60	56	67	68
Total	100	100	100	100	100	100
(N)	(1 898)	(754)	(690)	(101)	(238)	(66)
Listened to radio advertising						
Often or sometimes	35	36	36	36	34	27
Rarely or not at all	65	65	65	64	66	73
Total	100	100	100	100	100	100
(N)	(1 898)	(742)	(696)	(100)	(241)	(67)

Source: Lloyd (1990, 102).
Note: Percentages may not add to 100.0 because of rounding.

advertisements alone increased by approximately 100 percent, from $3.57 million in 1983 to $7.17 million in 1987. The figure was much higher again in 1990. Figure 5.1 demonstrates graphically the increase in party expenditure on election broadcasting between the 1974 and 1990 elections. Expenditure, especially by the Australian Labor Party (ALP) government, has jumped dramatically over the past two elections. Prior to this, the ALP was regularly outspent by the Liberal and National parties in tandem.

The cost of television advertising to the political parties is so great because television is an expensive medium. Public funding of political party campaigns, which is discussed below, has not solved the problem, and may even have exacerbated it. Mills comments,

> Public funding of election campaigns mainly means public funding of
> TV stations. Television airwaves belong, in theory, to the community;
> owners of TV stations are licensed by the public to use them under certain
> conditions. So public election funding means the Australian public is

spending large amounts of money to buy back their own airwaves –
for elections, probably the most significant civic function we have.

This is indefensible in principle, but it is made more pressing by
the reported incidence of TV stations charging political clients – that
is the taxpayer – more than they charge their commercial advertisers.
(1986, 189–90)

The Australian Broadcasting Tribunal's review of advertising time
on television (Australia 1989, 26, table 3.1) has shown how television
advertising rates grew at twice the rate of the consumer price index
during the mid-1980s (1982–86). These figures are reproduced in
figure 5.2. Because of factors such as the short warning time for elections (most are called before the required time) and the concentration
of advertising over the short campaign period, it seems that political
parties, but not commercial advertisers, are paying the full, "normal"
rate. Political parties cannot bargain effectively with television station
management, partly, as Mills notes (1986, 190) because "TV manage-

Figure 5.1
Party expenditure on election broadcast advertising

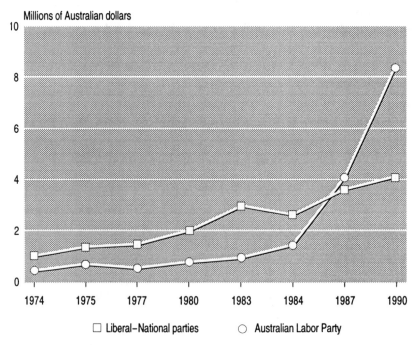

Millions of Australian dollars

Source: Ward (1990, 5, figure 3).

Figure 5.2
Index of television advertising rates compared to the consumer price index: 1980–86

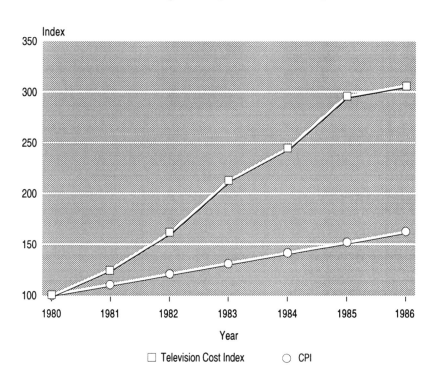

Source: Australia (1989, 26). Commonwealth of Australia copyright reproduced by permission.

ments, not without reason, wish to avoid the appearance of favoring one Party over another."

Some of the funds required for expensive advertising campaigns may come from public funding, which was one of the 1983 reforms introduced by the Hawke government. Funding is allocated to political parties on the basis of a certain amount per vote, adjusted every six months in line with the consumer price index. The rate for a House of Representatives vote is twice that for a Senate vote. Expenditure over and above that covered by public funding must be met by donations to party funds; otherwise the political party will suffer a shortfall. In the 1987 election, the ALP's $10.5 million expenditure was met 45.5 percent from public funding and 48.4 percent from donations. The National party's $4.1 million expenditure was met to the extent of 29.5 percent from public funding and 42.3 percent from donations. The Liberal party's $6.1 million was met 57.3 percent by public funding and 66.1 percent by donations (Hughes 1990, 151). As Hughes points out, these figures suggest a substantial shortfall for the Nationals, a small short-fall for the Labor party and a large surplus for the Liberals. Overall, 40.2 percent of reported campaign expenditure in the 1987 election was covered by public funding (ibid.). It would appear that in 1990, even after public funding and donations, the ALP was left with a substantial debt of, perhaps, $5 million, while the Liberal party emerged in a healthy financial situation.

Even after taking public funding into account, Australian political parties need to obtain large corporate funding if they are to survive financially. As the Joint Standing Committee on Electoral Matters (JSCEM) reported (Australia 1989, 25), "political parties have had to rely increas-ingly on donations from the corporate sector. Thus the democratic process has become increasingly dependent on who can raise the substantial funds needed to buy advertising on the electronic media – and in particular, television." While this view was held by the majority on the Committee, it was not held by the Liberal and National party members but by the Labor and Democrat members. Indeed, public funding was not supported by the Liberal and National parties when it was introduced by Labor and the Democrats in 1983.

The question of the quality and probity of paid political advertising is equally contentious in Australian election campaigns. The new Hawke government took up this issue after its election in 1983 (Mills 1986, 175–77; Hughes 1990, 147–51). The situation in 1983 was that section 161(e) of the *Commonwealth Electoral Act*, which made it an offence to publish material containing "any untrue or incorrect statement intended or likely to mislead or improperly interfere with any elector in or in relation to the casting of his vote," had been interpreted narrowly in the courts to refer to "the mechanics of marking a ballot paper rather than the choice of candidates or parties to vote for" (Hughes 1990, 147). The Hawke government, with the support of the Australian Democrats, set out to change that, and in the process (short-lived, as it turned out) "became the only democracy to endeavor to legislate for electoral honesty" (Mills 1986, 176).

The government endorsed the proposal of the Joint Select Committee on Electoral Reform (JSCER) and legislated for it to be an offence during an election campaign to

print, publish or distribute or cause, permit or authorise to be printed, published or distributed any electoral advertisement containing a statement

a. that is untrue; and
b. that is, or is likely to be, misleading or deceptive. (Hughes 1990, 147)

Almost immediately after this legislation was passed, Parliament began to have second thoughts about the whole idea, particularly the likely interpretation of "untrue" and "misleading or deceptive." The JSCER reconsidered and decided that "a decision as to whether a political statement is 'true' seems necessarily to involve a political judgement, based upon political premises" (Mills 1986, 177). While the *Trade Practices Act* did attempt to deal with misleading or deceptive commercial advertising, the JSCER decided that there were too many problems and impracticalities in trying to legislate fairness in electoral advertising (Hughes 1990, 48). They concluded,

> Political advertising differs from other forms of advertising in that it promotes intangibles, ideas, policies and images. Moreover, political advertising during an election period may well involve vigorous controversies over the policies of opposing parties ... even though fair advertising is desirable it is not possible to control political advertising by legislation ... The safest course ... is to repeal the section effectively leaving the decision as to whether political advertising is true or false to the electors and to the law of defamation. (JSCER, quoted in Hughes 1990, 148)

The new section was removed from the legislation prior to the 1984 elections, so it was never actually tested.

As Hughes shows (1990, 148), while the government and the Opposition have agreed that such a provision is unworkable, the Australian Democrats have not been convinced. They have attempted, unsuccessfully, on several occasions, to reintroduce the provision. The Democrats, as a minor party, are often imposed upon by one of the major parties. Such was the case during the 1990 elections, when former Democrat leader Don Chipp was clearly misrepresented, by selective editing, in an ALP advertisement that implied that he was in favour of Democrat supporters giving their second preferences to Labor.

The other aspect of election advertisement quality that has been the subject of continual discussion has been the allowable length of advertisements. Critics of unrestricted length argue that advertisements that are very short, say 30 seconds, are vehicles not for information but for propaganda. As the ALP submitted to the JSCEM, "Although short (30 second television) advertisements are useful for promoting images and conveying impressions they are a poor means of transmitting information or reasoned argument. On the other hand, advertisements of longer duration are likely to be better vehicles for presenting issue-related cases and policy choices; however, they might make programming more difficult and could risk boring viewers. Therefore, a suitable balance needs to be struck between these considerations" (Australia 1989, 53). For these reasons, the ALP suggested that paid advertising be available in two-minute modules only. The Liberal and National parties rejected this view, arguing that it would not lead to an improvement in communication, but only lose the attention of voters. The Liberal party further claimed that the cost implications of allowing no advertising of less than two minutes would discriminate against smaller groups (ibid., 102). The JSCEM recommended against any minimum time for political advertisements broadcast on radio or television (ibid., 103).

PUBLIC OPINION POLLING

Public opinion polling began in Australia in the 1940s and, for a long time, was carried out solely by the Morgan Gallup organization. Since 1971, there has been a "change from a monopolistic to a competitive structure in Australian polling" (Beed 1977, 226). Over the past 20 years, there have been a number of professional firms operating in competition. Public opinion polls are commissioned more often by the press than by the electronic media, but all media outlets publish their results frequently during election campaigns. They are also commissioned and used extensively by the political parties and pressure groups.

What the polls say about the fortunes and chances of the competing parties is often the major news reported by the media during an election campaign. Furthermore, the campaign strategies of the parties are often determined by what their "private" public opinion polls and the "public" public opinion polls tell them about their competitive situation and about the impact of the style of campaign they are running. Polls, it is thought, can generate their own momentum; there is argument about whether their publication should be regulated or unregulated. Attention is also directed to the polls' record in predicting election results and to the links between polling organizations and their commissioning newspapers.

The studies of recent Australian elections convey the importance, even centrality, of public opinion polling to election campaigns. For example, in a study of the 1977 campaign, Lloyd (1979, 250) writes, "As in 1975, the opinion polls were a dominating influence on media interpretation of the campaign ... The turnaround in the polls was the principal news story for the latter part of the campaign ... The polls were reflected in newspaper editorials and in the electronic media talk-backs and phone-ins and current affairs programs."

Table 5.5
Notice taken of opinion polls, and party support
(percentages)

		Vote				
	All voters	Labor	Liberal	National	Democrat	Other
Notice taken						
None at all	42	38	41	50	53	53
Some	47	50	47	43	40	40
Quite a lot	11	13	12	7	7	7
Total	100	100	100	100	100	100
(N)	(2 007)	(798)	(730)	(108)	(250)	(68)

Source: Lloyd (1990, 111, table 6.6).
Note: Percentages may not add to 100.0 because of rounding.

In a study of the 1980 campaign, which Labor lost after apparently leading just a week before polling day, Goot (1983, 140) concludes, "In the space of two weeks a 'dull' contest became a 'cliffhanger.' Central to this transformation were, of course, the polls. They dominated the press coverage and the television news; caused the Liberal Party to revamp its campaign and redouble its advertising, and both directly and indirectly affected the vote. The polls symbolized the campaign as contest in its purest form."

By 1990, Lloyd (1990, 110) could report that "the use of public opinion polls by the media has been a controversial aspect of recent election campaigns. In the 1984 and 1987 election campaigns the use of the polls in media news was excessive, and sometimes misleading. Some polls had methodological problems, and reputable polls were reported sensationally and inaccurately on occasions." This was not the case in the 1990 election campaign in which polls were used "with greater restraint and responsibility."

The 1990 Australian Election Survey investigated the extent to which voters, as distinct from the parties and the media, took public opinion polls seriously. It found that a majority of voters did take some interest in public opinion polls, especially supporters of the two largest parties, and that 11 percent of voters took quite a lot of interest. The results of this survey are given in table 5.5.

DIRECT-MAIL CAMPAIGNS

One of the developments of the 1980s in Australian election campaigns has been the use of direct mail. The major political parties have learned the techniques from American and Canadian professionals (Mills 1986, 192–97). The technique is used for both fund-raising and election campaign communication.

The Labor party's computerized direct-mailing operation, *Polfile*, is one aspect of the professionalism that has given the party an apparent competitive edge over its opponents in recent election campaigns (Ward 1990). The ALP has used telephone canvassing followed by computerized direct-mail targeting of electors in its approach to marginal electorates during the last two elections. Electors are contacted by telephone after cross-referencing of electoral rolls and telephone books. They are then classified by voting intention and by special interests. Once this is done, direct mailing swings into action. It has been claimed that in one marginal ALP electorate alone in the 1987 election, the sitting member sent 65 separate personalized sets of letters to electors selected through telephone surveying and classified according to interests (Warhurst 1988, 54).

LEADERS DEBATES

There have been only two publicly televised debates between political party leaders in Australian election campaigns, in 1984 and 1990. In 1983, Bob Hawke's challenge to debate the then prime minister, Malcolm Fraser, was declined. In 1984, Hawke debated the Liberal party leader, Andrew Peacock. In 1987, there was no debate between Hawke and Liberal party leader John Howard. In 1990, Hawke and Peacock, who was once again Liberal party leader, had a return bout.

In 1984, the government was riding a wave of popular support, and Hawke was expected to win the debate easily. As it turned out, in the absence of any objective evaluation, the conventional wisdom is that Peacock performed well enough in that debate, and in the campaign as a whole, to greatly reduce Hawke's margin of victory. The Liberal campaign leadership hoped for a similar result in 1990, but they were disappointed. Peacock was reportedly lacking in substance in comparison to the prime minister, especially on issues such as environment and health policy, which were the subjects of campaign debate at the time.

The structure of the one-hour, no-audience debate in 1990 has been well described in Lloyd's study (1990, 95):

> The candidates made brief opening and closing statements, with interspersed statements on economic policy, social policy and the environment. After each brace of policy statements, the leaders questioned each other and were questioned by the panel, with opportunities for

supplementary questions by politicians and journalists. In a later segment, journalists questioned the leaders on general issues. While the format allowed plenty of opportunities for interplay between the participants, it was cumbersome and had a high potential for embarrassment, even political disaster. Much depended on balance and timing, with the skill of the moderator paramount in ensuring fair treatment of each leader while keeping the show moving along.

The debate was not broadcast as widely by the media in 1990 as it had been in 1984. With the benefit of hindsight, Lloyd considers this to have been an error of judgement by media executives that is unlikely to be repeated. In 1990, the debate was telecast directly by the ABC and by the Special Broadcasting Service, but by only one of the three commercial television networks. The ABC also broadcast the debate nationally over radio.

The 1990 Australian Election Study indicates that a majority of the electorate (56 percent) watched the debate (Lloyd 1990, 97). As Lloyd says, this is a high percentage given that two of the three commercial networks did not broadcast it. He concludes: "With enormous spin-offs from secondary coverage by all media, the impact of

Table 5.6
Voter responses to the great debate
(percentages)

			Vote				
		All voters	Labor	Liberal	National	Democrat	Other
Watched							
Yes		56	60	57	55	44	41
No		44	40	43	45	56	59
	Total	100	100	100	100	100	100
	(N)	(2 007)	(799)	(729)	(108)	(249)	(68)
Performance rating							
Hawke much better		16	33	3	2	7	.12
Hawke somewhat better		30	46	16	13	33	27
Neither Hawke nor Peacock		38	19	51	50	53	50
Peacock somewhat better		12	2	24	28	7	12
Peacock much better		3	0	7	7	0	0
	Total	100	100	100	100	100	100
	(N)	(1 875)	(754)	(677)	(102)	(235)	(60)

Source: Lloyd (1990, 98, table 6.1).

Note: Percentages may not add to 100.0 because of rounding.

the debate was incalculable." It was one of the turning points of the campaign. The debate was popular with ALP and Liberal–National party coalition voters, but less so with Democrat and minor party supporters, which is not surprising given that only the two major leaders took part. The Australian Democrats' leader, Janine Haines, was rebuffed when she made a claim to participate. Table 5.6 records voter responses to the debate.

THE AUSTRALIAN ELECTORAL COMMISSION

The Australian Electoral Commission's (AEC) primary purpose is to "conduct parliamentary elections and referendums which accurately record voting intentions and are honest and equal in their treatment of electors" (AEC 1990, v). In accordance with this purpose, one of the AEC's goals is "to improve the Australian public's understanding of and participation in electoral matters." AEC's own research suggests that "lack of knowledge of basic facts about the political system contributes to problems with the mechanics of voting, which in turn causes informal voting" (AEC 1989, 3). Furthermore, its own research among young people revealed "poor enrolment figures and disinterest in the electoral system by young Australians" (ibid., 36).

The AEC itself runs a media campaign above and beyond its legislative responsibilities, for example, to advertise polling places and its usual advertising of enrolment, special voting requirements and formal voting requirements. A special campaign was undertaken during the election campaign period. Its purpose was to encourage young people to enrol. During the campaign period the AEC also placed radio and press advertisements about postal, pre-poll and absent voting and about formal voting requirements. "These advertisements were based on research into voter understanding of what constitutes a formal vote and focused on the most frequently made mistakes: the use of a tick or a cross instead of numbers, and the failure to number every square (unless using the top part of the Senate ballot paper)" (AEC 1990, 10).

The AEC also distributed to every household (6.1 million) a pamphlet containing "information on how to cast formal votes as well as more general polling information" (AEC 1990, 11). This information was about how to cast a vote, not about the choice of whom to vote for.

On polling day itself in the 1990 elections, mobile polling stations were used in the Northern Territory and in all states except Victoria. The purpose of using mobile polling stations was to reach isolated people who would be too far away from the nearest static polling station to be reasonably expected to cast a vote. Such isolated voters live in Aboriginal communities, on cattle stations and in small remote townships. In 1990, there were 266 such communities, including 14 734 voters served by the 147 localities visited by light aircraft and four-wheel-drive vehicles. Most hospitals and nursing homes were also served by mobile facilities (AEC 1990, 12).

The AEC undertakes many community awareness programs, most but not all of which occur outside election campaign periods (AEC 1990, 18–19). These include an Electoral Education Centre in Canberra, "established to provide educational sessions on the federal electoral system to groups of students on educational visits to the national capital"; public displays of electoral materials and information at shopping centres, schools, universities and colleges, and royal shows; school visits; and publications such as posters, fact-sheets, leaflets, newsletters and curriculum materials.

The Aboriginal and Islander Electoral Information Service (AIEIS) "provides electoral information to Aboriginal and Torres Strait Islander communities and groups" (AEC 1990, 19). AIEIS's responsibilities include assisting with Aboriginal enrolment and maintaining electoral rolls in Aboriginal communities. It tries to motivate Aborigines to participate in elections through what it calls its "pre-election motivation program." This program included a video, "Election '90 AIEIS," and a radio advertisement that were broadcast over the central Australian Aboriginal television station IMPARJA, and via the Broadcasting for Remote Aboriginal Communities Scheme (ibid., 20).

PAID ADVERTISING AND FREEDOM OF SPEECH IN 1991

On 19 March 1991, the Cabinet decided, on the basis of a submission by the Minister for Administrative Services, Senator Nick Bolkus, to legislate to ban all political advertising on television and radio. It would do this by amending the *Commonwealth Electoral Act* and the *Broadcasting Act*. It would need the support of the Australian Democrats for this legislation to pass through the Senate (Eccleston 1991).

The Cabinet decision draws together the threads of Australian debate over the last few years and is the culmination of several years' search by the Australian Labor Party for an answer to the dilemma it found itself in with electronic election advertising. The party's paid advertising was very professional and at least the equal of any other party in Australian politics, but it was worried about where the escalation of campaign expenditure, largely caused by electronic advertising, was leading. In particular, the level of expenditure threatened to drive it, and perhaps other parties, bankrupt. The party had emerged from the 1990 election campaign with a large debt, and as the party's popularity with the business community waned in the late 1980s and early 1990s, the scale and urgency of the problem grew.

The Labor party's submission in 1989, two years before, to the JSCEM's inquiry into the conduct of the 1987 federal election and the 1988 referendums had made its concerns clear (Australia 1989, 52–53). The party had argued then that the aggregate amount of time and the allocation of that time among political parties for political advertising on television and radio should be regulated. It advocated that each party should be given an allocation of electronic time for the term of each Parliament, and that paid political advertising outside of such a scheme should be prohibited. The Australian Democrats' submission to the same enquiry (ibid., 57–58) argued that the party's first preference would be for an extension of free time to political parties by commercial stations as a condition of licence: "As public facilities, they should provide a certain amount of time for the purpose of political advertising free of charge." However, the Democrats thought such a scheme was unlikely to be accepted, so they recommended as a second preference "that claims for public funding for radio and television advertising and production be limited to, at most, 10 percent of the monies available for public funding." The same would apply to paid advertising in the print media.

The Liberal party, in its submission to the JSCEM inquiry, advocated an entirely open market. "Broadcasting and televising of political advertisements should be on the basis of an unfettered commercial arrangement between the party and the network concerned" (Australia 1989, 55). It argued that "it is the right of any organization in a democracy to promote its ideas without arbitrarily imposed restrictions" (quoted in ibid.). Consequently, "there should not be any limit on the amount of time which any individual party, or the parties as a whole, may purchase for the purposes of campaign advertising" (quoted in ibid., 56). The junior coalition partner, the National party, concurred. It believed "that as any party's commercial advertising activity will always be dictated by its financial capacity it should be entirely a matter for political parties in conjunction with commercial organizations, to decide the amount of advertising they will place on commercial radio or television" (ibid.).

The idea of a complete ban on electronic advertising was first canvassed within ALP circles during 1990, after unsuccessful attempts by the ALP National Secretary, Robert Hogg, to construct a bipartisan agreement with the Liberal party. Hogg sought agreement to the introduction of a spending ceiling on electronic advertising by political parties according to each party's primary vote at the previous elections. Hogg also proposed unsuccessfully to the Liberal party that commercial stations be compelled to extend "free time" to political parties. In return the commercial stations would be compensated by lower licence fees.

The government's proposal, it was argued, would reduce the pressure for fund-raising by political parties and allow a "level playing field" for smaller parties, which lacked the financial resources of the three major parties. The Minister condemned the existing situation as inequitable and denied that the right of free speech was being infringed. "There is absolutely nothing free about electoral advertising. Only the duopoly of the Coalition and the ALP can really afford the $10 million needed each election" (Eccleston 1991).

The expense of electronic advertising, the Minister argued, led to the danger of corrupt practices, a danger pointed out, he said, by two recent state government inquiries, the Fitzgerald inquiry into corruption (Queensland), and the Independent Commission Against Corruption (New South Wales). These two commissions supported reform of campaign donation disclosure laws for this reason. So, the Minister continued,

> the Government is not prepared to continue with a situation which may lead to corruption.
>
> Clearly a situation has arisen in the United States where large lobby groups are outright buying support for their particular interests.
>
> This Government will not be waiting until we need a royal commission into federal political funding. (Eccleston 1991)

He admitted, however, that he had no evidence that there had been corruption in Australian federal politics.

The expense of electronic advertising undoubtedly makes the proposed legislation appealing to the Australian Democrats, who experience a severe competitive disadvantage under the existing system. It seems at this early stage to have the support of the leader of the Australian Democrats in the Senate.

There was an immediate negative response to the government's proposal. The major opposition parties are totally opposed as are representatives of the electronic and print media. The wide sweep of the proposal, which included political advertising by interest groups, also led to almost unanimous opposition from a wide assortment of community groups, including church and charitable organizations. The proposed legislation has been seen as a desperate attempt by a penurious party to save itself and as a clear assault on the basic right of each individual to freedom of speech (*Australian* 1991, editorial). It was criticized as possibly unconstitutional, and the Liberal premier of New South Wales promised that his state government would mount a constitutional challenge. Finally, it was criticized for being difficult to implement. How could "political" be defined, and where would the boundaries between political and non-political be drawn?

The government proposal also included fuller disclosure requirements for political donations. While strongly opposing the ban on paid advertising, the Liberal party leader, John Hewson, appeared to support the government's plans for further campaign donation disclosure. This reversed the traditional Liberal party position on this issue. Public funding was also to be expanded by increasing the rate of funding per Senate vote to that of the rate per House of Representatives vote, which is presently twice as much. This, too, undoubtedly appeals to the Democrats.

The immediate government response to the community backlash was to press on with a somewhat narrower version of the ban. The proposed legislation was to exempt charitable organizations that wish to mount broad "issues" campaigns, though not overtly partisan advertisements by such groups (Milne 1991). It would be up to the Australian Broadcasting Tribunal to determine what was a political advertisement. This still poses problems of implementation, especially in the heat of an election campaign. The Democrats appear to be vacillating in their support, so there is no guarantee that the legislation (in whatever form) will pass through the Senate. However, the government does appear confident that its broadcasting power ensures the legislation's constitutionality.[3]

CONCLUSION

This study has set out, in a dispassionate fashion which belies the intense emotion that surrounds the issues, the major elements that provide the structure for campaign communications in modern Australian federal elections. These structural elements include the pre-election electronic blackout, arrangements for free time on the electronic media for election broadcasts, developments in paid election advertising, public opinion polling, direct-mail campaigns, formal debates between party leaders and the role of the Australian Electoral Commission. The study concludes with a report on the (unfinished) public discussion of the Hawke government's proposal to ban all political advertising on television and radio. This public debate has revealed the intensity of the beliefs about campaign communication issues, beliefs that touch on themes central to democracy, such as free speech and unfettered citizen participation in politics. The remainder of this study provides a personal evaluation of the major issues and recommends some possible solutions to Australian dilemmas in this field.

The Australian system of campaign communication is one that, as in many others in countries around the world, empowers political parties and other professionals, impoverishes the political parties themselves, enriches the owners and managers of the electronic media, and disillusions many ordinary party members and citizens.

It is a system that favours the major parties and reinforces their dominant place in the electoral and party system. It also reinforces some of the other dominant aspects of Australian political life, such as centralization of policy making and over-concentration on the leaders of the major political parties.

For all the modern developments in campaign communication, it is doubtful that citizens are any better informed by the political parties than they were in the past. Rather, the style of communication seems to have contributed to a general alienation from the political parties and from party politics.

What to do? The current trend in Australian politics is toward deregulation of all aspects of economic and social life, so it is difficult to believe that wholesale regulation of campaign communication is the answer. It is also difficult to see that election communication should be far removed from other forms of communication in society. Therefore, I do not support the present government proposal for a total ban on advertising on the electronic media.

I would favour some upper limits on paid advertising on television by each political party. This would help to control the spiralling costs that the major political parties are facing, which is a major problem of the present system.

Another major problem is the imbalance between the major parties and the other parties and independents. The best solution to this imbalance would seem to be some extension of free time to the commercial electronic media. Just how such an extension could be implemented is unclear. Current suggestions all seem to involve variations of taxpayer funding. The alternative, some form of community service provision by the private owners of the commercial networks, appears impractical in the Australian political culture. It would be vigorously opposed by the media owners, whose support could only be bought by a countervailing reduction in government licence fees for television stations.

Optimistically, what may eventuate from the current proposal that is being discussed in Parliament is a general recognition of the weakness of the present system and an open discussion of the possible alternatives. Yet, in a pre-election climate with Labor declining right around the nation, such optimism may not be warranted.

ABBREVIATION

s(s).   section(s)

NOTES

This study was completed in July 1991.

I would like to thank Kah Ying Choo for her assistance with the research for this paper, Cathy Lynch for word processing the manuscript, and Alan Brideson (Australian Electoral Commission), Bev Forbes (Joint Standing Committee on Electoral Matters) and Kathryn Cole (Legislative Research Service, Department of the Parliamentary Library) for their advice and assistance with obtaining information. I would also like to acknowledge my indebtedness to a number of major sources, including academic studies of Australian Commonwealth elections since 1975, the publications of the Australian Electoral Commission and the Joint Standing Committee on Electoral Matters of the Parliament of Australia, and the expertise of Murray Goot, Clem Lloyd, Stephen Mills and Ian Ward.

1. For a full listing of results for House of Representatives and Senate elections between 1949 and 1987, see Mackerras (1989). The 1990 results can be found in Bean et al. (1990). A good general source is McAllister et al. (1990).

2. Australian elections are always held on a Saturday, so the blackout is always from midnight on the Wednesday prior to the election.

3. Just before the legislation reached the Senate in June 1991, it appeared that the Australian Democrats would not give their support, and it was, therefore, unlikely that the legislation would be passed.

REFERENCES

Aitkin, D., B. Jinks and J. Warhurst. 1989. *Australian Political Institutions.* 4th ed. Melbourne: Longman Cheshire.

Australia. *Broadcasting Act,* 1942, No. 33.

————. *Broadcasting and Television Amendment (Electoral Blackout) Act,* 1983, No. 37.

————. *Commonwealth Electoral Act,* 1918, No. 32, s. 161(*e*).

————. *Commonwealth Electoral Legislation Amendment Act,* 1983, No. 144, s. 114.

————. *Trade Practices Act,* 1974, No. 51.

Australia. Joint Standing Committee on Electoral Matters (JSCEM). 1989. *Who Pays the Piper Calls the Tune: Minimising the Risks of Funding Political Campaigns.* Inquiry into the Conduct of the 1987 Federal Election and 1988 Referendums. Report no. 4. Canberra: Australian Government Publishing Service.

Australian. 1991. "Media Ban Assaults Our Basic Rights." 20 March.

Australian Electoral Commission (AEC). 1989. *Sources of Electoral Information.* Research Report no. 1. Canberra: Australian Government Publishing Service.

———. 1990. *Annual Report 1989–90.* Canberra: Australian Government Publishing Service.

Bean, C., I. McAllister and J. Warhurst, eds. 1990. *The Greening of Australian Politics: The 1990 Federal Election.* Melbourne: Longman Cheshire.

Beed, T. 1977. "Opinion Polling and the Elections." In *Australia at the Polls,* ed. H.R. Penniman. Washington, DC: American Enterprise Institute for Public Policy Research.

Eccleston, Roy. 1991. "Outrage at TV, Radio Ad Ban." *Australian,* 20 March.

Goot, M. 1983. "The Media and the Campaign." In *Australia at the Polls,* ed. H.R. Penniman. Washington, DC: American Enterprise Institute for Public Policy Research.

Hughes, C.A. 1990. "The Rules of the Game." In *The Greening of Australian Politics: The 1990 Federal Election,* ed. C. Bean, I. McAllister and J. Warhurst. Melbourne: Longman Cheshire.

Inglis, K. 1983. *This Is the ABC.* Melbourne: Melbourne University Press.

Jaensch, D. 1989. *Power Politics.* Sydney: Allen and Unwin.

Lloyd, C.J. 1977. "The Media and the Elections." In *Australia at the Polls,* ed. H.R. Penniman. Washington, DC: American Enterprise Institute for Public Policy Research.

———. 1979. "A Lean Campaign for the Media." In *The Australian National Elections of 1977,* ed. H.R. Penniman. Washington, DC: American Enterprise Institute for Public Policy Research.

———. 1990. "The 1990 Media Campaign." In *The Greening of Australian Politics: The 1990 Federal Election,* ed. C. Bean, I. McAllister and J. Warhurst. Melbourne: Longman Cheshire.

Mackerras, M. 1989. *The Mackerras 1990 Federal Election Guide.* Canberra: Australian Government Publishing Service.

———. 1990. "Appendix A. Election Results." In *The Greening of Australian Politics: The 1990 Federal Election,* ed. C. Bean, I. McAllister and J. Warhurst. Melbourne: Longman Cheshire.

McAllister, I., M. Mackerras, A. Ascui and S. Moss. 1990. *Australian Political Facts.* Melbourne: Longman Cheshire.

Mills, S. 1986. *The New Machine Men: Polls and Persuasion in Australian Politics.* Ringwood: Penguin.

Milne, Glenn. 1991. "Hawke to Proceed on Political Ad Ban." *Australian,*
26 March.

Ward, I. 1990. "The Changing Nature of Australia's Political Parties."
Paper prepared for a colloquium on the Future of Non-Labor Parties in
Australia, University College of Southern Queensland, Brisbane, 28 July.

Warhurst, J. 1988. "The ALP Campaign." In *Australia Votes,* ed. I. McAllister
and J. Warhurst. Melbourne: Longman Cheshire.

Windshuttle, K. 1984. *The Media: A New Analysis of the Press, Television,
Radio and Advertising in Australia.* Ringwood: Penguin.

6

THE MASS MEDIA
AND ELECTION CAMPAIGNS
IN THE UNITED STATES
OF AMERICA

Doris A. Graber

I T IS DIFFICULT to generalize about mass media coverage of election campaigns in the United States because there are considerable variations in coverage, depending on the office at stake. Coverage differs for national, state and local campaigns, for campaigns involving executive or legislative positions, and for campaigns of major or minor political significance. There are sizable variations even in campaigns for the same office (Asher 1988; Kessel 1988). The closeness of the race matters, as does the array of other races that compete for media attention. Major national crises, such as Operation Desert Storm, can also deflect attention from campaigns. Changing newspeople and changing news trends, such as the current focus on public opinion polls, can alter coverage patterns. Nonetheless, certain general trends stand out, and they will be the focus of this study.

To put the study into an appropriate context, a number of shortcomings in campaign coverage research must be pointed out. Despite these flaws, the research on which this study rests is extensive and thorough, and provides a solid foundation. Most of the research data come from presidential and congressional campaigns, because such campaigns have been extensively studied. Far less is known about the media's role in gubernatorial campaigns. Similarly, almost nothing has been done systematically to study the role of the media in local elections. What little information is available suggests that patterns of news coverage resemble those of congressional elections, including variations in the amount of coverage, depending on the newsworthiness of a particular campaign. Routine campaigns receive slight coverage, while exciting races that involve controversial candidates or policies are amply covered.

At the presidential level, the fact that U.S. election campaigns are extraordinarily lengthy is an important factor that shapes media coverage. Presidential campaigns may begin two or more years before the election, and they are in full swing a good ten months before the date of the final election. The actual candidates are not formally selected until the close of the six-month primary election season and the subsequent nominating conventions. Conventions can take place as late as mid-August, less than three months before the November election date. High costs have discouraged researchers from studying media influence throughout the entire year-long campaign, stretching from the primaries to the final election. Before 1980, the early stages of presidential campaigns were wellnigh ignored, yet they often are the most crucial because they determine who will be eliminated before the final contests.

Other research gaps that hamper the analysis of campaign coverage include the dearth of content analyses. When campaign story content has been analysed, it has rarely been placed in the context of news coverage in general (Graber 1987a). For example, on average, even in presidential years, election news constitutes only a minor portion of total coverage, except when election returns are reported. Hence, stories dealing with other matters clamour for the voters' attention and colour the way in which campaign news is interpreted (Iyengar and Kinder 1987). Research on media impact has been flawed because the measurement of audience attention to campaign news is inadequate. Most surveys ask global questions about whether or not the respondent has followed the campaign in the media, and there are usually no questions about the specific stories that have come to the respondent's attention or about what the respondent has actually learned from exposure. When questions about learning are asked, they probe for specific, researcher-defined information, rather than seeking open-ended respondent-controlled answers.

Most research on campaign coverage has focused on newspapers and television. The role of news magazine and radio election information has been given little scholarly attention, and the impact of brochures, flyers, billboards, campaign rallies and in-home canvassing has been almost totally ignored. The explanation of this lies in poll results, which indicate that television and newspapers are the most widely used sources of campaign information. An average of 90 percent of the adult media audience claim to use television, and around 75 percent claim to use newspapers. By comparison, only 45 percent of the media audience claim to use radio (Asher 1988). The lack of research on radio coverage is particularly regrettable. When radio exposure comes from all-news stations, rather than from regular radio news broadcasts, it is often massive because news items are repeated throughout the day. Studies of learning in general, as well as studies of the impact of advertising messages, indicate that repetition is a powerful factor in increasing message retention and use.

The impact of several new technologies also needs to be studied, particularly as they hold promise of reaching audiences that currently are not adequately exposed to television and newspaper campaign stories. Examples are video and audio cassettes about the campaign; candidates, as well as organized bodies such as labour unions, have distributed such cassettes in recent campaigns. Desktop publishing is also a new technique that permits inexpensive production of professional quality campaign flyers that can be tailored to the varied needs of audience groups. Computer bulletin boards and electronic mail, as well as public-access channels on cable television, are other possibilities for narrowcasting.

Other newcomers to the campaign news scene are Cable News Network (CNN) and the non-profit cable Satellite Public Affairs Network (C-SPAN). The established major television networks have cut back substantially on some aspects of campaign coverage, such as the nominating conventions, which have lost audience appeal because the names of the nominees are already predetermined in most cases. CNN (with its round-the-clock news coverage) and C-SPAN (with its live congressional coverage) fill the gap. Given the relatively small though growing audience of these enterprises, their impact is still to be ascertained. Efforts to reach new audiences, such as high-school students, through special news programs presented as part of the curriculum, or attempts to present news bulletins regularly on rock music stations, also need to be assessed for effectiveness. Satellite capabilities now give local television stations ready access to national news sources. Local stations have therefore increased national election coverage substantially, while the national networks have reduced news coverage because of financial problems. Local news broadcasts are geared more closely to the interests of local audiences and may therefore have greater impact.

GENERAL FEATURES OF MEDIA COVERAGE

Legal Requirements

The First Amendment to the U.S. Constitution provides the legal context for campaign coverage. It stipulates that "Congress shall make no law ... abridging the freedom of speech, or of the press." This amendment, which also binds state governments and applies to public, semi-public and privately controlled publications, has given all mass media an exceptionally strong basis for resisting government controls. The basic philosophy is that restraints of the media, if needed at all, must come through the deterrent effects of fear of punishment for publishing harmful information after publication, rather than through "prior restraint." However, even though First Amendment rights are accorded a "preferred position" that requires their protection at all costs, the protection is not absolute. The courts have ruled that media freedom must occasionally give way to social rights, which the courts consider to be superior. Hence, there are restrictions to protect national security, community moral standards and market freedom. Most instances of judicial support for curtailment have involved conflict between the First Amendment and the Sixth, which guarantees an accused person a fair trial.

As mandated by the First Amendment, government does not, as a rule, regulate media messages. In the landmark case of *Miami Herald Publishing Company v. Tornillo* (1974), which dealt with an election campaign, the U.S. Supreme Court ruled that print press freedom to control news content could not be restricted; a Florida law that gave candidates the right to demand newspaper space to rebut attacks on their reputation was unconstitutional. This principle has been fully sustained for print media ever since. Electronic media which use the publicly owned air space to transmit messages are treated somewhat differently, for they are deemed to have public service obligations in return for the broadcast privileges granted to them. Section 315 of the *Communications Act of 1934* is their major source of constraint on campaign information. The guidelines for this Act are vague, stating that broadcast media shall "serve the public interest, convenience, and necessity." But regulatory authority does not extend to media content, except indirectly.

The crucial rules for broadcast media set forth in section 315 are the equal time rule, the fairness doctrine and the right of rebuttal. The equal time rule provides that broadcasters who permit a candidate for political office to campaign on their stations must give equal opportunities to all other candidates for the same office. The fairness doctrine encompasses a much broader array of situations, reaching beyond elections. It provides that broadcasters who air controversial issues of public importance must provide reasonable opportunities for the presentation of conflicting viewpoints. The right of rebuttal requires that an attack on the honesty, character or integrity of an identified person or group entitles the targets of the attack to reply. The broadcaster must notify the targets about the offending broadcast and must supply a transcript or summary. Then the target must be given a reasonable opportunity to respond. It is important to note that all of the regulations that mandate the electronic media to carry messages from actually or potentially aggrieved parties come into force only after a station has given access to one party.

The provisions mandating equal time for candidates exclude coverage provided through regular news programs and specifically exempt talk shows. The exempted talk shows now include the presidential and vice-presidential debates, which would become totally unwieldy if all declared candidates were to be included in the debate. (In 1988, for example, 39 candidates entered the presidential race.) However, the choices made by broadcasters must not favour or disfavour a particular candidate. Candidates who feel they have been unfairly shut out can appeal to the Federal Communications Commission (FCC), a five-member bipartisan body appointed by the president with the consent of the Senate.

Critics charge that the fairness doctrine and the rebuttal rule have impoverished public debate by suppressing controversy and that equal time provisions constrain election coverage. They contend that, predictably, broadcasters often close access to all of the protected groups and circumstances so as to avoid supplying remedial access. This has been particularly true in state and local elections, where many candidates are competing for offices that are of minor political significance. Moreover, critics point out that less than 10 percent of the 15 000 charges of unfairness are sustained in an average year, and they have therefore pressured the FCC to rescind section 315, especially the fairness provisions. To counter attempts to rescind the fairness rule, Congress passed a bill in 1987 that would make it a law; but President Reagan vetoed the bill, and subsequent attempts to pass such legislation have failed. In support of President Reagan's veto, the FCC proclaimed unanimously that the fairness rule was unconstitutional (*Congressional Quarterly Weekly Report* 1987), and this has put it in limbo. However, the other constraints remain in force, but are eased.

Several new proposals have been made for government controls of campaign messages. These include proposals to regulate advertising to make the identity of the sponsor of the advertisement more apparent. The intent is to increase the visibility of messages that identify the source. Such messages are obligatory, but they are often very small and are displayed so briefly that most viewers miss them. However, there is no agreement among experts about a sure-fire way to call attention to them. It has also been proposed to allow only advertisements that show the candidates speaking directly to viewers or debating with their opponents (*Washington Monthly* 1990).

Another suggestion is that stations should be obliged to give free air time to all candidates, since the federal government does not charge fees for station licences. Proponents of this point out that broadcasters earned $27 billion in advertising revenues in 1988. Recent proposals have also called for reorganizing and strengthening the Federal Election Commission (FEC). The Commission handles complaints about unfair and improper campaign and election practices. It has three members from each party, putting it into perennial deadlock along partisan lines because four commissioners must agree before any action can be taken.

More than half the states have laws against exit polling that prohibit asking voters who leave polling places how they voted, and then releasing this information immediately to the public. Nevertheless, these laws are rarely enforced since they are believed to violate First Amendment rights (Bates 1986). After the Reagan victories in 1980 and 1984 were broadcast nationwide before the polls had closed in West Coast states, the three major networks, as well as Westinghouse Broadcasting, agreed to delay election outcome projections for each state until its polls had closed. However, polling data from states where the polls have closed are still available. To stop this potentially damaging information leak, Congress tried three times, starting in 1986, to pass a *Uniform Poll Closing Act,* and although these attempts have failed, the prognosis for ultimate success seems favourable.

The only other controls that have a direct impact on the media coverage are limitations on campaign financing, which limit the amount of money that candidates may spend on the campaign and the sum that various donors may contribute. The purpose is to reduce excessive inequalities in financial resources. Since campaigns are costly, especially when it comes to procuring mass media coverage, wealthy individuals and groups can pay to get more coverage, giving them a greater opportunity to influence elections than financially poorer groups. Unfortunately, many of the laws regulating campaign financing can easily be bypassed, so the spectre of undue control remains. For example, while the contributions of individual donors are limited, the number of donors is unlimited. Moreover, many laws and regulations intended to curb campaign spending have been successfully challenged as violations of First Amendment freedoms.

Pressure to finance campaigns publicly has also borne some fruit. Since 1972, federal income taxpayers have been able to specify that $1 or $2 of their taxes should go to the federal campaign fund for presidential campaigns. This amounts to an indirect federal subsidy; the federal government forgoes tax revenues, but only at the direction of individual taxpayers. The law was intended to make candidates less dependent on special interests and to curb overall spending. Presidential candidates who accept federal money, as nearly all do, must accept limits on the amount of money that they raise privately. In recent years, it has also been proposed that acceptance of public funding should carry the obligation to participate in campaign debates among the presidential and vice-presidential nominees. New Jersey, for example, already has such a law. It mandates two one-hour debates during gubernatorial primaries and final elections for candidates who accept state funding.

According to John W. McGarry, chairman of the FEC, the spending limit for presidential candidates in the 1992 primaries is $33.6 million. A candidate who observes the limit may claim up to $13.5 million in federal matching money. The actual award is based on dollar-for-dollar matching of small private contributions that may not exceed $250. Currently, the public funding of presidential campaigns appears to be threatened for two major reasons. One springs from the financing law, which pegs expenditure limits to inflation and population growth but has kept the income tax deductions stationary since 1976. The other reason is that taxpayer contributions to the election fund have been lagging. For example, in 1989 only 19.9 percent of taxpayers authorized the deduction, compared to 28.7 percent in 1980. Meanwhile, campaign costs and the need for funding have risen sharply. These problems explain why proposals to extend public funding to congressional campaigns have made little progress. Most candidates, too, have shown little enthusiasm for public funding because they do not like some of the strings tied to spending the federal money.

Self-Regulation

The very limited legal constraints on campaign coverage are bolstered by self-regulation through established professional norms. Probably the strongest influence on who and what gets covered comes from the role perceptions of American journalists. These perceptions are fuelled by an unstable mixture of conflicting motivations. On the one hand, since most American media are privately owned and are operated for profit, journalists see themselves as business people. Their mission is to attract media audiences so that their enterprises, which depend heavily on advertising revenues, remain profitable. They give the audience what they think the audience wants, which is entertaining news, often dubbed "infotainment." There is ample evidence that their appraisal of public wishes is correct. When offered a choice between serious political programming and entertainment, most Americans opt for entertainment, despite protestations to the contrary. Attention spans for news items are short. The longer, more detailed newscasts on public television, which are available free of charge, are shunned compared to the attention given to more entertaining regular news programs.

Voter education is definitely not the goal for most journalists. As one producer put it when asked about possible ways in which he might plead for more time from his station for election reports, "The worst thing we could do is to use 'the educational gambit.' If I went in and used that gambit, I'd be thrown out. They would tell me to go to work for educational television or public broadcasting" (Semetko et al. 1991, 36).

At editorial conferences, where stories for newscasts are selected, election news is just another story that must compete for time on the basis of its newsworthiness rather than on the basis of public policy concerns. In the typical newscast, as described by an NBC producer, "The 'Nightly News' will normally have about three and a half to four minutes of campaign reporting, something like one minute and 45 seconds for each candidate plus some 30 seconds for comments by correspondents and (anchor) Tom Brokaw. This is less than 20 percent of the total amount of 22 minutes available to the show each night" (Semetko et al. 1991, 37–38).

On the other hand, this attitude that news production should be treated as a business venture is balanced by a sense of obligation to present stories that are important for the public to know. The notion that the media have a special civic obligation is embedded in American political culture. It explains why their business is the only one mentioned in the Constitution and given special status. Media are perceived as the eyes and ears of the public and as being obliged to supply information that the public needs. The print media, in particular, often provide more detailed election coverage since they have more space available for political news than the broadcast media. The media also serve as civic watchdogs – as a fourth branch of government that holds the threat of adverse publicity over errant public officials. As part of the watchdog function, the media periodically look behind the stories submitted by government officials, particularly during election contests when the danger of deceptive government messages is heightened.

Self-scrutiny by the media has become more common. Many newspapers now have reporters and columnists who specialize in assessing the quality of media coverage. However, it is more common for newspapers to critique television coverage than their own stories. In 1988, the balance was 58 percent television criticism to 26 percent newspaper criticism, with 16 percent of the stories critiquing both media. Subjects mentioned frequently included the negative coverage of vice-presidential candidate Dan Quayle, the propriety of designating George Bush as the presidential winner early on and the deficiencies in issue coverage (Buchanan 1991). In addition to self-criticism, there has been an upswing of media criticism by other sources, which the print media have reported extensively.

Another important development in monitoring the quality of media messages is the advertisement watch that a number of print and electronic media have instituted; the purpose is to scrutinize candidate advertising claims and to alert readers to misrepresentations. In some cases, media have investigated issues raised by candidate pronouncements so that they could supply factual data which had been excluded from the candidate messages; the purpose here is to clarify meanings that might otherwise fail to emerge. For example, a claim that a candidate favours tax reduction might be balanced by a story indicating the cuts in services that reduced taxes would entail. While the positive consequences of such advertising monitoring remain to be assessed, there appear to be some unintended undesirable results: press attention to questionable advertisements has increased public awareness of them, along with public familiarity, and often acceptance, of their messages (Owen 1991).

The major media have also improved the way in which they report polls. They routinely apprise the public of their polling methods and margins of error. Many write stories that put polling figures into proper perspective. The quality of poll conduct and interpretation has improved considerably. However, as pointed out in news stories, many smaller dailies and weeklies and smaller radio and television stations still fall short of acceptable standards.

Coverage Patterns
On average, in presidential election years, which are peak years for election coverage, presidential election stories constitute roughly 13 percent of the news in élite papers, such as the *New York Times* and the *Washington Post*, and 15 percent of the news on the three major television networks: ABC, CBS and NBC. This is roughly the same amount of news devoted to foreign affairs and coverage of crime news (Graber 1988). Campaign coverage is less in most publications that originate in smaller communities.

During the course of the year-long campaign, election stories are not featured with unusual prominence in terms of headline size, front-page or first-story placement, and picture inclusion, and they are only slightly longer than average. This means that they do not dominate the news. Rather, they compete with other news for the voters' attention.

Patterns of coverage by the print media and television are remarkably uniform in the types of situations that are covered and in the aspects of these situations that are stressed. They are also remarkably stable from election to election. This means that situations that are not part of the established patterns described below are not likely to be covered in any of the mass media. This leaves troubling information gaps. When major events occur, all news outlets concentrate on them, often neglecting other important stories that are happening concurrently. This is the "pack journalism" phenomenon that has been decried by many media analysts. (The term was coined to describe reporters who, like a pack of wolves, jointly attack the same news target.) Likewise, journalists use the same appraisal dimensions for all candidates, though the emphasis put on these dimensions and appraisals varies for individual candidates. For example, one candidate's ethics or energy policy positions may be discussed heavily and judged positively or negatively, while the ethics and comparable issue stands of another candidate may be ignored. These disparities make it difficult to compare candidates and make voting choices. However, in some media markets, the press, or organizations like the League of Women Voters, prepare and publish parallel columns of issue positions for each candidate so that these positions can be compared more readily.

The largest variations among the news media throughout the country are in the amount of election coverage and the evaluation of the merits of candidates and their programs. These variations, which explain why voters judge candidates differently despite similar news patterns, are related to the preferences of journalists or media owners and their desire to appeal to different audience predispositions. For example, newspapers in large urban areas, where liberal Democrats abound, are far more likely to support Democratic policies than their country cousins are. Small-town people have a more conservative bent, as do their media. By and large, media owners are a conservative, Republican lot whose views often prevail on the editorial pages, while their staffs are far more liberal (Lichter et al. 1986).

Content analyses of major newspapers and of television networks show that, on average, 60 percent of the substantive news in campaign stories focuses primarily on the candidates' personal and professional qualifications and 40 percent focuses on policy issues. When every issue in the story is coded (rather than a maximum of three issues per story, as is usual), the proportions tip more in the direction of issues (Graber 1983, 283–300). Table 6.1 presents the breakdown distinguished by one group of analysts for 1988, showing a somewhat higher than average issue content. Discussion of the candidates' qualifications includes personality traits, style characteristics and ability to project a favourable image, as well as professional skills. Usually, less than half of the comments in newspapers deal with professional skills, such as skills in handling foreign affairs, sustaining the economy and control-

Table 6.1
Presidential and vice-presidential coverage in campaign '88
(in percentages for each candidate)

Topic	Bush	Dukakis	Both	Quayle	Bentsen	Both
Character	26	20	8	39	45	19
Competence	22	21	13	48	31	38
Economic issues	16	13	23	1	2	10
Domestic issues	23	30	35	5	12	24
International issues	12	15	21	7	10	10
Total numbers of stories	541	329	454	368	58	21
Percent of stories	31	19	26	21	3	1

Source: Adapted from Buchanan (1991). Based on 1 771 stories from 18 media sources, 8 September to 8 November 1988. The media were the *New York Times, Washington Post, Christian Science Monitor, Wall Street Journal, Los Angeles Times, Newsweek, Time, U.S. News and World Report, National Journal, New York Daily News, Chicago Tribune, Houston Chronicle, Sacramento Bee,* NBC, ABC, CBS, CNN and PBS.

Note: Percentages do not add to 100 because of rounding.

ling crime. For television, the emphasis on professional skills is an even smaller proportion. The most frequently mentioned characteristics are trustworthiness, strength of character, leadership capabilities and compassion. Style and image projection characteristics trail.

Content analyses of election news have also shown that the coverage of policy issues is spotty, neglecting many important issues even when the candidates differ about the best ways to handle them. The issue positions of vice-presidential candidates remain virtually unexplored. The main emphasis is usually on domestic rather than foreign affairs. Domestic problems are more easily explained because audiences can be assumed to know and understand the basic context. It is also easier to arrange good picture coverage for domestic affairs. Issues that are complex, of long standing and lacking in violence are least likely to be covered. Many social issues, such as care of the elderly and inadequate housing, fall into this category.

Media issue coverage is much narrower than party platforms and does not stress the partisan aspects of the campaign. In recent elections, print media have featured some 25 issues and television around 20. Of these, only half were given extensive coverage. By contrast, party platforms have covered well over 50 issues. The media prefer narrow issues on which there is a clash of views, but the candidates prefer to discuss broad, consensual issues; two-thirds of the issues mentioned by candidates are broad, compared to one-quarter of issues mentioned by the media (Patterson 1982).

Television coverage of policy issues is even more limited than newspaper coverage. Stories are briefer and there is more emphasis on dramatic elements. The sources that are interviewed know that television news works in snippets and have learned to frame their remarks accordingly. Events therefore become fragmented and barren of context. Yet the public seems to prefer this approach, judging from the fact that audiences are quite small for the more probing newscasts on public television and for the occasional in-depth election analysis programs. Television news has become the primary source of election information for the majority of people, ranking well ahead of newspapers.

The large number of print stories that appear during major national campaigns make it possible to discuss various topics in some depth. Since print media have fewer worries about losing clients to competitors (because nearly all American cities are now served by only one daily newspaper), they often take advantage of their position of strength. Stories analysing the candidates, the issues and the conduct of the campaign, including information about the nature of advertisements and the significance of various polls, can all be reported at some length.

Television news must use different strategies. To keep audiences amused through fast-paced news, the usual election story is compressed into 60 to 120 seconds. To save time, television newscasters create stereotypes early in the campaign. Thereafter, they build stories around these stereotypes. These televised stereotypes are the most pervasive election information made available to the electorate. The brevity of television news stories gives little chance for in-depth reporting and analysis. Stories therefore present simple, graphic images that illustrate selected themes about the candidates and the campaign. Like print news stories, they are selected for their presumed attractiveness to the audience. This means that they must contain new information that is exciting because of its significance, its human drama or its element of surprise. When these qualities fade, journalists switch attention to fresher targets.

The most attractive themes are shared by television and print media, as well as being reported by nearly all individual media outlets. The result is pack journalism. A large number of news stories are initially collected by major wire services such as the Associated Press (AP) and United Press International (UPI) or by the wire services of major papers such as the *New York Times* and *Los Angeles Times*. Skilful communications directors of the candidates have met with increasing success in recent campaigns in creating appropriate news material, thereby tempting journalists to publish news that benefits their candidate (Morrison 1988; Runkel 1989).

Issue coverage by news sources is supplemented by issue coverage contained in political advertising in newspapers, on television and radio, or disseminated through videotapes, bumper stickers and billboards. In earlier elections, when television commercials often lasted for five minutes, the major campaign issues were covered more extensively in these commercials than in network newscasts (Patterson and McClure 1976). In the 1972 presidential campaign, between 18 September and 2 November, more than 65 minutes of advertising time were used by the Nixon campaign to report on the candidate's foreign policy stands regarding Vietnam, China, the Soviet Union and U.S. allies. The television networks spent an average of 15 minutes on these commercials, and most viewers remembered more from them than they did from news items in regular broadcasts. Simplicity of content in commercials, the excellent packaging and the frequent repetition of advertising messages explain the better retention.

In recent campaigns, most commercials have been compressed into 30-second spots and their issue content has diminished (Kern 1989; Nesbit 1988). This does not mean that their ability to convey memorable information has diminished, especially early in the primary season when voters form their initial opinions about many of the contenders. When voters are asked what they know about the candidates, responses frequently refer to facts gleaned from advertisements. This is especially true for voters who are politically uninvolved and therefore naïve. During the 1988 campaign, most voters remembered Vice-President Bush's advertised charge that Governor Dukakis was soft on crime and furloughed murderers.

The memorability of these charges was further increased by ample press commentary about the controversial content. A study of 569 voters from Iowa, New Jersey and Virginia, which tested recall of the content of 1988 campaign advertisements, showed that 96 percent of the respondents remembered the content of Bush's commercials, as compared to 90 percent for Dukakis's commercials (Owen 1991, 45). Considering that the sample population ranked above average in education and that it was responding to a mail questionnaire, the high memory rate is likely to be above average. Nonetheless, it provides support for other findings that point to the high retention of information contained in commercials.

However, except for low-information, low-involvement campaigns, advertisements appear to have limited persuasive appeal, although people learn facts from them (Patterson and McClure 1976; Robinson

1981; Owen 1991). Reactions to advertisements seem perceiver-determined: people see in them what they want to see (Owen 1991), and commercials for a candidate whom they oppose are not likely to impress them favourably. The persuasive appeal of commercials is also undermined because people are exposed to a mixture of supportive and opposing advertisements. This makes them cynical. There is little scholarly corroboration for candidate claims that they won or lost because of certain commercials. Election choices hinge on a combination of many factors so that it is impossible to isolate a single one. Nonetheless, candidates and their handlers believe in the power of commercials to sway votes, particularly as partisan ties have steadily lost strength. Advertising campaigns have therefore been escalating, especially since cable television provides a new and somewhat cheaper outlet and makes it easier to tailor messages to the needs of smaller, more homogeneous audiences.

The similarities in overall patterns of coverage spring from a strong consensus among journalists about what is newsworthy and should therefore be covered. For most journalists, the criteria of newsworthiness reflect their views of the type of stories that media audiences would like to read and watch. Producing audience pleasers means concentrating and even spurring conflicts, keeping score about who is ahead and who is behind, and reporting whatever dramatic incidents or juicy personal details may emerge. Complex stories that are stuffed with data, especially statistics, are shunned. Journalists are less concerned about covering what audiences ought to know, in terms of the criteria derived from democratic theories. However, concerns about keeping voters well informed do account, at least to a minor degree, for some of the "meat" that is included in coverage.

Instead of a "campaign model," where coverage would be a mirror of the actual campaign, coverage follows the "incentive model" where the appeal of the story to its prospective audience is the incentive that prompts journalists to cover it (Hofstetter 1976). The incentive model is clearest in media geared to specialized audiences, such as ethnic groups or economic interest groups. Their media unabashedly focus on stories that are of special interest to that particular audience.

News patterns are not dominated by what the candidates wish to publicize, although they are drawn from what the candidates say and do. The fact that newspeople's preferences govern story choices mutes the candidates' influence on campaign coverage but by no means obliterates it. Candidates and their staffs have become increasingly adept at generating the kind of story materials and photo opportunities that journalists find irresistible. Even so, candidates perennially complain that their discussions of policy issues are ignored. During the 1980 presidential primaries, for example, five of the eleven major party candidates devoted more than half of their speeches to issues. Reagan and Kennedy speeches had more than 70 percent issue content. Yet media coverage failed to reflect this substantial emphasis on issues. Candidates also point out that media coverage routinely lags behind the acceleration of campaign activity before the primary and general elections, when candidates want to present their case to the voters and when newspeople are holding back on coverage because they are waiting to report the election outcome.

Concerns about Quality of Coverage

Analysts of campaign coverage are concerned that it is riveted too much on discussions of candidate personalities at the expense of a focus on issues. When issues are discussed, the overriding consideration is newsworthiness rather than intrinsic importance. For instance, prison furloughs for convicted murderers rank ahead of discussions of a staggering national debt or relations with a crumbling communist empire. Even when ample time is available to explore serious issues in depth, as happened when presidential nominating conventions were covered in full, the emphasis has been on brief, rapidly paced, freshly breaking events. In fact, the amount of coverage for particular issues often seems to be in inverse proportion to their significance. For example, huge amounts of coverage were given to candidate Carter's interview with *Playboy* magazine in 1976, in which he discussed his sexual urges, and to Senator Bentsen's essentially meaningless statement in 1988 that vice-presidential candidate Quayle was no John F. Kennedy. Whatever symbolic meaning these stories may have carried about Carter's character and Bentsen's assessment of Quayle's presidential calibre – and obviously there was some – they did not merit the amount of television time and newspaper space devoted to them.

Especially on television, stories lack the necessary context that would help the voter determine how important a particular quality or issue is in relation to the job that the incumbent will have to perform. There has been very little systematic analysis of the essential requirements for the various governmental jobs and for ways to test which of the candidates best meets these requirements. In other professions and trades, precise standards and evaluation criteria have been developed, but this has not occurred for legislative and executive officials.

In presidential elections, coverage deficiencies are most noticeable during the primaries, when high quality is crucial. The media concentrate their attention on the front runners, thus handicapping the campaigns of the less well-known candidates from the start. This makes the ability to win in early primaries a key qualification for a successful candidacy. For example, in 1980, 81 percent of primary election coverage went to the four front runners; the remaining 19 percent was shared by the six second-tier contenders. At a time when the electorate should be made familiar with the diverse candidates, there is less emphasis on discussing personal qualities than later on. Most emphasis goes to horse-race and hoopla.

Critics have also warned that campaign coverage has become excessively negative, as illustrated in table 6.2, causing voters to become cynical and disinclined to vote. From a purely quantitative perspective, evaluative comments are not as bountiful as neutral statements. Yet from a qualitative perspective, when impact is considered, negative statements are most memorable and influential, followed by positive ones; neutral statements come last. In the negative vein, electoral politics is depicted as a disreputable activity undertaken by politicians to fool the public, and the media are pictured as the public's defenders who try to uncover the truth. Journalists speculate about the venal motivations that prompt candidates to choose policy positions and build political coalitions. The pervasive cynicism is bound to rub off on the media audience, even though it is partly balanced by serious and more respectful coverage.

The predominance of comments about the candidates' personal failings, incompetence and mismanagement is hardly fair to capable candidates whose personal strengths, skills and professional successes are slighted. It undermines their ability to command a following after the election, especially from voters in the opposing party. In 1988, for example, the chief Democratic contenders during the primaries were

Table 6.2
Candidate evaluation in post–Labor Day network television news, 1984

Candidate	Score
Ronald Reagan	-33
George Bush	-55
Walter Mondale	-10
Geraldine Ferraro	-28

Source: Data from Clancey and Robinson (1985, 53).

Scores constitute the balance between all explicitly positive and negative references to the candidate. Neutral comments have been omitted. $N = 625$ news stories from the ABC, CBS and NBC early nightly news.

derisively referred to as "the seven dwarfs." During the general election, 87 percent of the stories about candidate Bush were negative or were a mixture of positive and negative remarks, while for candidate Dukakis the comparable score was 62 percent (Buchanan 1991). The lead paragraph in a 1980 *Time* magazine story summed up the Reagan/Carter race in a typically downbeat mood: "For more than a year, two flawed candidates have been floundering toward the final showdown, each unable to give any but his most unquestioning supporters much reason to vote for him except dislike of his opponent" (King 1981). Negative comment comes primarily from selecting sources with negative opinions about a candidate (for instance, soliciting appraisal of a candidate's pro-nuclear energy stand from nuclear foe Ralph Nader). While negative news is pursued, good news and favourable appraisals are shunned lest they be interpreted as flattery. Cynicism is chic.

Another complaint is that the bulk of campaign coverage usually goes to horse-race events – who is ahead and behind and what happened on the campaign trail. Such coverage trivializes elections, making them seem like fleeting contests. In 1988, 60 percent of the combined content of newspaper and television stories dealt with the horse race or candidate squabbles, with most media hovering near the mean. These figures are based on content analyses of campaign coverage in 18 news sources: the *New York Times, Washington Post, Christian Science Monitor, Wall Street Journal, Los Angeles Times, Newsweek, Time, U.S. News and World Report, National Journal, New York Daily News, Chicago Tribune, Houston Chronicle, Sacramento Bee,* NBC, ABC, CBS, CNN and PBS. These media were analysed between 8 September and 8 November 1988. By comparison with the coverage of campaign events, coverage of policy issues was sparse, amounting to roughly 30 percent for issues and candidate qualifications combined (Buchanan 1991). The remaining coverage was devoted to news about voters and about the nature of media coverage.

The emphasis on horse-race coverage has been enhanced by the growing popularity of featuring public opinion polls. Polls have become an increasingly important aspect of campaign coverage, especially since major media institutions now have their own polling divisions. Examples are the CBS–*New York Times* poll, the NBC–Associated Press poll and the ABC–*Washington Post* poll. These polling divisions become hyperactive during campaigns and their results are featured by the organizations that are footing the bill. During the final week of the 1984 presidential election, for instance, the *New York Times* devoted one-third of its election coverage to poll reports (Patterson and Davis 1985). The polls become benchmarks for voters, who use them to identify potential winners and losers and, if so inclined, switch their votes to jump on or off the bandwagon or change their minds about the need to cast their votes (Owen 1991). Polls are also used by potential candidates to determine whether to enter the race or to stay out. For example, Reagan decided to challenge Ford in 1976 because Ford's ratings were low in the period before the Republican nominating convention (Broh 1983). Similarly, Carter's low poll ratings in the 1980 campaign encouraged Edward Kennedy to challenge him. Low poll ratings, besides suggesting lack of voter support, also portend diminished financial resources and volunteer help.

The complaints about too much horse-race coverage at the expense of stories about candidate qualifications and policy issues must be put into context. When campaigns are lengthy, candidate qualifications and policy issues, once they have been covered, are no longer news. The only genuinely new happenings are the unfolding events of the campaign. They may be trivial, but they are new and exciting. Races make hearts pound. Americans love them. The basic language about campaigns refers to combat and games; it does not refer to discourse, argument, reasoning or contemplation. Candidates "run" for election or "compete" for them. They don't "stand" or "sit" for elections, as the metaphors suggest in other countries. Networks, ever eager to boost audience size, feel compelled to make political stories entertaining. For television, this means brief stories with attractive visuals, and preferably reporting something new – a formula that spells "horse-race."

The desire to keep audiences attentive also explains why campaign stories frequently feature predictions about future events, even when they are useless for preparatory action. Predictions heighten the drama and bring people back to find out whether the predicted event did in fact happen. For example, voters gain little from the many election outcome forecasts that abound on the day before voting takes place. There is little harm in such news, of course; but when there are frequent, justified complaints about insufficient time and space to present important news, why waste that precious resource on idle speculation?

Lower-Level Races

Coverage patterns for lower-level races are broadly similar to those for national races, but there are distinctions because these campaigns are much shorter and less well financed. Coverage is much sparser, therefore, and focuses on matters that are of particular local concern. The substance and amount of coverage depend on the race. Hotly contested ones receive the most attention. When the outcome seems certain, there is much less attention on the horse-race and on the personality traits of candidates, and more attention is focused on the record of the incumbent and the claims of the challengers. As well, reporting of poll results is less common than on the national level (Entman 1992).

Television coverage is sparse for campaigns that dip below the statewide level, especially when the boundaries of media markets and electoral districts do not match well. It is considered wasteful to use free or paid media to discuss a campaign that interests only a fraction of the audience reached by a medium. Local elections make more use of radio commercials, billboards and flyers than is true of nationwide campaigns. Except for nonpartisan elections, they often put greater stress on identifying the candidate's party. The chief goal is usually to gain name recognition or, failing that, to ride into office on the strength of a party label. However, local patterns are not homogeneous; they vary from state to state and from race to race.

THE MEDIA AUDIENCE

Ideal versus Real Voters

How well do the media educate voters? The answer depends on the definition of "well educated." An idealistic definition posits voters who have been informed by the media about all of the major political issues of the day, the policy options available for dealing with them and the policy positions taken by all candidates for a particular office. Voters would also know their own policy preferences. As rational decision makers, they would determine which candidate reflects their positions most closely, and they would then vote for that candidate. Roughly 12 percent of the electorate meet these criteria (Neuman 1986).

Assuming some diligence in exposing themselves to élite newspapers, news magazines and telecasts, such voters can find the necessary information in the American media for top executive positions, such as the presidency or governorships, and for major national and state legislative posts; but for lower-level positions, such information would be hard to find.

The vast majority of voters do not come close to the ideal pattern, and they lack the inclination to do so. For example, when the National Opinion Research Center asked people in its 1982 General Social Survey to rate matters that were important to them, family and children ranked at the top (6.77 on a 7-point scale); politics and public life rated 4.02, below relatives, friends and acquaintances, career and work, leisure time, and religion and church. During the early months of the 1988 presidential campaign, 69 percent of the respondents to a nationwide Gallup poll had paid attention to a human interest story about a small child trapped in an abandoned well; 40 percent had followed the 1987 stock market crash closely; 37 percent had paid close attention to the U.S. Navy's escort of Kuwaiti tankers in the Persian Gulf; but only 15 percent claimed close attention to the Republican race (Buchanan 1991).

One can raise questions about the soundness of the traditional model of the ideal voter, since it flies in the face of the realities of the civic virtues and cognitive capacities of average Americans. Average voters do not want to spend much time learning about electoral politics, and even when they do make the effort, the complexity of modern politics makes clear-cut decisions impossible. Forming opinions about complex issues like defence policy or monetary policy is well beyond the reach of the average voter. Besides, most policy options have advantages as well as disadvantages and bring unequal benefits and sacrifices to various groups of citizens. The fact that controversies about these policies are widely aired in the media is an added complication. If the experts disagree about the appropriate assumptions and remedies in major policy areas, how can ordinary citizens expect to reach defensible conclusions?

Given the multitude of issues with which modern governments deal, voters are likely to have major areas of disagreement with every candidate. Moreover, it is uncertain which of the issues discussed during a campaign will require action during a candidate's term and what obstacles are likely to affect the implementation of such action, making it impossible to stick to campaign pledges. New and unforeseen issues may arise later on. For this reason, it may be wiser and simpler to concentrate on general impressions of the character and capacities of the candidate or to use party affiliation as cues.

An Informed Electorate?

In view of the limited interest in election news, it is not surprising that the biannual surveys conducted by the Survey Research Center at the University of Michigan show that, on average, only 16 percent of the electorate reach genuinely high scores when judged on their ability to give up to five responses to open-ended questions about liking and disliking parties and presidents (Kessel 1988; Smith 1989). Fifty-nine percent score below the mean in knowledge about candidates and parties (Kessel 1988); only slightly more than half of the respondents are able to comment on the strengths and weaknesses of more than one candidate. During the 1980 presidential primaries, only 17 percent of the respondents increased their knowledge during the primaries, which occur from February to June; another 10 percent actually lost ground over the course of the primaries (Keeter and Zukin 1983). By early September 1988, nearly half of the respondents did not know who the

1 5 9

M A S S   M E D I A   A N D   E L E C T I O N S   I N   T H E   U . S . A .

vice-presidential nominee was on the Democratic ticket (Buchanan 1991). The fact that citizens also report being interested in the campaign obviously does not mean that they learn a great deal new.

However, the situation is not as dismal as it may seem. Although most people retain little specific knowledge from exposure to the media, they do gain impressions and draw conclusions which they are able to recall later. Thus, dissatisfaction with a series of candidates sponsored by one's party over several elections may crystallize into a feeling that the party fields poor calibre candidates, even if one does not remember who these individuals were. Studies of inferential reasoning also indicate that voters have schemata about many aspects of elections, such as the stands of the parties, from which they are able to draw inferences (Conover and Feldman 1986). This explains why they may retain conclusions drawn from long-forgotten facts. People often vote for the candidate who espouses positions that they prefer, even when they cannot recall what positions their chosen candidate has taken or the specifics of the policy (Graber 1988).

Knowledge about the candidates reflects media coverage but is a much abbreviated and blurred version. Facts and figures are rarely recalled. When they are, mistakes are common. Most voters pay attention to only a narrow array of issues which have special salience for them. Complex policy alternatives are remembered far less often than policies that involve simple yes or no choices. When people are asked about what they have learned and why they would vote for a candidate, three out of four answers concern personality traits (Graber 1989); they revolve around human qualities such as trustworthiness, strength of character and will, and compassion for people in all walks of life.

Basing decisions largely on personality criteria makes sense, because this is one area in which voters have developed judgemental expertise. They are particularly astute in interpreting the body language visible on television. Notwithstanding candidate efforts to project idealized images and media efforts to deflate these images, the realities of the situation become apparent to most voters over the course of a lengthy campaign. Even though voters often evaluate candidates differently, this does not mean that they disagree about their characteristics (Owen 1991). When voting choices are not based on personality characteristics, they are often based on stereotypical party cues. When party cues are lacking and when media coverage is scant, as happens in primary elections or in nonpartisan elections at the local level, voter turnout is usually very low.

When people mention issues, they stress domestic economic and social problems proportionately much more than the media do. People usually do not refer to campaign events and they touch much more lightly on foreign affairs and general domestic issues. Although people find campaign hoopla entertaining, they make little effort to commit it to memory. Focus groups conducted during the 1988 elections suggest that the public considers horse-race coverage excessive. However, the focus group participants did not express great interest in exposing themselves to the news about issues and about candidate qualifications that was provided by public television stations, CNN and the major national newspapers (Buchanan 1991).

Media impact on the vote is greatest for heavy consumers of media fare who are ambivalent about the candidates (Weaver et al. 1981). Messages are most potent if they concern a significant unforeseeable event that appears as a genuinely new consideration. Major foreign policy successes or disasters and major scandals are examples. Thus, there seems little reason to fear that campaign coverage will lead to massive swings in votes. However, since many elections are very close, a shift of even a small percentage of the vote can change the election outcome.

This fact explains the concern about media impact on election outcomes. The concern extends to possible bandwagon or underdog effects from broadcasting election returns and projections while the polls are still open on election day. The precise balance between these countervailing effects remains uncertain (Tannenbaum and Kostrich 1983). To forestall them, in states which have no legal prohibitions, voluntary restraints by media organizations have been recommended and have partly been implemented. Moreover, it remains controversial to what extent journalists should alter news production out of a concern with the impact that their stories are apt to have. In the case of exit polls, concern about possibly adverse consequences from such polls and from early forecasts seems excessive to some observers, who point out that voters are bombarded throughout the election year with information designed to sway their vote. Why, they ask, should there be squeamishness on the last day of the campaign about potentially persuasive information?

The issue is further clouded by the fact that the actual impact of such early disclosures is in dispute. Various studies have come to different conclusions, possibly because impact varies. One recent study suggests that roughly 20 percent of the registered voters who did not vote in 1988 stayed away because exit polls indicated that the winner had already been determined. While their votes would not have changed the outcome of the presidential contest, they could have affected other contests for which these people would probably have voted if they had gone to the polls (Lavrakas and Holley 1990).

BEYOND VOTER EDUCATION

The major impact of media coverage springs from the effects of news stories on the viability of the candidates, rather than from producing well-educated voters. Media are most influential early on, when impressions of parties and candidates are shaped. Name recognition bestowed by news stories and a winner image are the crucial factors that permit front runners to emerge. Front-runner status then attracts money and other campaign resources. The media also determine to a large extent by what crucial issues each candidate's competence will be judged. They do this by focusing the voter's attention on selected individuals and by highlighting selected aspects of their personalities, careers and policy positions. By moulding the images of political reality, the media shape the political and emotional context of the election that leads to subsequent voting decisions (Hadley 1976).

When the media highlight dramatic events, often out of proportion to their significance, they become the highly influential occurrences that have been called "medialities" (Robinson 1981). Medialities may be scandals involving the candidate's personal or official life, or events like the stock market crash of 1987. The way such stories are featured gives them exaggerated importance. The media can also destroy candidacies by publishing information that reflects adversely on the candidate's character, even if it does not genuinely relate to the candidate's fitness for office. For example, news that the candidate used a prohibited drug decades earlier may ruin the candidate's chances. Information about marital infidelity, divorce, out-of-wedlock children or even cheating in college may be highlighted and may lower poll ratings, thus reducing the candidate's ability to attract campaign resources.

Campaign conduct has become media-centred because candidates believe that media coverage is crucial. Gaining coverage involves spending large blocks of time cultivating relations with media personnel, accommodating to media beats and deadlines and, most importantly, doing and saying things that provide good story material. The ability to cater to human-interest concerns or to the fascination with political conflict is important. News coverage is viewed as a matter of exchange. The media exchange their ability to publicize candidates and issues in return for story material supplied by candidates in readily usable ways.

Audiovisual messages are deemed particularly potent in conveying favourable images of candidates, because they are akin to personal encounters between candidates and voters. They can convey impressions about the candidates' personalities and capabilities far more rapidly and completely than any other medium. For example, the apprehension that John F. Kennedy might be too young and inexperienced for the presidency was allayed by his performance in the televised debate with Richard Nixon. Similarly, the fear that Ronald Reagan might be too old for the rigours of the presidency was allayed by the vigour he displayed during the televised debate with Walter Mondale (Rosenberg and McCafferty 1987).

A much-quoted anecdote captures how highly televised effectiveness is regarded. CBS television reporter Leslie Stahl condemned candidate Ronald Reagan during the 1984 campaign for falsely posturing as a man of peace and compassion. Her indictment was accompanied by pictures that showed Reagan "basking in a sea of flag-waving supporters, beaming beneath red-white-and-blue balloons floating skyward, sharing concerns with farmers in a field, picnicking with Mid-Americans, pumping iron, wearing a bathing suit and tossing a football ... getting the Olympic torch from a runner, greeting wheelchair athletes at the handicapped Olympics, greeting senior citizens at their housing project, honoring veterans who landed on Normandy ... joshing with the press corps, impressing suburban school children, wooing black inner-city kids" (Schram 1987). Stahl's attack on the candidate fell flat. Indeed, one Reagan assistant actually thanked Stahl for broadcasting four and a half minutes of favourable pictures, because "that's all the American people see" (ibid.). This observation is supported by the fact that during the 1984 presidential campaign, favourable pictures coincided with favourable poll results even when verbal media commentary was predominantly negative for a candidate (Graber 1987b).

In recognition of the potency of pictures, candidates now rely on experts to hone their television skills and to create appealing visuals. The television age has put a premium on candidates who perform well on that medium. This makes it more difficult, though not impossible, for candidates who lack these skills to be selected initially and to prevail if they are selected. Walter Mondale attributed his inability to defeat Ronald Reagan to the disparity in television skills. While it is difficult to establish just how much this disparity contributed to his defeat, analysts agree that it was a factor. The candidate who is able to hire the best team of media experts, which usually means the candidate who has most money available, enjoys a tremendous advantage. Currently, media expenses, including the cost of commercials and of gaining news exposure, are the single largest cost item for candidates at all levels, taking between 30 to 50 percent of their budgets.

PROBLEM AREAS

Structural and Political Bias

What are the major inadequacies in campaign coverage at the present time? High on the list are problems of unequal coverage for various contenders. These problems are primarily matters of structural bias that arise from technical difficulties, rather than political bias based on ideological considerations. For example, it is easier to interview a New York–based candidate about a breaking news event for the early morning news than a Los Angeles contender who would have to be contacted well before dawn. Both types of bias are troubling because they affect the outcome of campaigns. Political bias is rare because the media are not under party control. To appeal to broad audiences, they try to keep explicit partisan views out of news stories. It is therefore not surprising that only 1–4 percent of news stories show traces of political bias (Graber 1989). Editorials, of course, are intrinsically biased because they express value judgements. While the élite press leans toward liberal views, the majority of the press has usually leaned in a conservative direction on its editorial pages, despite the fact that liberals predominate among rank-and-file reporters and editors (Lichter et al. 1986).

As part of their editorializing, the news media explicitly endorse various candidates. Their willingness to take sides raises questions about partisanship possibly creeping into news stories. The impact of editorial endorsements varies. Republican presidential candidates have received most of the endorsements in the 20th century, yet, in spite of this, Democrats have won close to half the elections. Endorsements seem to be more influential when they come from élite media and refer to lower-level offices rather than the top spots. Below the presidential level, the media tend to give somewhat more coverage to their endorsed candidates.

However, for the most part, electronic as well as print media geared for the general public try to produce balanced coverage of all major candidates for the same office. But the standards used in striving for fairness and balance are debatable. Newspeople traditionally aim for rough parity in the number of stories about each candidate and rough parity in the number of overtly favourable and unfavourable stories, irrespective of the comparative newsworthiness of the candidates or their comparative merits. Fairness, as currently interpreted, does not mean that competing candidates are discussed along identical dimensions, despite complaints by various politically disadvantaged groups, such as women and African Americans, that such disparities are unfair to them. African Americans contend that too much attention is focused on their race, while women believe that coverage often ascribes political interests to them based on stereotypes. Current fairness conventions do not require that the candidates' friends and enemies are quoted in equal proportions or that their stories get similar time, space or placement, nor do they require proportionate coverage of major political orientations. For example, during the 1984 Democratic National

Convention, 85 percent of the interviews with Democrats featured liberals, even though liberals constitute a much smaller proportion than this in the Democratic party in Congress. Only 56 percent of the Democrats are liberals (Adams 1985).

Coverage varies because the newsworthiness of candidates varies, as does their willingness to talk to reporters (Graber 1986). Media markets often do not coincide with electoral districts, and consequently the appeals of candidates who are of interest to only a small fraction of the audience in that market tend to be slighted. Charismatic candidates get more coverage than lacklustre ones. Incumbents have a distinct advantage over challengers; even when they attract the same number of campaign stories, they usually get additional attention through coverage of their official duties (Stovall 1984). This is particularly true for top offices such as president and governor, but it is also a factor at the legislative level. Challengers in contested congressional elections receive the least coverage (Goldenberg and Traugott 1984). As table 6.3 shows, in both House and Senate races, most of the coverage of challengers deals with campaign events, whereas incumbents receive most coverage of their political attributes (Clarke and Evans 1983).

The most damaging inequalities in coverage occur during primary contests when many candidates are competing for the same office. The media, in a political triage operation, bestow the lion's share of coverage on the candidates that appear to have the best chance of winning. Usually, these are the incumbents or otherwise already well-known candidates. The emphasis that the media place on early victories makes coverage more manageable, but it also creates a psychological momentum that increases the winning candidates' chance of gaining subsequent victories. Without media legitimation, political unknowns have little chance, and they are forced out of the race prematurely.

Table 6.3
Median number of local newspaper paragraphs mentioning selected themes in 14 tight congressional races, 27 September to 7 November 1978

Themes	Incumbent news	Challenger news
Campaign organization	22	27
Personal characteristics	10	13
Political attributes	49	4
Issues/ideology/group ties	29	12

Source: Clarke and Evans (1983, 61).

The impression that early front runners are likely to win is enhanced by the fact that polls early in a campaign primarily measure name recognition rather than popularity. Thus, well-known candidates benefit because the voters simply do not know the others. Early in the campaign, media coverage and high poll ratings go together and bring in money, but after a while, winning primary contests counts for more. Winners get the coverage and losers do not, except when these results defy expectations. However, the substance of coverage tends to be unfavourable for front runners who are often attacked. (For example, Senator Gary Hart, who received favourable coverage initially, was attacked after he trounced Vice-President Mondale in the 1984 New Hampshire primary election.) Nevertheless, most candidates prefer unfavourable coverage to no coverage at all.

At times, unknown candidates can beat the odds. This happened when Jimmy Carter campaigned for two years before the presidential primaries so that he could gain name recognition. Such tactics have served to stretch out overly long campaigns even further. Another tactic used by candidates to gain a winner image and enhance name recognition is to concentrate on early campaign events, such as the New Hampshire primary and the Iowa caucuses. Winners in these contests increase their chances of gaining early name recognition. For example, after Governor Carter won the New Hampshire primary in 1976, he received the lion's share of media coverage, for although he had garnered only 30 percent of the vote, this exceeded expectations and was therefore considered a major victory (Bartels 1985; Orren and Rockefeller 1987). The same manoeuvre failed to clinch the nomination for Senator Gary Hart, who finished second in the Iowa caucuses and beat Vice-President Mondale in New Hampshire. In the end, the Vice-President received the nomination.

An Embarrassment of Riches

The fact that American elections involve a plethora of offices at the state and local levels makes it difficult to cover all of them and sustain audience interest. Consequently, the media are forced to be selective, and this results in unequal coverage, along with the distortions it brings to the electoral process. Campaigns for the top offices get the most attention at the expense of important but less elevated offices. For example, Americans receive a great deal of information about presidential campaigns but comparatively little about congressional campaigns. A comparison of television coverage of the 1988 presidential campaign with the 1990 congressional campaign showed that only 170 stories were aired during the 1990 congressional races; but when the

1988 presidential race was added, the total swelled to 2 201 stories (*Media Monitor* 1991). Similarly, campaigns for state legislative office rarely receive much coverage, whereas gubernatorial contests are reasonably well covered. In states with long ballots, where the heads of various administrative agencies as well as judges are elected, coverage for individual candidates is extremely sparse.

A major gap in coverage is the slight attention given to vice-presidential candidates, except when they appear to be particularly unfit as happened initially in Vice-President Quayle's case. In a typical presidential campaign, 95 percent of the coverage goes to the presidential contenders and only 5 percent to the vice-presidents – who stand a very good chance of becoming president, but who ride into office under their president's name. Efforts to keep coverage balanced between candidates for the same office do not extend to third-party candidates; they are usually ignored, except for a few prominent ones like George Wallace of the American Independent Party, Robert La Follette of the Progressive Party and John Anderson of the National Unity Campaign.

Another facet of the unequal coverage problem is the relative coverage of various contests during primary campaigns. Early contests are covered excessively, while later ones are slighted. In the 1984 primaries, for example, Iowa and New Hampshire, which represent less than 3 percent of the U.S. population, received almost one-third of the total media coverage in the major television networks and the *New York Times*. New York, California, Pennsylvania, New Jersey and Illinois, which have 31 percent of the U.S. population, received another one-third. This left primaries in the remaining 43 states, where two-thirds of all Americans live, with slightly over one-third of the coverage (Adams 1987). Given the impact that news about winners and losers has on the outcome of the campaign, the ballots cast by voters in the well-covered states become much more influential than ballots cast in other states. Candidates therefore make special efforts to woo voters in these states, including promising them favoured treatment if the candidate wins.

Legislation has been proposed to rearrange primaries so that coverage inequities could be reduced. For example, a large group of states might share the opening of the primary campaign by holding their primaries on the same day. However, states which stand to lose political clout by such an arrangement are likely to block such reforms, arguing that those Southern states which hold combined primaries on "Super Tuesday" in early March have been disappointed in their hopes of attracting more equitable coverage.

Buying Access through Advertising

One common way to gain access to the media is to buy advertising space or time. Many campaign managers believe that campaigns can be won or lost through advertising, making expenditures for creating advertisements and publishing them eminently worthwhile (Kern 1989). For instance, in 1988, voters allegedly learned the cutting edge issues through commercials. Commercials can be carefully constructed to maximize the chances that they will attract voter attention to concerns favoured by their sponsors, and can be coordinated with news and constantly monitored through focus groups and polls. They have the advantage of repetition. On the minus side, they are a comparatively discredited, suspect source.

Television advertising is generally deemed the most effective form of advertising, but it is also the most costly. In 1988, the Bush campaign spent approximately $35 million on television advertising for 37 spots, and the Dukakis campaign spent $30 million for 47 (Owen 1991, 34). The chance of using commercials therefore depends on the ability to raise funds. Minor candidates in national elections – and sometimes even major candidates – have lacked the money to be competitive in advertisements. Below the national level, less well-financed races have also been unable to afford television advertisements. Yet these are the offices that receive the least news coverage, and commercials are thus their best means of getting their message to the voters, who lack alternative sources of information about candidates (Graber 1989). The impact of advertisements can be decisive, especially when elections are close and involve many uncommitted, comparatively disinterested voters (Robinson 1981; Owen 1991).

Federal Election Commission data show that during the 1990 midterm elections, in which incumbent members of Congress achieved a 95 percent re-election rate, the incumbents held a 20 to 1 financial advantage over their challengers during the crucial final weeks of the campaign. By mid-October, incumbents had a combined war chest of $120 million, compared to $6 million remaining in the coffers of their challengers. Most challengers had less than $25 000 available. Only fifteen challengers won. Of these, seven had spent more than $297 000 by mid-October – nearly four times the average spending of challengers.

The best-financed candidates do not always win, but because folklore says they do, folklore has become a self-fulfilling prophecy. Candidates who have money troubles are generally viewed as weak, so support for them is likely to dwindle, and candidates who see their chances of raising money as slim are not likely to run. The outcome is that people who have money to give, such as political action committees (PACs) or individual wealthy benefactors, known as "angels," gain in influence over election outcomes. However, the growth of cable television may reduce the disadvantages springing from limited funding, for cable television is less expensive and can be targeted to smaller audiences.

REFORM SUGGESTIONS

There has been a great deal of dissatisfaction among the American public and among politicians and scholars about the manner in which recent American election campaigns have been run. The 1988 campaign brought much of this criticism into the open and produced many widely publicized suggestions for reform. The concluding section of this study presents the gist of these reform proposals grouped according to the political actors who could be most instrumental in carrying them out.

Candidates and Campaign Consultants

To improve campaigning, candidates should agree about matters to be avoided, such as inappropriate remarks about race, religion or ethnicity, irrelevant ad hominem attacks, and misleading and inflammatory rhetoric. Even though negative advertising has proven effective in tarring opponents with unfavourable images, candidates should eschew this tactic as a dangerous breach of ethics that can reduce campaigning to a mud-slinging contest that harms the democratic process. If consultants recommend such tactics, candidates should countermand them. Since voluntary constraints are unlikely to be sufficient to curb the practice, incumbents should support some of the legislative measures designed to curb abuses by linking candidates more closely to commercials for their campaigns. Incumbents should also support greater powers and financial resources for the FEC to investigate abuses and initiate punitive actions. It seems incongruous that "truth in advertising" is the law of the land in the United States when it comes to commercial messages and that these laws are strictly enforced, yet there are no constraints on misleading the public through skewed or irrelevant campaign messages.

More positively, candidates should agree which key issues need to be addressed by all candidates for the benefit of the voters. They should engage in meaningful debates about domestic and foreign policy issues with or without media moderators. In fact, some scholars and politicians would make debates mandatory as a way of presenting the issues to voters and showing them where each candidate stands. This recommendation is based on considerable evidence that debates slightly raise the knowledge levels of the least informed, although they do little for the well informed.

Several changes in the format of candidate debates have been proposed (Kraus 1988; Jamieson and Birdsell 1988); critics have charged that at present they are merely parallel press conferences and that they should be replaced by a genuine debating format. In the reformed version, the candidates might ask each other questions. Alternatively, members of the general public, rather than the press, might ask questions. In the past, when members of the audience have been the interrogators, their questions have run along different lines from the questions asked by journalists during debates. Another reform calls for removing the stringent limits on the time available for answers. Candidates cannot give balanced answers to complex questions within 60 to 90 seconds. However, increasing response time begs the question about how far the audience's attention span can be pushed.

Candidates could make a major contribution to curbing escalating campaign costs by self-imposed and mutually agreed limits on the number and cost of advertisements of all kinds. They could refuse to take contributions from PACs, as some members of Congress are already doing. However, this would not stop such committees from organizing on a candidate's behalf and spending money to promote the candidacy.

All such limitations would require an imbalance of sacrifices in that incumbents, who are currently able to raise money most easily, would have to forgo opportunities for the benefit of challengers. It is also within the power of incumbents to pass legislation to mandate some of these reforms, but it is unlikely that they would act in such a self-denying way, since the First Amendment provides a convenient cloak with which they can justify their reluctance to restrain expenditures that might finance more campaign messages. However, voter disgust with excessive spending and scandals linked to campaign funding could overcome this reluctance.

Campaign consultants can contribute to improved campaign news by universal acceptance and observance of their current code of ethics so that none can benefit from behaviour that others have foresworn. Like the medical profession's credo, "Above all, do no harm," consultants should avoid campaign practices that debase politics, that lead to uninformed voting and that make it more difficult to attain good government after the election. They need to deal with violations through professional sanctions imposed on violators, rather than through retaliating in kind. Other professions have succeeded in controlling abuses through self-policing. There is no reason why consultants cannot do likewise.

The Media
The media can improve campaign coverage by a more aggressive questioning of candidates about significant issues that the candidates

have ignored. Usually, there are many important issues, such as the budget crisis in 1988, which all candidates shun for reasons of political expediency. Where resources permit, reporters should research these topics and present the missing information to the public. Journalists should also provide more excerpts from candidates' statements on issues, rather than summarizing them briefly. More coverage should be given to third-party candidates and to vice-presidential contenders. The former deserve a hearing for their political views, and the latter need to be assessed as potential presidents. In state and local elections, more coverage should be accorded to lower-level offices, including some free television time. Reporters should also assess what the voters want to know and should provide information accordingly.

Media coverage would be more useful if journalists organized information better for easier comparison. For example, they could list important issues along with the stands of all candidates on those issues. Such box scores should be featured repeatedly throughout the campaign, because different voters tune into the campaign at different times. Moreover, many quickly forget what they have heard.

Journalists should also offer more ample evaluations of the political significance of the differences of candidates and their programs. They should carefully examine the validity and relevance of claims that are made by the candidates and stated in advertisements, and they should question priorities that seem misplaced. Editorial pages should be used more extensively to condemn undesirable campaign behaviour. At the same time, the tone of coverage should be less cynical, with fewer implied accusations of the "When did you stop beating your wife?" variety. Poll coverage should be placed in a better context: voters need to be alerted to the fact that an understanding of polls requires an understanding of the political context in which they were taken. They need to be made aware that questions can be posed in such a way that they channel answers in predetermined directions.

The major media organizations, which are now running their own polls and which feature them endlessly throughout the campaign, should reconsider the merits of doing so. With the box scores of various tallies changing repeatedly, often within a very brief span of time, the information is little more than trivia. Worse, it can create false images that distort the outcome of the campaign. When media pay for the production of such information, they commit themselves to its publication, irrespective of its value. This is a very uncomfortable position for a conscientious editorial staff. If excessive poll coverage were to be curbed, the space and time freed up could be used for more valuable coverage.

During debates and other important broadcasts, the electronic media should provide candidates with a captive audience by avoiding counter-scheduling. This would prevent citizens from taking refuge in entertainment fare and ignoring political broadcasts designed to educate them. The sizable number of viewers who watch television nightly without too much concern about particular programs could be enticed to watch political broadcasts if nothing else were available. However, while most of the suggestions for media changes are feasible and are unlikely to arouse major opposition, this last suggestion could be problematic. With the spread of video recorders and videotape libraries, the force-feeding of politics by eliminating competing broadcasts would be less likely to be successful.

Political Parties

Political parties could contribute to reform by restructuring the calendar for primaries in order to reduce the disproportionate influence of early primaries on the campaign. They could work toward lowering campaign costs by shortening campaigns, and they could strive to educate and train novice candidates better about the fundamentals of running good campaigns, including the media aspects. They could help by financing campaign messages of resource-poor candidates. They could also monitor the quality of campaigning by candidates running under their party banner. They could take action against candidates who violate accepted standards of good campaigning. They could also make greater efforts to gain publicity for party platforms and to articulate national priorities when candidates fail to do so. Since neither the media nor the candidates have made voter education a priority, the parties need to fill this gap (Patterson 1989).

Compared to other democracies, election turnout rates in the United States are low. For the 1988 presidential race, they stood at 50.15 percent; and for the 1945–81 period, the U.S. rate was 59 percent, compared to 77 percent in Britain and 87 percent in West Germany (Orren 1987). In addition to the political cynicism that pervades the campaign and discourages voting, U.S. voter registration requirements are a major hurdle. The two reasons combined explain why only about 61 percent of the eligible voters are registered. Among voters who consider the trouble of registering for elections worthwhile, 75 to 80 percent vote in presidential elections. To improve the situation, the parties, with the assistance of the media, could mount a major campaign for eased registration procedures, such as allowing registration by mail or at various public agencies and reducing the length of waiting periods. The major obstacle to the success of this proposal is the fear that eased registration would sharply increase illegal additions to the voters lists, leading to massive election fraud. Election outcomes would then be in doubt. In the small number of states where voters can register when they apply or renew their drivers' licences, average voter turnout has increased by 10 percent. The parties could also lend their support to the passage of a *National Voter Registration Act* that would ease the registration process and make it more uniform. If a compromise could be reached about the appropriate provisions of such an Act, it would probably be passed.

Media Audiences

Since the real or imagined desires of media audiences are a major influence on coverage, audiences are powerful shapers of media content. They can increase the chances of getting better campaign coverage by keeping in touch with media personnel and requesting coverage that is missing or too sparse; they can voice protest when coverage seems bad; and they can bring pressure on media personnel by patronizing "good" media and encouraging others to do likewise. Since mass media need mass audiences, this type of support or disapproval is a potent weapon. Media audiences can also complain to candidates and political parties when campaign information is poor, inadequate or objectionable. Although all of these steps are uncomplicated, they will founder on the shoals of public apathy.

The academic community can contribute to better campaign coverage by researching what types of knowledge are essential for informed voting choices and what information is detrimental to informed voting. It would seem, for example, that negative information about candidates is appropriate and even desirable when it is accurate and relevant and is presented in a context that is not likely to mislead. On the other hand, scurrilous information that lacks relevance to the job the candidate seeks and that misleads or diverts attention or stirs hatreds would seem to be inappropriate and harmful; hence, it should be avoided, even if it seems to elicit voter support.

Research could determine which characteristics or past-performance data predict how candidates will perform in the future. Media coverage could then emphasize this type of information. Audience needs and desires must also be studied more carefully to attain a better fit between them and the substance and format of information that is made available. Current knowledge about information processing already points the way to numerous reforms. For example, better coordination between television pictures and text, so that they reinforce each other, would facilitate comprehension, as would more parallel presentation of the candidates' policy positions in print news stories. The knowledge gained through research and dialogue could then be translated into guidelines for the political actors who dispense campaign information. Such guidelines must be realistic in terms of the characteristics of various media and in terms of audience attention and comprehension.

The role of entertainment media in disseminating political information needs to be studied much more carefully. Because of their large and often devoted audiences, entertainment programs may have substantial potential for informing voters. This potential should be examined seriously.

The changing demographics in the United States provide added impetus for such an examination. The traditional formats for election broadcasting – as exemplified primarily in news and public affairs programming – are designed for what could become an increasingly narrow segment of the electorate. Many voters may be more attuned to gaining information through other formats, such as the standard entertainment programs of television, or storytelling modes.

Obviously, the agenda for reform of media coverage of campaigns is large. Its implementation will require considerable effort by politicians, journalists and ordinary citizens throughout the United States, but the stakes are high, and the momentum for reform has been growing in strength. In line with the American public's strong aversion to government interference with the media, most reform proposals call for voluntary action. This speeds and eases the possibility for adoption. It therefore seems reasonable to expect that the 1992 presidential election campaign will benefit from at least some of the reform proposals spawned by the dismal performances in 1988 and 1990.

ABBREVIATIONS

ch.	chapter
Stat.	United States Statutes at Large
U.S.	United States Supreme Court Reports
U.S.C.	United States Code

BIBLIOGRAPHY

This study was completed in June 1991.

Adams, William C. 1985. "Convention Coverage." *Public Opinion* 7 (December/January): 45.

———. 1987. "As New Hampshire Goes. ... " In *Media and Momentum: The New Hampshire Primary and Nomination Politics,* ed. Gary R. Orren and Nelson W. Polsby. Chatham: Chatham House.

Asher, Herbert B. 1988. *Presidential Elections and American Politics: Voters, Candidates, and Campaigns since 1952.* 4th ed. Chicago: Dorsey Press.

Bartels, Larry M. 1985. "Expectations and Preferences in Presidential Nominating Campaigns." *American Political Science Review* 79:804–15.

Bates, Stephen. 1986. "Lawful Exits: The Court Considers Election Day Polls." *Public Opinion* 8 (Summer): 53–54.

Brady, Henry E., and Richard Johnston. 1987. "What's the Primary Message: Horse Race or Issue Journalism?" In *Media and Momentum: The New Hampshire Primary and Nomination Politics,* ed. Gary R. Orren and Nelson W. Polsby. Chatham: Chatham House.

Broh, Anthony. 1983. "Presidential Preference Polls and Network News." In *Television Coverage of the 1980 Presidential Campaign,* ed. William C. Adams. Norwood: Ablex.

Buchanan, Bruce. 1991. *Electing a President: The Markle Commission Research on Campaign '88.* Austin: University of Texas Press.

Cantril, Albert H. 1991. *The Opinion Connection: Polling, Politics, and the Press.* Washington, DC: Congressional Quarterly Press.

Clancey, Maura, and Michael Robinson. 1985. "The Media in Campaign '84: General Election Coverage, Part I." *Public Opinion* 7 (December/January): 49–53.

Clarke, Peter, and Susan Evans. 1983. *Covering Campaigns: Journalism in Congressional Elections.* Stanford: Stanford University Press.

Congressional Quarterly Weekly Report. 1987. 28 March, 27 June, 8 August.

Conover, Pamela Johnston, and Stanley Feldman. 1986. "The Role of Inference in the Perception of Political Candidates." In *Political Cognition: The 19th Annual Carnegie Symposium on Cognition,* ed. Richard R. Lau and David O. Sears. Hillsdale: Erlbaum.

Devlin, L. Patrick. 1989. "Contrasts in Presidential Campaign Commercials of 1988." *American Behavioral Scientist* 32:389–414.

Entman, Robert M. 1992. "Super-Tuesday and the Future of Local News." In *The Future of News,* ed. Philip S. Cook, Douglas Gomery and Lawrence Lichty. Baltimore: Johns Hopkins University Press.

Goldenberg, Edie N., and Michael W. Traugott. 1984. *Campaigning for Congress.* Washington, DC: Congressional Quarterly Press.

Graber, Doris A. 1983. "Hoopla and Horse-Race in 1980 Campaign Coverage: A Closer Look." In *Mass Media and Elections: International Research Perspectives,* ed. Winfred Schulz and Klaus Schoenbach. Munich: Oelschlaeger.

———. 1986. "Mass Media and Political Images in Elections." In *Research in Micropolitics*, vol. 1, *Voting Behavior*, ed. Samuel Long. Greenwich: JAI Press.

———. 1987a. "Framing Election News Broadcasts: News Context and Its Impact on the 1984 Presidential Election." *Social Science Quarterly* 68:552–68.

———. 1987b. "Kind Pictures and Harsh Words: How Television Presents the Candidates." In *Elections in America*, ed. Kay Lehman Schlozman. Boston: Allen and Unwin.

———. 1988. *Processing the News: How People Tame the Information Tide.* 2d ed. New York: Longman.

———. 1989. *Mass Media and American Politics.* 3d ed. Washington, DC: Congressional Quarterly Press.

Hadley, Arthur T. 1976. *The Invisible Primary.* Englewood Cliffs: Prentice-Hall.

Hofstetter, C. Richard. 1976. *Bias in the News: Network Television Coverage of the 1972 Election Campaign.* Columbus: Ohio State University Press.

Iyengar, Shanto, and Donald R. Kinder. 1987. *News that Matters: Television and American Opinion.* Chicago: University of Chicago Press.

Jamieson, Kathleen Hall. 1989. "Context and the Creation of Meaning in the Advertising of the 1988 Presidential Campaign." *American Behavioral Scientist* 32:415–24.

Jamieson, Kathleen Hall, and David S. Birdsell. 1988. *Presidential Debates: The Challenge of Creating an Informed Electorate.* New York: Oxford University Press.

Keeter, Scott, and Cliff Zukin. 1983. *Uninformed Choice: The Failure of the New Presidential Nominating System.* New York: Praeger.

Kern, Montague. 1989. *30-Second Politics: Political Advertising in the Eighties.* New York: Praeger.

Kessel, John H. 1988. *Presidential Campaign Politics: Coalition Strategies and Citizen Response.* 3d ed. Chicago: Dorsey Press.

King, Anthony. 1981. "How Not to Select Presidential Candidates: A View from Europe." In *The American Elections of 1980*, ed. Austin Ranney. Washington, DC: American Enterprise Institute for Public Policy Research.

Kraus, Sidney. 1988. *Televised Presidential Debates and Public Policy.* Hillsdale: Erlbaum.

Lavrakas, Paul J., and Jack K. Holley, eds. 1990. *Polls and Presidential Election Campaign News Coverage: 1988.* Evanston: Northwestern University Press.

Lichter, S. Robert, Stanley Rothman and Linda S. Lichter. 1986. *The Media Elite: America's New Powerbrokers.* New York: Adler and Adler.

Media Monitor. 1991. 5 (January): 1. Washington, DC: Center for Media and Public Affairs.

Miami Herald Publishing Company v. Tornillo, 418 U.S. 241 (1974).

Morrison, Donald, ed. 1988. *The Winning of the White House 1988.* New York: Time.

Nesbit, Dorothy Davidson. 1988. *Videostyle in U.S. Senate Campaigns.* Knoxville: University of Tennessee Press.

Neuman, W. Russell. 1986. *The Paradox of Mass Politics.* Cambridge: Harvard University Press.

Orren, Gary R. 1987. "The Linkage of Policy to Participation." In *Presidential Selection,* ed. Alexander Heard and Michael Nelson. Durham: Duke University Press.

Orren, Gary R., and Nelson Rockefeller. 1987. "New Hampshire: Springboard of Nomination Politics." In *Media and Momentum: The New Hampshire Primary and Nomination Politics,* ed. Gary R. Orren and Nelson W. Polsby. Chatham: Chatham House.

Owen, Diana. 1991. *Media Messages in American Presidential Elections.* New York: Greenwood Press.

Patterson, Thomas. 1982. "Television and Election Strategy." In *The Communications Revolution in Politics,* ed. Gerald Benjamin. New York: Academy of Political Science.

———. 1989. "The Press and Its Missed Assignment." In *The Elections of 1988,* ed. Michael Nelson. Washington, DC: Congressional Quarterly Press.

Patterson, Thomas, and Richard Davis. 1985. "The Media Campaign Struggle for the Agenda." In *The Elections of 1984,* ed. Michael Nelson. Washington, DC: Congressional Quarterly Press.

Patterson, Thomas, and Robert McClure. 1976. *The Unseeing Eye.* New York: Putnam.

Robinson, Michael. 1981. "The Media in 1980: Was the Message the Message?" In *The American Elections of 1980,* ed. Austin Ranney. Washington, DC: American Enterprise Institute for Public Policy Research.

Rosenberg, Shawn, with Patrick McCafferty. 1987. "The Image and the Vote: Manipulating Voter Preferences." *Public Opinion Quarterly* 51 (Spring): 31–47.

Runkel, David R. 1989. *Campaign for President: The Managers Look at '88.* Dover: Auburn House.

Schram, Martin. 1987. *The Great American Video Game: Presidential Politics in the Television Age.* New York: William Morrow.

Semetko, Holli A., Jay G. Blumler, Michael Gurevitch, David Weaver, with Steve Barken and G. Cleveland Wilhoit. 1991. *The Formation of Campaign Agendas: A Comparative Analysis of Party and Media Roles in Recent American and British Elections.* Hillsdale: Erlbaum.

Smith, Eric R.A.N. 1989. *The Unchanging American Voter.* Berkeley: University of California Press.

Stovall, James Glen. 1984. "Incumbency and News Coverage of the 1980 Presidential Campaign." *Western Political Quarterly* 37 (December): 628–38.

Tannenbaum, Percy H., and Leslie J. Kostrich. 1983. *Turned-on TV/Turned-Off Voters: Policy Options for Election Projections.* Beverly Hills: Sage Publications.

United States. *Communications Act of 1934,* June 19, 1934, ch. 652, 48 Stat. 1064 (codified as amended in scattered sections of 47 U.S.C.).

———. *Constitution of the United States of America,* 1788. First Amendment, 1791.

Washington Monthly. 1990. "The Other Essential Campaign Reforms." 22 (September): 34–35.

Weaver, David H., Doris A. Graber, Maxwell E. McCombs and Chaim E. Eyal. 1981. *Media Agenda-Setting in a Presidential Election: Issues, Images, and Interest.* New York: Praeger.

7

MASS MEDIA
AND ELECTIONS
IN CANADA

Frederick J. Fletcher
Robert Everett

THE CANADIAN SYSTEM of campaign communication is the product not only of indigenous evolution in the context of its own political and media institutions, but also of the influence of external models. The British model influenced the development of both the political system, including parliamentary practices and elections, and the mass media system. For example, the mandated role and philosophy behind the British Broadcasting Corporation had some influence on the Canadian Broadcasting Corporation, especially in the early years of broadcasting. More recently, Canadian political journalism has been influenced by American experience. Indeed, campaign communication in the United States and Canada is more similar than their distinct political institutions and processes would lead one to expect. The emulation effect seems quite clear. Other industrial democracies, including the United Kingdom, have been similarly influenced by American electoral campaigns and media coverage but have not always responded in the same ways.

The purpose of this study is to trace some of these external influences on campaign communication in Canada and, more generally, to examine Canadian practice in a comparative context. The other chapters in this volume have provided an overview and critical assessment of campaign communication in eight countries. Here, an attempt is made to discuss Canada along the same lines.

THE POLITICAL SIGNIFICANCE OF CAMPAIGNS

The essential feature of election campaigns is the contest among the major parties for voter support, but that contest, fought in the ridings and more importantly in the media, has a number of consequences beyond the vote. The political significance of campaigns must be assessed, not only in terms of voter choices and election outcomes, but also with regard to the quality of the public debate, the information environment provided for voters, and the images of parties, leaders, issues and institutions that emerge. Campaigns should promote a constructive engagement of citizens, foster their interest and confidence in and understanding of the electoral process, and provide a stimulus to participation.

With respect to voter choice and electoral outcomes, the best evidence now suggests that campaigns are of increasing importance. There were major shifts in party preferences during the campaigns in 1984 and 1988. These shifts reflect the growing volatility of voters' party preferences in Canada. Party identification appears to be weaker, and an increasing proportion of voters makes its choice during the campaign. The choice, however, appears to be based largely on the national campaigns, with local candidates having only modest effects in most ridings. The limited role of local candidates appears to be the result of various tendencies in the electoral process toward campaigns that revolve around national themes, even though important regional differences remain (Fletcher 1987, 346). Commentaries on other countries identify similar tendencies. For example, Warhurst (1991) notes that Australian campaigns are waged by parties that are "centralized and shaped by national considerations."

Despite the national focus of campaigns, elections remain regional in significant ways. Examination of federal elections since 1945 makes it clear that they remain strongly regionalized despite increasing centralization of campaign planning and media coverage. These patterns usually coincide with provincial boundaries and reflect linguistic and regional economic differences. The basic themes of the national campaigns often resonate differently by region, leading to increasingly sophisticated regional targeting by campaign planners.

Nomination battles remain essentially local, despite some centralizing developments. Two key reforms of the 1970s – the printing of party labels on the ballot and the accompanying requirement that the national party leader endorse all nominees – have increased central influence on the nomination process. Recent controversies have produced some tightening of the rules. Nevertheless, the nominations process remains relatively informal and local in all the major parties. Nomination contests, though increasingly common, are not normally fought in public. Media attention is usually relatively slight, except where controversy is drawn to the attention of the media by the participants, or in traditionally safe seats where nomination by the dominant party is tantamount to election.

RESEARCH PERSPECTIVES ON THE MEDIA'S POLITICAL SIGNIFICANCE

Even more than in the United States, the assumption of limited campaign effects, based on early election studies in that country, has discouraged serious study of the media and elections in Canada. In making the inevitably difficult choices regarding variables upon which to focus, the first major surveys of electoral behaviour in Canada in the 1960s paid limited attention to the potential effects of media coverage of campaigns (see Meisel 1975). The focus tended to be on such variables as party identification, relationship of partisan choice to socio-economic cleavages, and other such factors. Revisionist approaches were slow to take hold, and, as late as 1979, the authors of the major work on voting in Canada to that date were unable to detect any significant relationship between paying attention to campaign coverage and switching parties between the 1972 and 1974 federal elections (Clarke et al. 1979, 290). In a later work, however, the same authors found at least the potential for media and campaign influences. In short, largely as a consequence of the time at which voting studies began in Canada, little work has been done on the relationship between media and campaigns at the federal or provincial levels. This is true of the limited number of studies of constituency-level campaigns as well. One result of this evolution has been a division of labour between students of the media, who have focused on campaign coverage itself, and scholars of voting behaviour, who have given little sustained attention to media effects.

Campaigns are signal events in contemporary representative democracies. A national election campaign produces bursts of intensive, comprehensive activity and broad recognition of its importance. Among the attributes of campaigns are "specific and overt aims and a limited timespan," which make possible some "assessment as to their effectiveness" (McQuail 1987, 258). Although research results are far from conclusive in terms of mass media effects, the campaign at least satisfies the minimal prerequisites for investigation: an attentive media "audience," deliberate attempts to persuade by partisans, and coverage that approaches saturation levels. Moreover, the wealth of data from polls and focus groups is being mined for insights into the complex of variables – including media use – that feature in electoral decisions. In part, it is the mix of these variables that cautions against unqualified statements of media effect over the short term.

Where the question has been posed in voting studies, it has been asked in terms of the relationship between gross amount of (reported) exposure to media messages and actual conversion in party preference. Few attempts have been made to develop more precise measures of media use or to specify types and conditions of influence more clearly. The actual information environment in which voters make their choices and form their opinions about the system has been very little studied. As Siune (1991) argues, caution in this vein is warranted, given that the impact of television, for example, is contingent on variables such as interest, knowledge, education and durability of partisanship.

Nevertheless, existing research has some important things to tell us. In a 1977 study of Ontario voters, it was found that while only 28 percent of respondents reported using the media as a basis for their vote decisions, more than two-thirds turned to the media to find out the main issues in the campaign. Moreover, 88 percent said they looked to media coverage to find out what sort of persons the leaders were (Drummond and Fletcher 1980, 105–108). In a Decima poll reported in *Maclean's* (1988), 51 percent reported finding the media coverage helpful in their vote decisions. In addition, 45 percent said the leaders debates were helpful, and 26 percent found the party television spots provided useful information. Although these data are not sufficiently comparable to indicate a trend, they do suggest that voters themselves see media coverage as important and helpful.

As far as information flow is concerned, there are several studies that demonstrate a relationship between media use and level of campaign information. In the 1977 Ontario study, knowledge of the names of local candidates and capacity to make specific comments about party leaders were both related to attention to campaign news and advertising, as were level of interest and probability of voting. There was a clear syndrome of interest, exposure and turnout. In general, respondents reported much less exposure to local candidate information than to information about the provincial parties and leaders. These findings are reported in Drummond and Fletcher (1980, 105–108, 114).

There is ample evidence that campaigns increase voter information. A clear example is the 1985 Ontario provincial election, in which the opposition party leaders improved their recognition factors dramatically in only a month of active campaigning (Fletcher 1990, 208). Lambert and his colleagues found a modest but potentially important relationship between media use and information holding in the 1984 National Election Study, despite having to rely on variables not well designed to answer such questions (Lambert et al. 1988). The lesson here, perhaps, is that much more research is needed to understand the flow of information in campaigns, especially at the constituency level. In particular, new concepts are required to link information flow, attitudes toward the political process, and various modes of participation. Variations among regions and constituency types might well be a focus of study.

The influence of other forms of campaign communication also remains largely uncharted. Customarily, candidates release brochures in three waves, and, overall, they seem to have considerable success in communicating the names and party affiliations of local candidates. The impact of other forms of campaign activity is unclear. Palda (1985) demonstrates a clear relationship between spending and electoral success, and Krashinsky and Milne (1985; 1986) make a strong argument for an incumbent effect. Palda (1985, 537) relates the incumbent advantage to pre-election communication through subsidized mailings and constituency offices. However, Black (1984) found that the relationship between canvassing and reinforcement, conversion and turnout is very complex. Its impact varies with the competitive situation in the riding ("competitive contacting ... fosters reinforcement") and the activity of the dominant party (Black 1984, 372). It would be both theoretically and practically worthwhile to be able to specify the conditions under which various aspects of the constituency-level campaigns have measurable effects.

The influence of news coverage and comment is also difficult to specify. While it is true that late deciders and transient voters are more willing to ascribe influence to the media than are other voters, the pattern of influence remains uncertain. Editorials and pundits have limited readership and, except in low information situations such as municipal elections, appear to have limited influence. Their primary effect appears to be on the morale of campaign workers. Sorting out the independent influence of the media in news coverage is difficult since parties have considerable capacity to influence the agenda. Nevertheless, there are, as will be seen, conditions under which debates among party leaders can have considerable influence. There is reason to suspect that the same is true for local candidates' debates and other elements in constituency-level campaigns. It would be useful to examine local campaigns in the ridings targeted by the three larger parties in order to identify the factors associated with targeting and the impact of the mix of national and local elements in the campaigns. (The decision to target a specific constituency by a national party appears to be based on competitiveness, voter volatility, and media fit.) The influence of campaign communication on turnout and voter information is important in the context of democratic theory.

Even as the media take on greater importance – for both parties and voters – in election campaigns, other forms of communication continue to play a role in linking citizens and candidates. New technologies and techniques have been employed for soliciting funds, encouraging party memberships, maintaining contact with constituents, and communicating with voters. American parties (in particular the Republicans) and Political Action Committees first grasped the possibilities of direct mail communication, computers, polling, focus groups, and new publishing formats in the 1970s. Subsequently, they have been adopted elsewhere. These techniques should not be viewed in isolation from media strategies. During election campaigns, daily canvassing and focus groups are used to make quick adjustments in media strategy and to gauge reaction to commercials. Yet they also affect front-porch encounters between party workers and constituents when intelligence is gleaned from voters and fed into computer banks or when literature is targeted at specific groups. In many countries, it is assumed that acceptance and application of these techniques (together with the availability of funds) will lend a "competitive edge over opponents" (Warhurst 1991).

To date, Canadian voting-behaviour specialists have conceded the possibility of media influence while remaining sceptical regarding direct influence. For example, Clarke et al. (1991) argue that opinions formed around debate performance had a modest impact on voting decision in 1988. Another study indicated that the truly "attentive" audience for election coverage is 50 percent or less of the public and that reinforcement, rather than conversion, results from exposure (MacDermid 1991). Evidence of the media's social power rests not only on the convictions of communications specialists, but on the practices (and spending) of political parties. Major party strategists believe that news coverage and broadcast advertising are the keys to electoral success.

CAMPAIGN COMMUNICATION IN THE CANADIAN MEDIA

The major elements in the Canadian campaign communication system can be classified in terms of the extent to which parties and candidates can communicate their election appeals without mediation. The messages can be essentially unmediated – free-time broadcasts and spots – or partially mediated – broadcast interviews and leaders debates – or mostly mediated. The mostly mediated messages are those presented as news and commentary. Messages presented in newspapers and magazines appear to be the most mediated, with television news more open to influence by the parties.

Unmediated Communications

As with most comparable countries, Canada has developed rules for the allocation of free-time spots and paid advertising. These regulations

have changed over time, a feature which is also shared with other jurisdictions. This tendency toward change is evident in underlying principles, mechanisms for determining or adjudicating allocation, and the
specific formulas used in the allocative process. Adjustments of this
kind are not simply refinements made in a spirit of democratic renewal,
but are subject to political pressures and have their origins in a number
of considerations, among them:

- the introduction of new technology, along with shifts in audience preferences, tastes and habits;
- increases in the number of private, entertainment-oriented media
  outlets, challenges to the monopolies of national public broadcasters, and erosion of the public interest ethos in broadcasting;
- the participation of parties in the allocative process, particularly
  parliamentary parties, which translates into demands for greater
  input, control or access;
- shifting assumptions about the impact of various kinds of content,
  as well as their limitations and flaws; and
- a conscious attempt to create a "flexible" system.

In addition, there is a reluctance to intervene directly in news judgements, even where press freedom is not constitutionally protected. The
regulations tend to apply primarily to alternative forms of candidate-
to-voter communication, such as broadcast advertising and free time.

The actual public policy created out of the interaction of these forces
differs from country to country. At one end of the spectrum, every political party in Denmark receives equal allocations of time, provided it
can obtain the signature of 1/175 of the total number of voters in the
preceding election (Siune 1991). An obvious exception to this regulatory regime is the United States, where there are no allocations of time
per se and where the environment is the least regulated (Graber 1991).
Various attempts to impose spending limits, to establish rules of fair
access, or to legislate a right of reply for candidates have been struck
down by the courts or abandoned in the spirit of deregulation during
the Reagan years. And in Europe, the rapid growth of private broadcasting over the past decade, alongside the public systems, has brought
new opportunities to purchase time for partisan advertising during
campaigns. Often this advertising is available only at the local level.

A 1981 survey of 21 democratic countries by the American
Enterprise Institute disclosed that 18 countries had some form of free-
time allocation and that Canada was one of only four (Australia, Japan
and the United States are the other notable exceptions) to permit paid

political advertising (Taylor 1990, 272). With the growth of private broadcasting in Europe in recent years, however, paid time has become increasingly available alongside free time. The rules for the allocation of free time among parties differ quite widely. The most common pattern is for the time to be allocated among the parties represented in the national legislature on the basis of the number of seats held or the share of the popular vote received in the previous election (or a combination of the two). However, most countries make some provisions for minor parties, especially when they achieve some prominence (as for the Greens in Germany). Only Denmark provides equal time for all competing parties (Siune 1991). The allocation rules for free time are often also applied to paid time, as has been the case in Canada since the 1974 reforms. The rules place considerable weight on previous election results, making it difficult for new parties to gain access to time.

Canada's regulations grew with the national broadcasting system and were incorporated into the central tenets of the system beginning in the 1930s. Regulation of political broadcasting began in 1936 with the passage of a *Broadcasting Act* that required the CBC to prescribe time periods to be devoted to political broadcasts (by private and CBC stations) and to ensure that times were assigned equitably to all parties and candidates. Sponsors were to be identified and all dramatized political commentary was banned. By the time these rules had been proclaimed, radio had featured in two election campaigns. In 1930, the leaders of the Liberals and Conservatives spoke over the air on the eve of the election. Five years later, the Liberals were stung by the barbs of "Mr. Sage," a fictional character invented by the (unnamed) Conservatives to pillory Prime Minister King. Emphasis within the guidelines reflected unique Canadian political dynamics. (The ban on dramatization was dropped from the *Broadcasting Act* in 1968 but remained in the regulations as a caution against "excessive theatricality.")

In performing its regulatory function, the CBC enunciated principles (in formal statements in 1939, 1944 and 1948) that are still operative: all parties must be offered equal and fair opportunities to explain their positions on the issues of the moment; no one should be permitted by virtue of position or wealth to dominate the airwaves; the right to respond to ideas is inherent in the concept of free speech. (See Soderlund et al. 1984, 118–19; LaCalamita 1984.) The underlying principle was that of a reasonably "level playing field" for the contestants.

Initially, the parties were not allowed to purchase time on television. Their unmediated messages were confined to the free-time broadcasts using identified speakers (the infamous "talking heads"). The failure of such programs to attract substantial audiences gradually brought changes. As Dalton Camp put it, "if the format was right for politics [in that it promoted issue-oriented discussion], it was wrong for television." It soon became clear that "if the parties were to use television, it would have to be on television's terms" (1981, xv). Television campaigns, whether mediated or unmediated, had to be organized by television's rules. These rules, however, were not technologically determined but, rather, emerged from the professional practices of journalists and advertising specialists. More informative campaign television may well be possible.

New campaign regulations adopted in the 1970s were designed to provide registered political parties with a reasonable opportunity to communicate their appeals directly to the public. The rules restrict paid advertising to the final half of the eight-week campaign, regulate the allocation of paid and free time, limit campaign spending, and provide for reimbursement from the federal treasury of half the costs of radio and television commercials purchased by the registered parties. The advertising reimbursement provision was dropped in 1983 in favour of a general subsidy, a result in part of lobbying by the print media. (For a useful discussion of the regulations, see Seidle and Paltiel 1981; see also LaCalamita 1984, 563.)

All broadcasters, including the CBC radio services, which normally do not run advertisements, are required to make available prime time spots (radio: 6:00–9:00 AM, noon–2:00 PM, 4:00–7:00 PM; television 6:00 PM to midnight; see *Canada Elections Act* s. 99.4(*b*)), at normal rates for up to a total of six and one-half hours, divided among the parties according to a formula based on seats held in the House of Commons when the election was called, share of popular vote in the previous election, and the number of seats contested. Free time – on both public and private networks – is allocated on the same basis. The actual time allocations are negotiated by the agents of registered parties and the broadcasters under the supervision of the broadcasting arbitrator. This position was created in 1983 to mediate between broadcasters and political parties. The arbitrator is appointed with the unanimous consent of the registered parties or, failing that, by the chief electoral officer. The parties are free to establish any time allocation upon which they can secure unanimous agreement among themselves. Should consensus prove elusive, the arbitrator applies a formula based on share of seats, proportion of popular vote, and percentage of seats contested in the previous election.

The new rules permitted the parties to reach substantial numbers of voters with unmediated communications. The free-time broadcasts on CBC English television, for example, had an average audience of 620 000 in 1979 – a figure that grew to 830 000 in 1988. On both CBC and

CTV, free time was made available across a spectrum of programming, including public affairs (such as "The 5th Estate" and "W5"), daytime drama, situation comedies and sports. The party advertisements, not surprisingly, reached a much larger audience: 77 percent of respondents in a national survey in 1979 reported having seen or heard a party spot during the campaign. The comparable proportion in 1988 was 62 percent. This decrease suggests that it would be useful to trace audience patterns over time, since political broadcasts in Canada increasingly face competition from other programming.

Because free-time telecasts have smaller audiences, thought to be made up largely of already committed supporters, they have taken second place to advertising spots and news coverage, which are believed to reach more "switchable" voters. Indeed, the leaders of all the major parties turned down offers of free-time telecasts in 1953 (Soderlund et al. 1984, 18), but have since used them to provide further exposure for key campaign themes, often using extended versions of their spots, or "soft" features on their leaders. Cable systems – which have a high level of penetration in Canada – and some broadcasters also provide free time to local candidates.

From the point of view of promoting discussion of issues and philosophies, the arrangements for 1988 were problematic. Among the items negotiated between the agents of the parties and the broadcasters was the duration of free-time units. These were agreed to be two minutes for the three major parties and one minute for all other registered parties. As a consequence, the broadcasts were essentially indistinguishable from paid advertisements. In fact, the networks treated them like spots. A requirement that free-time broadcasts be longer, perhaps a minimum of five minutes, might have produced a difference in both form and content, requiring a sustained argument. Such a change might have added to the range of information available to voters.

Because of the Conservative landslide in 1984, the 1988 allocation of access to both free and paid time was even more skewed than usual. The Conservatives were allocated 50 percent of all available paid time; the Liberals could purchase 22.8 percent, and the New Democrats 17.2 percent. The remaining 10 percent was divided among the remaining 10 registered parties (totals ranging from three to seven minutes). The free-time allocations were roughly similar. The consequence of these allocations was to give the governing party a substantial advantage over the others and to require the minor parties to rely on other means to have a significant role in the campaign debates. Minor parties receive relatively little coverage in news and public affairs as well, with the result that minority viewpoints are little heard during campaigns, unless their proponents are able to afford advocacy advertising of the type that emerged in 1988. The minor parties are limited by the paid-time allocation formula in the amount of time they can purchase (usually less than five minutes per broadcast outlet), as well as by their usually limited funds.

It is true, however, that the new rules helped to equalize access to the airwaves among the established parties. The new limits reduced spending by the two major parties, while the public funding and tax credits for contributions permitted the NDP to increase its expenditures substantially. While the two largest parties continued to have a decided advantage, accounting for 78.6 percent of all advertising expenditures in 1979, the first election under the new scheme, this was a decline from their 91.1 percent share in 1974. The NDP was able to increase its share from 6.8 to 20.3 percent. By 1980, the NDP had increased its share to 24 percent. During the 1988 campaign, the NDP actually outspent the Liberals and Conservatives in television advertising, accounting for 35.7 percent of all expenditures on televised spots. By careful targeting, the NDP has in the past three elections been able to compete on even terms in key areas where it had a realistic chance to win.

In an attempt to close a loophole in the spending limits provisions, spending restrictions were tightened to prohibit anyone but a registered party or candidate (and their official agents) from incurring expenditures designed to promote or oppose a particular candidate or party. Approved by all three parties in the House of Commons in 1983, the amendments effectively precluded spending by interest groups during the campaign. Just prior to the 1984 campaign, the section was declared unconstitutional by an Alberta provincial court and the federal government elected not to appeal. The matter remains unresolved, and, as one legal scholar noted, "the wild card of massive infusions of paid political messages sponsored by 'parallel campaigns' run by political action committees heretofore strictly regulated looms large on the regulatory horizon and threatens to sweep aside the restricted system as it has evolved to 1984" (LaCalamita 1984, 578). The problem, as the chief electoral officer acknowledged in his 1984 report, is to strike an acceptable balance between "adequate control of election expenses and the freedom of expression of Canadians" (Canada, Elections Canada 1984, 24). The parties, with their access to advertising limited to the last four weeks of the campaign and restricted by spending limits, could easily be overwhelmed by wealthy groups, shattering the principles that have been accepted since the 1930s.

One questionable effect of the new rules was to promote the use of television and radio spots. As Seidle and Paltiel put it: "An indirect consequence of the reimbursement to parties for time purchased on the electronic media was that the national campaign committees were encouraged to spend a greater proportion of their budget than ever before on this form of advertising. 'Fifty-cent dollars' are hard to resist, and parties were given an incentive that accentuated the long-term trend in Canadian election campaigns away from the use of the print media to ... radio and especially television advertising" (1981, 277). Expenditures on television advertising by the major parties jumped from $1.2 million in 1974 (45 percent of all advertising expenditures) to $3.6 million in 1979 (55 percent) and $4.6 million in 1980 (62 percent). The 1984 figure was 54 percent, a decline that can probably be accounted for by the repeal of the partial reimbursement provisions. In 1988, expenditures on print, television, and radio advertising by the three largest parties represented approximately 53.4 percent of all expenses. On average, television advertising accounted for 31.9 percent of total campaign expenditures by these parties. In addition, the major parties received free-time television allocations worth an estimated $6 144 997.

In recent elections, while the national parties have spent more than 80 percent of their advertising dollars – more than half of their total expenditures – on broadcast advertising, mostly television, local candidates spent less than one-quarter of their advertising budget on the electronic media. In 1988, the figure fell below 10 percent for candidates of the three main parties. There is a further distinction in that local campaigns are far more likely to rely on print media, weekly newspapers in particular, while national advertising is concentrated on television and radio. It is, perhaps, not surprising that the national campaigns have tended to dominate the public consciousness, despite spending somewhat less overall than the aggregate of local candidates ($7.5 million versus $8.6 million). The proportion of total funds disbursed by the national offices of the three major parties has increased from about 30 percent of total campaign spending in 1974 to 47 percent in 1984 (calculated from data in Paltiel 1975, 186–99). These figures support the general impression that campaigns have become more centralized.

Measures of campaign effort and campaign expenditure in individual ridings are not readily available, though we do know that all three national parties are increasingly targeting their messages to marginal ridings. The flow of information to the voter regarding the party leader and the local candidate varies greatly from riding to riding. Though no systematic studies have been done, observers have noted that the emphasis on party, leader and candidate varies on the basis of estimates by campaign organizers of the relative voter appeal of each in the particular region or individual district. The interaction of local, regional and national campaigns in shaping the information environment of individual voters needs closer examination.

The history of Canadian regulations and practices identifies a number of features shared with other countries. Although precise rules and conventions vary, the bulk of free time is allocated based on standings in the legislative assembly or share of the popular vote in the preceding election, with some minimum and often minimal allocations to small, new or non-represented parties. The rules favour established political parties, an advantage that is heightened when paid time is also available.

Partially and Fully Mediated Communications

As far as ostensibly nonpartisan campaign information is concerned, the national media – loosely defined as the prestige dailies, such as the *Globe and Mail, Le Devoir* and *La Presse,* the *Toronto Star* and the Montreal *Gazette,* and the major television networks, as well as the Canadian Press (CP), the Southam News service (SN, which provides specialized news, analysis and commentary to the 17 member papers of the Southam chain), CBC Radio, and a few syndicated columnists – tend to set the tone for election coverage. The national campaigns of the parties are oriented primarily to the national media. They rely on a "trickle-down effect" to reach the regions (though they do monitor key regional outlets and sometimes target particular regions for attention). The national late evening newscasts on television carry almost no local coverage. Even the highly rated supper hour newscasts produced by local stations tend to use syndicated reports on the leader tours as the focus of their campaign coverage.

In addition to the style-setting national media, the system encompasses regional media consisting of metropolitan dailies and regional television networks, local dailies and broadcasters, community newspapers and low-power radio stations, and magazines (in particular, the news magazine *Maclean's*). These media essentially compete for the attention of Canadians with American media, including a transcontinental string of border stations. This is a factor which has to be taken into account, because these foreign media distract and may well disorient some voters (Everett and Fletcher 1991, 163). The division of labour is far from perfect, with news organizations at all levels offering a mix of national, regional and local coverage. The trend, however, has been toward metropolitanization of major dailies and television stations, with local coverage often left to smaller radio stations and community weeklies. A television station based in Vancouver, for example, will use retransmitters to cover much of the province, tailoring its local news to cover as many as 20 ridings in a federal election, precluding sustained coverage of any routine local race. Recent closings of regional CBC stations in the wake of cuts in government funding will complicate coverage in places such as southern Ontario and Calgary.

The system is completed by cable television. Just over 70 percent of Canadian households subscribe to cable television, primarily to obtain clear signals from the American networks, and penetration is much higher in the major urban areas. Most cable systems cover relatively few constituencies and are a potentially efficient means of local campaign communication. The cable systems deliver anywhere from 12 to more than 40 channels, including American and Canadian off-air stations, pay-TV systems, speciality services, and a community channel. Major Canadian urban centres have a vast array of services to choose from, with the result that campaign messages are always competing with a variety of entertainment programs. It is impossible to saturate the television medium with political messages, as is sometimes done in Europe, by broadcasting the same program on all channels.

The major news organizations generally avoid overt partisanship in their news coverage. The last vestiges of a party press vanished in the 1960s, though some Canadian newspapers still have visible partisan leanings. In many European countries, however, the party press still exists. The broadcast media generally strive for a nonpartisan image, but there are a number of exceptions here also. In Canada, major private broadcasters and the publicly owned CBC usually avoid overt favouritism. The CBC's four principal networks – English radio, English television, French radio, French television – reach most of the country. The CBC also operates a Northern Service, an indispensable means of political communication in the territories and northern reaches of the provinces, and an all-news channel, which may be expected to offer some new coverage formats for the next federal election. In their news coverage, CBC outlets do not differ significantly from their private sector counterparts, except that they tend to devote more resources and time to public affairs coverage and are sometimes more venturesome. All these outlets are subject to frequent accusations of partisanship, but the bias often seems to be in the eye of the beholder. However, there are certain patterns of coverage that require careful examination in terms of their effects on the process and in terms of fairness.

The major news outlets tend to focus on the national campaign, though they also offer profiles of local ridings and coverage of the all-candidates meetings that are a feature of local campaigns. Editorial endorsements are common only in the larger dailies and appear to have little influence in federal elections. The major dailies have overwhelmingly favoured the Conservatives in recent federal elections and have almost never endorsed the NDP. During the 1988 federal election campaign, which ultimately turned in large measure on party policy toward free trade with the United States, only two major dailies editorialized against the proposed deal. This is often explained by the increasing concentration of ownership of the major media, especially ownership by large conglomerates with many non-media interests; but clear evidence is lacking. For a general survey of election coverage practices in Canada, including the role of ownership, see Fletcher (1981b, 79–102). There is some indication that concentration of ownership has weakened local coverage (Canada, Royal Commission 1981, 163–79).

On a day-to-day basis, the key style setters are the senior members of the parliamentary press gallery, based normally in Ottawa. The gallery's membership tripled between 1974, when there were 125 journalists, and 1990 (estimate by Taras 1990, 71), but some two dozen high-profile reporters and commentators continue to have substantial influence over the focus and tone of political coverage, especially during election campaigns. Their dominant role in campaign reporting helps to ensure knowledgeable coverage but also permits long-established attitudes and common opinions to affect coverage. The substantial influence on the coverage by national political specialists suggests the need for a careful look at their attitudes and work patterns, as well as the ways in which the major news organizations go about covering elections (see Gilsdorf 1990).

In many other democratic countries, the news media are closer to government or to the leading parties. In this respect, the Canadian media are closer to those in the United States. In most countries, however, the major national media and the leading correspondents establish the agenda and interpretive framework for election coverage.

JOURNALISTIC NORMS AND PRACTICES

The information flow in election campaigns is influenced significantly by the rules of the news game and by practices specific to election campaigns. In addition to standard news values, which favour items that are simple, direct, personal, dramatic, and new, a number of other norms have emerged or been confirmed over the past decade. These include fairly well-established rules of proportionate allocation of attention among the major parties, especially on television; increased number of direct appraisals of how leaders are performing; increased attention to party strategies (and strategists); and a decreased acceptance of off-the-record briefings and covering for gaffes. There was increasing attention to issues from 1974 to 1980, with some of the major news organizations establishing issue teams and analysing party positions systematically. This pattern of coverage was less evident in 1984, largely because of the nature of the campaign, but returned in 1988 as news organizations tried to deal with the Free Trade Agreement.

Data on allocation of attention among the major parties make it clear that coverage tends to be divided roughly according to standings in the House of Commons when the election is called. This is a conscious policy of the broadcast media, with most organizations monitoring their own coverage (as they know the parties do). Newspaper coverage also tends to follow these guidelines, though the editors of most of the large dailies deny it. Coverage of local candidates appears also to be largely on a proportionate basis, usually in riding profiles and coverage of all-candidates meetings, but some newspapers do pay approximately equal attention to all "serious" candidates.

This pattern of proportional coverage is a response not only to pressure from the major parties but also to the balance requirements imposed upon broadcasters. Section 3(d) of the 1968 *Broadcasting Act* specifies that programming presented by Canadian broadcasters "should provide reasonable balanced opportunities for the expression of differing views on matters of public concern." This has been interpreted by the CRTC to mean that equitable coverage of participants in the campaign in news and public affairs broadcasting is required along with the more precise requirements for free and paid time noted above. As the CRTC has expressed it, "The purpose of these requirements is to ensure the public's right to be informed of the issues involved so that it has sufficient knowledge to make an informed choice from among the various parties and candidates. This right is a quintessential one for the effective functioning of democracy, particularly at election time" (1988, 7–8). The Commission emphasizes that "equitable" does not mean "equal," but that "all candidates and parties are entitled to some coverage that will give them the opportunity to expose their ideas to the public" (ibid., 8). The document makes clear that these requirements apply to all forms of programming but declines to make specific requirements for news and public affairs on the grounds that each broadcaster is unique in terms of responsibilities and resources. The broadcasters have responded to this responsibility by developing a convention of proportionate treatment for the three major parties. In this sense, the allocative decisions made for regulated broadcasters influence other media outlets and practitioners. This pattern has been noted in other democracies as well. One example is the 1983 British election. Although trailing in the polls and out of the electoral race, the Alliance received a relatively high share of attention in newspapers, a reflection of their electronic media allocations (Semetko 1991).

Although regulations have an ancillary effect in keeping notions of fairness and equity in the minds of journalists, the impact on coverage is not always positive. While the convention does have the virtue of ensuring that the third major party does not disappear from the coverage as well as limiting the incumbent advantage, it also opens the news organizations to manipulation, since the parties can orchestrate the coverage by providing only one nugget of news each day. To meet its largely self-imposed quota of coverage for each party, each news organization is almost forced to use that nugget, which is transformed into a "sound bite" when it is aired during newscasts. Over time these clips have grown smaller: Gilsdorf and Bernier (1991) estimate they have shrunk from 30 seconds to 12 in Canada, while Taylor reports that the average length of candidates' sound bites on American television news has fallen from 42.2 seconds in 1968 to 9.8 seconds in 1988 (1990, 258, citing Adatto 1989). In addition, of course, the convention makes it difficult for the third party – or any party – to make gains, because the coverage pattern tends to persist with little regard to the quality or substance of the campaign. Minor parties are sometimes lumped together in a single report or tagged on to reports about the more prominent parties. However, major gains in the polls will bring coverage, as has been the case for the Reform party since 1988. Minor and emerging parties have an even more difficult time getting attention in the United States, but the campaign discourse is considerably more open in most European countries.

In the wake of the election campaigns of the 1970s, when charges of manipulation were rife, Canadian journalists developed a relatively high level of awareness of overt or clumsy attempts to control coverage. This is somewhat ironic, given that the concentration of media attention on leaders gives the parties a means and a motive to pitch campaigns in terms of personalities, style and managerial acumen. Even as "spin-doctor" has become a pejorative term, synonymous with calculating partisan impulses, the media continue to rely on official sources for campaign material. In the same decade, books about the kind of journalism practised on campaigns in the United States (Crouse 1974) and Canada (Cocking 1980, writing about the 1979 campaign) turned a critical eye on the pack. Journalists are now including media-related phenomenon in the coverage. Advertisements are replayed and analysed; behind the scenes glimpses of life on the campaign trail are becoming familiar. During the 1988 and 1990 American elections, the print media began to publish critiques of television advertisements and the veracity of candidate utterances (Graber 1991). This is consistent with the self-regulatory principles of the U.S. media and doubtless helps newspapers to find a niche in the midst of electronic campaigns. These so-called truth boxes – assessments of advertisements set off from other newspaper copy by a box – are costly and contested by party strategists but may have checked some abusive practices (Wolinsky et al. 1991).

Taras has said of the 1988 Canadian federal election that journalists "displayed an uncharacteristic reluctance to discuss party advertising strategies, challenge the appropriateness or truthfulness of the 'facts' presented in the ads or make judgements" (1990, 227). This seems to be an exaggeration, for it is clear that some commentary and analysis was inspired by the advertising (Kline et al. 1991). Ironically, too much attention to the strategies, however critical, runs the risk of accentuating an already overblown angle on elections, especially if context is missing.

Other journalistic practices that have been examined include the increasing attention to public preference polls; the notable increase in the amount of direct appraisal of leader performance in the coverage; the greater attention to the personal lives and qualities of party leaders; and the increasing focus on the party leaders at the expense of other aspects of the campaign. These trends are present in most other industrial democracies as well.

It should be noted that campaign coverage, like all journalism, is profoundly affected by news-gathering routines, prevailing professional standards and values, and source–reporter relations, all of which help to explain the nature of news about elections. During election campaigns, the source–reporter relationship is at least as important as at other times and is probably more visible. Party tacticians, pollsters and "spin-doctors," once consigned to the back rooms, are caught by the media spotlight. In part, this visibility stems from a conscious effort by journalists to supply background information, to report a source's obvious or clumsy attempts to control them, and to prevent accusations of having been manipulated. However, it is consistent with reliance on those who can speak with authority. The implications of this relationship are worrisome. Ericson et al. note that the development of negotiated source–journalist relationships tends to frame the news in a way that is consonant with institutional preferences, simultaneously narrowing the bounds of legitimate debate and constricting policy options (1989, 1–27).

In summary, the Canadian system of campaign communication is relatively nonpartisan and open to a variety of messages. However, electoral regulations and journalistic practices tend to focus attention on the three major parties and their leaders at the expense of minor parties and other groups. The advent of party registration, along with other changes in society, has led to a dramatic increase in the number of parties without representation in the House participating in election campaigns, from two in 1974 to nine in 1988. However, they have little access to the national media. The focus on the national campaigns is very strong, and local candidates get little coverage in the major media, making it difficult for a local candidate to overcome an incumbent or to buck a national tide. Certain types of media appear to counter, or at least hold out against, this trend. Weekly, local or small-circulation newspapers are more open to communications initiated by minor parties (Hackett 1991), as are community cable channels (Desbarats 1991). Even so, these media are not always exploited or promoted in a way that would enhance their contribution to campaign communication.

MAJOR TRENDS IN COVERAGE

Dominance of Television

By 1979, television had become the dominant source of campaign information for voters. A clear majority of voters (52 percent) reported getting most of their campaign information from television; 30 percent mentioned newspapers and 11 percent radio (Carleton School of Journalism 1979). Newspapers continued, of course, to be the most complete sources of information and to influence broadcast news, but the radio and television news organizations became increasingly autonomous in their news judgements during the 1970s and devoted more resources to public affairs. The federal campaigns of 1957 and 1958 were the first in which television was extensively used, but modern image politics did not come to Canada until the 1960s, when the national parties turned to private polling and the use of advertising agencies, initially employing specialists imported from the United States (Soderlund et al. 1984, 19–25).

Television's dominance as a vehicle for campaign communication appears to rest on the interaction of a number of basic social, political and economic factors. Newspaper readership is in gradual decline, and limited literacy is a persistent barrier to printed text for many Canadians. Significantly, party officials are convinced that television advertising is both effective and cost-efficient, an assumption which spurs their increased attention to advertising strategies (Romanow et al. 1991). Television's constant presence in the home and multifaceted use makes it attractive, and the medium itself can convey a sense of animation, trigger emotion, and accentuate conflict.

The trend toward television dominance among voters in campaign settings is evident in virtually every industrial democracy. In Germany, television is considered the most trustworthy medium and is especially important as a source for information and commentary about national politics (Schoenbach 1991, citing Berg and Kiefer 1987). Data compiled from recent Danish surveys indicate that while the percentage of those who deem television to be the most important source of news about campaigns in national elections does vary somewhat, it is consistently above that of other media (Siune 1991, citing surveys in 1987, 1988, 1989 and 1990). Comparable findings regarding the reliance on and trust in television have been reported about Australia (Warhurst 1991), the United States (Graber 1991) and the United Kingdom (Semetko 1991). In Canada, television is the primary source of information for 47 percent of the population, ahead of newspapers (31 percent) and radio (15 percent) (Adams and Levitan 1988). This ranking, if not the precise numbers, is found in most industrial democracies.

More important than the fact of television dominance are its implications for the campaign process. Attention to television – either as the sole media source or in conjunction with newspapers, radio and magazines – constitutes a powerful incentive to concentrate on the development of positive televised images and sophisticated advertising strategies. Campaigns are run for television by the national parties, primarily because party strategists believe it is the best medium for reaching uncommitted voters. The strategists believe, with some support from Canadian voting studies (Clarke et al. 1984, 132–35), that the floating voters tend to respond to image politics, for which television is particularly well suited. Campaigns, therefore, have become contests of television performance. This conclusion is borne out by studies of other countries. For example, content analyses in Britain and the United States report that 78 percent of the visuals are "initiated by parties or candidates (i.e., conducting planned campaign engagements)" (Semetko 1991). Influenced by television, the national campaigns tend to focus on party leaders, downplaying not only local candidates and potential cabinet members, but also policies and issues. One consequence – with repercussions for the balance of power in the parliamentary parties – is that "at election time, the leader has [tended to] become the party" (Snider 1985, 148–49). The evolution of television campaigning in Canada has clearly contributed to a decline in significance of local candidates.

Issues, approaches, perspectives, even the geography and timing of the leaders' campaign tours are dictated by the needs of television. Because the other news organizations also focus their coverage on the leader tours, television tends to shape the news in other media. Unless a special effort is made to develop alternative material, newspaper coverage tends to become captive to the television-oriented campaign. Indeed, a major consequence of television dominance is to permit the party strategists to control the campaign agenda as long as they provide the brief, dramatic statements required by television. The responses of journalists have tended to revolve around revealing the marketing strategies of the parties rather than seeking a more balanced approach to coverage. If it is true, as many communication theorists argue, that emotional appeals are best suited to television and rational appeals to print, the dominance of television has altered campaigns significantly.

Horse-race Journalism

The term "horse-race journalism" has resonance in a number of jurisdictions. In Canada, an early use of the term was that of Wilson (1980–81). Simply put, horse-race journalism implies a fascination with the final electoral outcome and the jockeying done by parties leading up to polling day. As Schoenbach (1991) notes, this sort of coverage attributes undue importance to the relative fortunes and standings in public opinion polls of leaders and parties. A related phenomenon is the accent on trivial incidents and colourful spectacles served up along the trail. Campaigns are constructed around daily pseudo-events staged by parties against the appropriate backdrops. While television finds the visuals irresistible, print journalists fish for angles that will enliven coverage, sometimes to offset the drudgery or counter the careful packaging.

These characteristics are distressing because they overshadow or animate so much of the coverage at the expense of substantive issues. Data from one content analysis from the 1988 American campaign indicate that only about 30 percent of content is based on either candidate qualifications or issues, as opposed to campaign events, voter profiles, poll standings, and the nature of media coverage (Graber 1991, citing Buchanan 1991).

Focus of the Coverage

Although analysts offer differing estimates of the magnitude of the dominance of the three major party leaders as a focus of coverage, the general consensus is that they are at the centre of the national campaigns, causing some observers to comment on the "Americanization" or "presidentialization" of Canadian electoral politics. (See, for example, Soderlund et al. 1984, 127ff.) Whether or not leadership itself is an issue, the lead items on television newscasts and newspaper front pages generally derive from the leader tours. For the most part, other actors are quoted in reaction to the statements of the party leaders. Local candidates and interest group leaders tend to be virtually absent from high-profile coverage.

Such determined attention to the party leaders and their doings allows them to set the campaign agenda, with the result that campaigns tend to focus on the issues of strategic advantage to the major parties. Issues that do not fit this category, because the established parties tacitly agree to ignore them for tactical reasons, may never be raised, especially given the difficulties faced by non-party groups in gaining news coverage during campaigns. Because newspapers have followed television in their coverage of the national campaigns, careful analysis of party policy or neglected issues is not common (though it is by no means unknown).

Negative Tone

Among the major findings of content analysis of media coverage of election campaigns has been the discovery of a clear trend toward more negative coverage of parties and leaders. Early studies of newspaper coverage, in 1962 and 1974, found that positive references tended to outnumber negative references for both parties and leaders. "The predominant role of the press in the 1962 election appears to have been that of cheerleader for all of the major parties," according to Qualter and MacKirdy (1964, 150–51; the 1974 reference is to Clarke 1984, 136). By 1979, however, the major parties and their leaders were both reported in negative terms, and, in 1980, all three parties and leaders received more negative than positive references. Except for the Liberals, the trend was reversed in 1984, but appears to have reappeared in 1988. Coders for a Carleton University study found that all three major parties and their leaders received more unfavourable than favourable coverage in 1988 (Frizzell et al. 1989, 89). Regional differences were slight in 1979 and 1980 but were significant in 1984 and 1988, a phenomenon worthy of further study.

The 1984 figures are the only ones in recent elections to show sufficient difference in both direction and magnitude for the major parties and leaders to suggest a major public impact (Fletcher 1988, 174–75). Whether the media follow the poll results or influence them, it seems likely that such strong differences in media perception at least reinforced voter leanings. This seems especially plausible in the light of the finding that voters switching away from the governing party are likely to cite negative assessments of the party or leader (Clarke et al. 1984, 142–43). The 1984 National Election Study found the media portrayal reproduced in the perception of its respondents, namely a generally positive attitude toward Mulroney and a generally negative assessment of Turner (Kay et al. 1985, 32).

What accounts for the negative trend in the tone of coverage and comment on the major parties and their leaders? With respect to the media in general, there is a predilection for "bad news." In terms of political reporting, two specific factors have been suggested: the nature of television and a growing cynicism among political journalists. Soderlund and his colleagues (1984) suggest that television may have a tendency "to seek out the confrontational aspects of party strategies"; television may be "more prone to carry the film clip in which one party leader attacks the other leader and his party, rather than being inclined to feature those parts of speeches devoted to the explanation of party policy. Politicians have reacted to this propensity by structuring their remarks to feed this appetite" (ibid., 87). In 1980 and 1984, the pattern for television and newspaper front pages was not very different, suggesting common news values, or that television coverage was setting the tone, as some have argued. As far as journalistic cynicism is concerned, interviews confirm that reporters' attitudes are a factor. Reporters and news organizations have reacted to the manipulative tactics of the parties – especially the two major parties – by turning to the evaluation of these tactics as a defensive measure, giving the coverage an appearance of cynicism (Fletcher 1981a, 291–92). The generally positive, or only mildly negative, coverage of the NDP and its leaders is usually attributed to its third-party standing. Since it has been deemed unlikely to form a government, the incentive for critical scrutiny is lacking. The NDP simply gets less attention.

The lack of overall negativism in 1984 makes it clear that party strategies do play an important role. The campaigns of 1979 and 1980 were marked by attack and counterattack, with both parties focusing on the leadership issue. This was much less true in 1974, when the differences between the leaders were generally framed in policy terms. Once again in 1984, the leaders generally refrained from direct attacks on one another. One might conclude, therefore, that the parties do play a major role in determining the tone of the coverage. Partisan attacks returned in 1988, and the coverage was once again judged negative.

In short, the negativism apparent in the coverage of recent Canadian national election campaigns is attributable to changes in journalistic norms, especially the emergence of an "appraisal of performance approach" to the coverage of party leaders, as well as to party strategies and the interaction between the two. Some have speculated that the negative tone of political coverage in general is threatening the legitimacy of the national parties and national institutions, but the linkage is difficult to draw. It seems likely, however, that the negative tone of media coverage may be implicated in the finding that "every political leader in the past two decades has declined in public esteem from the benchmark established in his first election as leader" (LeDuc and Price 1990, 14). It is interesting to note, however, that seeing the leaders in a less mediated situation – leaders debates – tends to improve their standing in the eyes of voters (ibid.).

The cynical tone of campaign coverage is a matter of concern in other democracies as well, but particularly in the United States. As a recent study for the Kettering Foundation (1991, 55) put it, "citizens are tired and frustrated by the nature and tone of today's political debate." For this, they blame both politicians and the media.

Media Polls

Perhaps the most obvious trend in media coverage of national election campaigns over the past decade has been the proliferation of media-initiated polls. During the 1979 and 1980 Canadian campaigns, there were eight and 10 national polls, respectively, and many regional and local ones. In 1984, there were 12 national polls. Polls were mentioned in 16 percent of election items on network television news in 1980 and 20 percent in 1984 (calculated from Soderlund et al. 1984, table 3-7, and Romanow et al. 1985, table 3). They were the occasion for 9 percent of the front page stories in our daily newspaper sample in 1980 and 12 percent in 1984. In addition, they formed the context for virtually all horse-race-oriented reports. Although they clearly reinforce the horse-race approach to election coverage, they are one element of media content that is outside of party control. In 1980, the Conservatives put their private pollster on the spot by asking him to refute media polls showing his party trailing. In 1984, Turner was put on the defensive by his sudden decline in public support in early published polls and suffered a further decline in his fortunes. Indeed, the electorate was so volatile in 1984 that several observers have speculated that the poll results played a critical role in the outcome (Romanow et al. 1985, 17). As one journalist put it, "the party that was able to persuade the voters it was going to form a national government might emerge as the winner" (MacDonald 1984, 281). The 1988 National Election Study found evidence that a "politics of expectations" was at work and that the polls contributed to strategic voting (Blais et al. 1990). Journalists have often confided that the coverage is influenced by the polls.

In 1988, the number of national media polls climbed to 22. Analysis of the 1988 election coverage by Frizzell shows that polls were the main topic of anywhere from 4.7 percent to 7.8 percent of the stories in major daily newspapers. Polls were the primary focus of 8.9 percent of election items on CBC national newscasts, 14.9 percent on CTV, and 11.4 percent on Global. The figures are not alarming, particularly when newspapers are covering the story and doing so in a relatively straightforward manner. The real problem is that poll standings leak into other forms of coverage, including background commentary and issue analysis (Frizzell 1991). This emphasis may well crowd out other reports of importance.

The infamous Gallup poll of 7 November 1988, which put the Liberals at 43 percent, a 12 percent lead over the Conservatives, caused such consternation in the Conservative camp that they moved quickly to refute it, using their own numbers from Decima. They were concerned primarily about the morale of their own workers, but also with a possible bandwagon effect. The 1988 Canadian National Election Study did find evidence of influence on voter expectations (Blais et al. 1990). Over a longer term, a poll like this one, which appears to have been inaccurate, can also raise concerns about fund-raising and change the nature of campaign coverage. In this case, it may have worked to the benefit of the Conservatives, galvanizing support for their position.

There was also a proliferation of local polls in key ridings. This development gave those races a profile that they would not otherwise have had. Many of them were technically deficient. Their impact on levels of voter interest, turnout and vote decision is not known.

The proliferation of public opinion polls is by no means unique to Canada. In Britain, the number of polls published during the three-week campaign went from a mere five in 1970 to more than 70 in 1987. In many industrial democracies, the polls have become a staple of campaign coverage, with both positive and negative consequences.

Debates

Televised leaders debates have become an important element of election campaigns in many democracies since the Kennedy–Nixon debates in the United States in 1960. Canada saw its first debate in the Quebec provincial election of 1962 and at the federal level in 1968. By the 1970s, televised leaders debates had become common in European elections, and they now seem fairly well entrenched in many countries, though their organization and formats remain informal and subject to negotiation among the parties and broadcasters (Bernier and Monière 1991).

In Canada, televised debates among the leaders of the three major national parties were an important feature of the 1979, 1984 and 1988 campaigns. The programs were important not only in their own right – with very large audiences – but also as heavily covered political events. The debates dominated the news for the next few days and were discussed right up to polling day. The single debate in 1979 had grown to three in 1984, two organized by the television networks (broadly following the 1979 format), one in each official language, and one organized by the National Action Committee on the Status of Women, Canada's most powerful women's lobby group, to focus on issues of particular concern to women. Only the network debates were held in 1988.

The two major English television networks, CBC and CTV, which had failed to gain party agreement to a leaders debate in 1974, were joined in 1979 by Global, an Ontario-based network. The networks proposed that a nonpartisan moderator and a panel of journalists be used to keep things focused and moving. After lengthy negotiations, an agreement was reached. The parties agreed to a round-robin format, with opening and closing statements by each of the three leaders. Each 30-minute segment pitted two of the three leaders against the other, discussing questions raised by the journalists.

In 1979, the debate attracted a total audience of 7.5 million, nearly half of the English-speaking population. Its impact was limited by the fact that it was exclusively in English. In 1984, there were two network debates, one in each official language, and the privately organized women's issues debate, covered by the networks as a news event. More than two-thirds of adult Canadians watched at least one of the three 1984 debates (Kay et al. 1985, 23). The 1988 debates attracted similar attention (LeDuc and Price 1990, table 1).

Aside from heightening interest in the election, the 1979 encounters had little impact. A careful analysis of survey data concluded that it had no impact on voter choice, although Conservative leader Joe Clark was generally viewed as having performed least well (LeDuc and Price 1985).

The network debates in 1984 and 1988 both had dramatic effects on the campaigns. There were immediate vote swings – away from Liberal leader Turner in 1984 and toward him in 1988 – and in each case the dynamics of the campaign were altered. The debates changed party strategies and media coverage and also precipitated short-term shifts in vote intentions. In addition, they appear to have stimulated interest in the campaigns and to have had a measurable effect on levels of information about leaders and issues, especially among voters with limited knowledge of and interest in politics. Interestingly, it appears that all leaders who participate in debates gain in public esteem. (For fuller discussions of debate effects, see LeDuc and Price 1990 and Fletcher 1987. On the educational impact of the 1984 debates, see Barr 1989.)

In general, the debates added little to the campaign agenda, because participating journalists focused on issues already on the table. Their major contribution, it appears, was to give the leaders an opportunity to communicate their central priorities and to probe the weaknesses of their opponents. While the exchanges did not add much to the information of the highly attentive public, they appear to have improved the information environment significantly for many other voters.

It is this educational effect that makes it worthwhile to consider mechanisms for ensuring that leaders debates take place. While it institutionalizes the leader focus of national campaigns, an unfortunate consequence in the eyes of some, it does provide an important forum for discussion of the major issues of the campaign. LeDuc and Price (1990, 2) suggest that the debates are becoming institutionalized, both in probability of occurrence and in form. It is important, therefore, to consider the appropriateness of the format as well as such matters as frequency and timing. A very real problem is the exclusion of minor party leaders from the debates. To exclude them means omitting the perspectives of significant numbers of citizens from the debates. To include them means to create a logistical nightmare and, probably, to lose much of the audience. Some form of compensatory time may be the answer.

It is worth noting that debates among local candidates have become increasingly common in recent campaigns. Some local stations carry debates, usually as part of their newscasts or public affairs programming, as do many community channels on cable. A survey commissioned in 1990 showed that 86.5 percent of community channel operators provided free time to registered parties and approximately 50 percent produced or covered local all-candidate debates (Desbarats 1991).

CAMPAIGN STRATEGIES

National campaigns in Canada revolve around leader tours and media advertising. The leader tours and speeches are supplemented by news releases from party headquarters, tours by the "B teams" of party notables, and constituency-level activities. In recent elections, all three major parties have exercised considerable central control over the campaigns at all levels, though advertising campaigns have usually been divided between French and English, with quite different campaigns in the two official languages (reflecting differences in political culture and issues). While the details of organizing the constituency campaigns are often left to provincial organizations, training materials and briefing materials are generally produced centrally. In recent elections, computerized communications systems have been used to produce frequent policy

updates for local candidates, providing constituency-level organizations with prepared answers for almost any conceivable question
regarding party policy. Local candidates are left to canvass and exploit
local media while the national campaigns dominate the highly visible
prestige media.

With the exception of the poorly organized Liberal campaign of
1984, recent campaigns have been carefully crafted exercises designed
to enhance the strong points in the images of each party and leader and
to draw attention to the weak points of the other. The advertising
campaigns – mostly 30- and 60-second spots – were carefully targeted
to particular regions, usually expressing concern for regional issues
and promising general solutions. Confined by law to the last four weeks
of the campaign, the spots were targeted at the floating vote and used
themes that had been successful in the public campaigns. In 1979 and
1980, the spots were frequently negative, attacks by one major party
on the leader of the other. They reflected the leader-oriented and generally negative tone of the campaigns. The free-time broadcasts were
often expanded versions of the spots and were only marginally more
informative. The 1988 campaign was basically similar.

There has been very little research on political advertising in
Canadian elections. There is some evidence that Canadians are unhappy
with negative advertising, but little is known – outside the parties, at
least – about its effectiveness. Practitioners certainly assume that advertising is effective. Recent studies of campaign advertising by Kline
(in Leiss et al. 1990, 389–404) and Taras (1990) have shed some new
light on questions about the content of the spots, the strategic considerations taken into account by the parties, and their effects. A survey
of media coverage of campaign advertising since 1977 suggests that
five key themes have passed into the public domain via newspaper
commentary: critiques of image manipulation; political marketing and
strategies; issues surrounding regulation; freedom of expression (especially in terms of third-party advertising); and economic and "structural" issues (in the case of the latter, relationships between media and
government through advertising) (Kline et al. 1991). Although most
practitioners are convinced of the advantages of negative advertising,
few pause over the possibility of any long-term harm to the political
system and citizen attitudes (Romanow et al. 1991).

The leader tours are designed to sell the party and leader through
the news coverage. The two major parties have over the past four elections followed a policy of tight control over access to the leader,
attempting to force the news organizations to cover the message that
the leaders try to dispense each day. The general pattern has been for

each leader to provide photo opportunities and some nugget of policy each day – usually carefully related to the overall theme of the campaign. Within some limits, the leaders have been able to focus media attention on their agendas, especially on television. Of course, attention does not always mean favourable coverage.

In many other democracies, campaign strategy and coverage are even more leader-oriented. In systems that feature proportional representation, the party, usually personified by the leader, is the central focus of campaigns, with local candidates generally not significant. In the U.S., the focus on the presidential race sometimes obscures the strong candidate orientation. While advertising during Canadian elections usually features the party and the leader, U.S. advertising is focused on individual candidates. In this context, Canada is more typical of other democracies. Nevertheless, in the British-style parliamentary systems, local candidates still count for something.

For the local candidate, the campaign is normally an exhausting round of canvassing, neighbourhood parties and all-candidates meetings, with media playing a minor role. The figures for the 1974 federal election appear typical: 18 percent of voters were contacted personally by one or more candidates; 34 percent were canvassed by a party worker; 78 percent remembered seeing campaign literature or receiving a telephone call (Clarke et al. 1979, 292). In the post-election survey in 1988, 48 percent of respondents reported being contacted by a candidate or party worker, and 86 percent remembered receiving a pamphlet (National Election Study 1989). The differences from 1974 to 1988 are slight. The literature is far from clear on the effectiveness of these efforts.

The options open to local candidates are restricted by centralized control of campaigns and spending limits. The effects of the imposition of spending limits in 1979 have been summarized by Seidle and Paltiel (1981, 264): constituency campaigns were much more carefully planned, as organizers faced hard decisions about the cost-effectiveness of various measures; television and radio advertising were often avoided, especially in urban areas, as too costly; spending tended to be primarily for brochures and signs and, to a lesser extent, newspaper advertising; energy had to be diverted to detailed record-keeping.

The experience of 1979 and 1980 was that the limits were very restrictive. The average permitted expenditure in 1979 was $26 924 and rarely exceeded $30 000 (calculated on a sliding scale based on number of voters in the constituency). In 1979, Liberal and Conservative candidates spent 80 and 78 percent of their limits, while NDP candidates spent 35 percent. However, NDP incumbents spent

78 percent of their limits, and it is believed that NDP candidates in the 55 ridings identified as priority ridings by the party spent nearly as much as their opponents. As noted, the spending was primarily on non-broadcast advertising (49 percent), including a wide range of media. (See Seidle and Paltiel 1981, 265–72.)

The rules, as well as the realities of media markets, limit the use of media by local candidates. Time donated by local broadcasters to candidates must be declared as campaign spending if its commercial value exceeds $100 and must be made available on an equitable basis to all candidates. For this reason and because television is generally viewed as an inefficient medium for reaching voters in specific ridings, the vast majority of television spots – with their substantial audience reach – promote the national parties, especially the leaders (LaCalamita 1984, 555–57). The increase in careful regional targeting in 1984 did little to change the nonlocal character of the advertising content. There has been little public research on the nature and effectiveness of targeting.

The amount of free media available to local candidates depends heavily on the location of the riding in relation to media organization, the competitiveness of the riding, and the presence of a high-profile candidate. Interviews with incumbents at both the federal and provincial level uncovered two patterns worthy of further investigation: urban incumbents were much more anxious for news coverage than rural candidates; and many incumbents felt that coverage by major news organizations whose reporters dropped into a riding for a feature or riding profile was so unpredictable and potentially damaging that they should be avoided. Urban incumbents in large ridings with transient populations felt that news coverage was their only hope of maintaining name familiarity, despite the risks. Many rural members felt that they received enough publicity through the routine channels of constituency newsletters and community events and that they could avoid the risks of mediated coverage.

As noted above, a number of structural factors limit the effectiveness of constituency-level campaigns. This gap is increasingly filled, however, by the mandatory community channels carried by most Canadian cable television systems. While commercial advertising is forbidden on the community channels, many of them provide extensive coverage of local politics and offer free time to candidates during election campaigns, though they have no legal obligation to do so. During campaigns, they are bound by the same rules as broadcasters: programs must be confined to the 29 days prior to voting day (when advertisements are permitted); and time must be offered on an equitable basis to all competing parties and candidates (Soderlund et al. 1984, 121).

As early as 1972, cable operators in many communities began to see a role in the coverage of public affairs. Filling the time on the community channel was often a problem, and community programmers saw an opportunity to gain goodwill by covering municipal council meetings and other public hearings. Incumbents, always looking for exposure, began to offer monthly reports or to do interview and phone-in shows, just as they did on local radio stations. (Many also wrote columns in local weeklies.) At times, challengers have been able to develop a public affairs show as a basis for gaining name familiarity. Provincial parties increasingly provide pretaped programs for incumbents to offer to local cable systems. Within the rules noted above, many cable systems offer blocks of time to candidates during elections, organize debates and/or cover all-candidates meetings. The structure of the systems frequently permits them to offer programming to subscribers in one or in a few ridings.

There is an increasing trend to targeting marginal ridings. It is becoming normal practice to concentrate resources on the target ridings and to coordinate national, regional and local campaigns very closely. Krashinsky and Milne (1986, 339) found that this practice appeared to have helped the NDP hold a number of marginal seats in 1984 in the face of the Conservative national tide. The selection of targets and the nature of the media campaign in these contested ridings deserve a high place on any research agenda concerned with election communication.

Campaigns have become increasingly important to the outcome of elections, and parties have grown more sophisticated in their campaign strategies. The media focus on leader tours allows the parties to influence both the issue agenda and the tone of the coverage and to coordinate their public messages with those in their spot advertising. The negative tone of recent campaigns appears to have been influenced by both media and party. While national campaigns hold the spotlight, local candidates must struggle with a media structure which is usually not geared to reach their potential voters efficiently and within restrictive spending limits. The cable-delivered community channels fill a void here, but little is known about their audiences or the extent to which they are available and utilized by local candidates.

CAMPAIGN PROBLEM AREAS

The objectives of election campaigns are best served when regulations and practices strike a balance between the freedom of the parties to market their candidates and programs as they see fit and the need to provide voters with sufficient information to make a reasoned choice. The goal is to facilitate debate within a framework of fairness that maximizes information availability and the legitimacy of the process. The media play a crucial role in monitoring the parties and leaders and providing a critical perspective on their activities and proposals. However, the parties deserve a reasonable opportunity to communicate their appeals directly.

The Local–Regional–National Information Balance

It is arguable that in a parliamentary system based on territorial representation, the growing emphasis on the national campaign at the expense of local candidates is problematic. Similarly, the increase in regional targeting of national campaigns may be undermining the consensus-building that comes from national debates. The problem is to find a suitable balance. At present, however, there are few incentives for parties to devote resources below the national level. The media focus on leaders and condense issues in terms of national relevance. Current spending rules sometimes restrict local campaigns. Community channels on cable may help break the dominance of the national campaign in the future, but this may be contingent on other media reflecting the dimensions of the campaign, the regional or local variations of national issues, and the importance of elected legislators.

Regulation of Broadcasting

The general principles for regulation of election broadcasting seem to reflect well the values of Canadians. There are, however, problems of implementation. The actual allocation of free and paid time does not seem to represent a "level playing field." Minor parties, those not represented in the House at the time of dissolution, in particular, are disadvantaged. Canada faces a dilemma, in common with other countries, of how to distinguish between coverage of significant political events involving partisans, and more or less overt campaigning conducted by those in office. Gerstlé (1991) has noted that the chief aspirants in the 1988 French presidential election campaign were the incumbent and the prime minister, a rivalry which complicated journalistic decisions about balance. Many Americans would be surprised to learn that 39 candidates contested the presidency in 1988 (Graber 1991), some representing parties that in other countries are plausible, if not principal, contenders. Regulations will have to take this factor into account and be sensitive to advantages (in familiarity and access) enjoyed by office holders. The increased number of registered parties has not broadened campaign debates significantly at the national level because of their lack of access.

Advertising

A number of issues are associated with recent trends in campaign advertising. From the standpoint of content, party advertisements are increasingly negative and devoid of substantive appeals. By their very nature – 30-second or one-minute segments – television and radio advertising encourage sloganeering and punchy jolts. This is particularly evident in the United States, where advertising is a major feature of campaigns at all levels.

One dilemma that must be taken seriously is the prohibitive cost associated with advertising. In the absence of subsidies and with limited free-time allocations, minor parties face severe disadvantages. Although costs are daunting, it is not only minor parties that will encounter funding difficulties. Many established parties are grappling with deficit financing. Advertising is coveted for its potential to inform and persuade voters, even though existing research remains ambiguous about persuasive effects. However, a more tangible and verifiable problem is that advertising campaigns lend a certain cachet to parties. If a party is unable to mount an advertising campaign of some kind, it is unlikely to receive attention in news coverage. Without this sort of visibility, parties will be unable to present themselves as viable alternatives.

Interventions by advocacy groups in the election of 1988 sparked a debate in Canada, and there will be keen interest elsewhere in the public policy response. Advertising by organized interests that endorsed policies, parties and candidates aroused considerable concern. The issue is not simply one of uneven distribution among interest groups of the funds needed to purchase advocacy advertising. Especially in Canada, the potential of unlimited advocacy advertising threatens to undermine the system of regulated competition that depends upon limits on party and candidate spending. If advocacy groups can spend as they see fit and align themselves with parties freely, the existing spending limits are unenforceable and the likely outcome is a money-driven system like that in the United States.

Media Practices

While the news media generally take seriously their responsibility to cover election campaigns fairly, their standard practices have raised concerns among observers. Problem areas include the narrow focus on leaders, the limited range of issues given significant coverage, the negative tone of much coverage (a result of media–party interaction), the proliferation of media polls, the increasing injection of reportorial assessments into the coverage, and the limited external accountability of the print media (broadcasters have to justify their coverage to the CRTC if complaints are made). Press councils and broadcast standards councils, while potentially significant, are limited in their scope and authority. The dominance of television is a concern to many observers, especially those who accept the premise that television communicates emotional appeals well but rational appeals poorly.

Public Opinion Polls

Media-sponsored polls are a major aspect of campaign coverage and appear likely to continue to grow in importance. They can draw attention away from issues or frame them in questionable ways. Inaccurate polls could conceivably alter election outcomes. On the other hand, they provide voters with important information which many appear to use to make strategic vote decisions. It seems unreasonable to deprive voters of information available to party strategists (and to anyone else who can afford access). Self-regulation would help ensure sound technical standards and appropriate reporting, and the quality of poll reporting might be improved by a requirement that all polls be deposited in a shared database available for scrutiny and re-analysis by any interest parties, including news organizations other than the sponsoring agency (Entman 1989, 131).

Debates

Leaders debates are now a familiar and expected facet of campaigns, an established, if not legally mandated, form of campaign communication. This has positive and negative implications for contemporary campaigns. The educational value of such debates seems clear. LeDuc and Price (1990, 16) report that debates enhance the public image of all participants, and they have a galvanic effect on activists and citizens.

As shown by the 1988 campaign, perceived success in a debate may unleash personalized negative advertising. News coverage of debates often revolves around emotional encounters, and journalistic assessments tend to concentrate on presentation skills. Using metaphors derived from sports or combat, journalists evaluate candidates' stamina and stress, knockouts and stumbles. In short, debates become part of the "winners and losers" framework. Even those who did not watch a debate can form an opinion based on follow-up coverage, poll results, and the "social consensus" of debate performances (see Johnston et al. 1991, 12–13). Under the existing conventions, debates tend to be of a general nature, covering many issues (an exception being the debate on issues of special relevance to women in 1984). Only major party leaders have been included, and they have been permitted to claim comprehensive issue competence even when small parties (such as the Greens) have unique electoral platforms.

Focus of Coverage

The focus in the five most recent elections has been on the contest between the leaders of the two major parties, with polls, debates and party strategies all getting significant media attention, especially on television. Polls were mentioned in 20 percent of all network television election items in 1984, debates in 12 percent, and campaign strategy in 7 percent. These figures are all higher than in 1979 and 1980 (calculated from Romanow et al. 1985, table 3 and Soderlund et al. 1984, tables 3-1 and 3-2). Polls and party strategists also received more attention in newspaper coverage, and pollsters and strategists became familiar to radio and television interview show audiences. The trend continued in 1988 and deserves careful scrutiny.

New Technologies

The multiplication of channels entails special problems for Canadian election communication, especially the fragmentation of the citizen audience. According to some observers, these risks may be offset by thoughtful use of new technologies. As Desbarats (1991) argues, the dilemma of a lack of diversity in campaign coverage could be resolved through content carried on systems that are not geared to a mass, national audience. This possibility may be particularly relevant to cable.

Although cable is not new to Canada, it is largely untried as a deliberate, imaginative vehicle for campaign communication at the community level. There is both a tradition of access on which to build and a new range of channels (speciality services and satellite signals) which could extend and diversify the communication system. In addition, it may be possible to promote election period communication using computer links, desktop publishing and videocassette. Depending on circumstances, these may be able to either link media and office-seekers or permit citizens to bypass conventional mass media. The crucial factor in shaping future campaigns will be the extent to which new technologies are used to broaden public debate or to narrow it into a dialogue between special interests and government.

Citizen Responses to the Electronic Campaign

In numerous attitude surveys and voting analyses, researchers are detecting unmistakable signs of disquiet among citizens, ranging from what could be described as malaise or diffuse fears about the integrity of the campaign communication process, to responses suggesting apathy and alienation. Turnout has dropped to exceptionally low levels in the United States (barely 50 percent in the 1988 presidential election), and, in other countries, many elections, especially those described by

Schoenbach (1991) as "second-order" (i.e., European, state and local), are characterized by reduced electorate participation or the ritualized exercise of a duty. Negativism in advertising worries Graber (1991), who argues that duelling by means of personal attacks exacerbates cynicism about politicians and politics. Even when citizens are alert to campaigns and appreciate the importance of elections, they are not necessarily learning about the issues.

While it would be inaccurate to blame media campaigns for under-lying attitudes toward politics, it seems clear that they do little to dispel negative impressions. Campaign studies will continue to explore the plausibility, causes and extent of phenomena such as bandwagon or underdog effects, tactical voting, outright alienation or temporary disin-clination to vote. While many discount the importance of local candi-dates in federal elections, 27 percent of respondents in a 1988 survey claimed that local candidates were the most important factor in their decision. Although the figure may be unreliable as a true, isolated vari-able, it hints at a desire to exert more control over members of Parliament (Price and Mancuso 1991, 201–204). It may also suggest uncertainty about the messages received during campaigns. At this stage of research, it is imperative to learn more about how people perceive their infor-mation environment, assess media performance, and articulate their information needs.

CANADIAN ELECTIONS AND CAMPAIGN COVERAGE

There are many weaknesses in the Canadian campaign communica-tion system, despite its strengths. Perhaps the major problem is that it has evolved as media technologies and practices have changed, and parties have adapted with new techniques of political marketing without much thought being given to the consequences for democracy. Canada is not alone in facing this dilemma. Most of the studies reported in this volume indicate that concerns about election conduct, media coverage and the political system in general are widespread. Recent public inves-tigations in Australia and New Zealand, as well as private studies in the United States, are relevant examples (Warhurst 1991; Kettering Foundation 1991). If these anxieties are not confronted, public confi-dence in the electoral process may suffer.

The literature on the role of the media in recent elections indi-cates that campaigns are far from edifying and less than gratifying, at least from the standpoint of scholars in the field. There is some despair that news organizations will not amend their practices nor suspend their traditional news judgements. Parties have been reluctant to abandon tactics that they believe reap benefits in the polling booths. The approach to regulation in most representative democracies has tended to favour established parties. Taken together, these attributes of contemporary elections lead to fears about the foundation on which mandates are forged.

As in many other facets of its political make-up, Canada has a mixed system of regulation and practice in terms of media and elections. Like the United States, Canada permits paid advertising, and recent campaigns have featured nationally broadcast debates where leaders field questions from journalists. As is the case for most European countries, free time (and purchased slots where permitted) are divided among competitive parties. The precise formula used in Canada is relatively complex and has produced, dramatically so in 1988, an exceptional imbalance. Few countries extend allocation rules to apply to private broadcasters, as is true of Canada, but regulations will likely be drawn as more countries have experience with mixed ownership systems. Regulations in Canada and many other jurisdictions act to limit, if not exclude, minor parties and reinforce journalistic propensities to highlight personalities, major parties and institutional frameworks.

Canada is distinct in the web of media networks that spread over the country. To take one example, television programming is carried in French and English, in the languages of native peoples, and on multilingual channels; it is transmitted by public, private and provincial educational channels which can be national, regional and local; and it is beamed over the air, through cable and via satellite. Despite the impressive reach of this network, the Canadian system co-exists with American media, whose programming is almost as widely available as domestic productions. Canadian campaigns have been coloured by this fact. The emulation effect is substantial at both the élite level, where campaign tactics are borrowed, and at the level of citizens, whose expectations are influenced by American values. The virtues of the Canadian system include considerable diversity and a reasonably high level of professionalism. Like democracy, effective electoral communication requires diversity and continual re-evaluation.

ABBREVIATIONS

c.	chapter
en.	enacted
R.S.C.	Revised Statutes of Canada
s(s).	section(s)

NOTE

We wish to acknowledge the advice of Peter Desbarats, whose careful reading of the draft led to many helpful suggestions for revision.

BIBLIOGRAPHY

Adams, Michael, and J. Levitan. 1988. "Media Bias as Viewed by the Canadian Public." In *Canadian Legislatures*, ed. Robert Fleming. Ottawa: Ampersand.

Adatto, Kiku. 1989. "TV Tidbits Starve Democracy." *New York Times*, 10 December.

Axworthy, Thomas S. 1991. "Capital-Intensive Politics: Money, Media and Mores in the United States and Canada." In *Issues in Party and Election Finance in Canada*, ed. F. Leslie Seidle. Vol. 5 of the research studies of the Royal Commission on Electoral Reform and Party Financing. Ottawa and Toronto: RCERPF/Dundurn.

Barr, Cathy Widdis. 1989. "Televised Campaign Debates: Their Impact on Voting Behaviour and Their Contribution to an Informed Electorate." Paper presented at the Canadian Political Science Association annual meeting, Quebec.

Bell, David V.J., and Catherine M. Bolan. 1991. "The Mass Media and Federal Election Campaigning at the Local Level: A Case Study of Two Ontario Constituencies." In *Reaching the Voter: Constituency Campaigning in Canada*, ed. Frederick J. Fletcher and David V.J. Bell. Vol. 20 of the research studies of the Royal Commission on Electoral Reform and Party Financing. Ottawa and Toronto: RCERPF/Dundurn.

Berg, Klaus, and Marie-Luis Kiefer. 1987. *Massenkommunikation III*. Frankfurt: Metzner.

Bernier, Robert, and Denis Monière. 1991. "The Organization of Televised Leaders Debates in the United States, Europe, Australia and Canada." In *Media and Voters in Canadian Election Campaigns*, ed. Frederick J. Fletcher. Vol. 18 of the research studies of the Royal Commission on Electoral Reform and Party Financing. Ottawa and Toronto: RCERPF/Dundurn.

Black, Jerome H. 1984. "Revisiting the Effects of Canvassing on Voting Behaviour." *Canadian Journal of Political Science* 17:351–74.

Blais, André, Richard Johnston, Henry E. Brady and Jean Crête. 1990. "The Dynamics of Horse-Race Expectations in the 1988 Canadian Election." Paper presented at the Canadian Political Science Association annual meeting, Victoria.

Buchanan, Bruce. 1991. *Electing a President: The Markle Commission Research on Campaign '88*. Austin: University of Texas Press.

Camp, Dalton. 1981. *An Eclectic Eel*. Ottawa: Deneau.

Canada. *Broadcasting Act,* R.S.C. 1985, c. B-9, s. 3.

———. *Canada Elections Act,* R.S.C. 1970, c. 14 (1st Supp.), s. 99.4; en. 1973–74, c. 51, s. 14; now R.S.C. 1985, c. E-2, s. 307.

Canada. Elections Canada. 1984. *Statutory Report of the Chief Electoral Officer of Canada.* Ottawa: Minister of Supply and Services Canada.

Canada. Royal Commission on Newspapers. 1981. *Report.* Ottawa: Minister of Supply and Services Canada.

Canadian Broadcasting Corporation. 1979. *Research Report,* TOR/79/31. Ottawa.

Canadian Radio-television and Telecommunications Corporation. 1988. "A Policy with Respect to Election Campaign Broadcasting." Public Notice CRTC 1988-142. Ottawa: CRTC.

Carleton School of Journalism. 1979. CBC Poll, 30 April to 10 May 1979, unpublished summary. Ottawa.

Clarke, Harold D., Jane Jenson, Lawrence LeDuc and Jon Pammett. 1979. *Political Choice in Canada.* Toronto: McGraw-Hill Ryerson.

———. 1984. *Absent Mandate: The Politics of Discontent in Canada.* Toronto: Gage.

———. 1991. *Absent Mandate: Interpreting Change in Canadian Politics.* 2d ed. Toronto: Gage.

Cocking, Clive. 1980. *Following the Leaders: A Media Watcher's Diary of Campaign '89.* Toronto: Doubleday.

Crouse, Timothy. 1974. *The Boys on the Bus.* New York: Ballantine.

Desbarats, Peter. 1991. "Cable Television and Federal Election Campaigns in Canada." In *Election Broadcasting in Canada,* ed. Frederick J. Fletcher. Vol. 21 of the research studies of the Royal Commission on Electoral Reform and Party Financing. Ottawa and Toronto: RCERPF/Dundurn.

Drummond, Robert J., and Frederick J. Fletcher. 1980. "Political Communication and Orientation to Legislators among Ontario Voters." In *Parliament, Policy and Representation,* ed. Harold D. Clarke et al. Toronto: Methuen.

Entman, Robert. 1989. *Democracy without Citizens: Media and the Decay of American Politics.* New York: Oxford.

Ericson, Richard V., Patricia M. Baranek and Janet B.L. Chan. 1989. *Negotiating Control: A Study of News Sources.* Toronto: University of Toronto Press.

Everett, Robert, and Frederick J. Fletcher. 1991. "The Mass Media and Political Communication in Canada." In *Communications in Canadian Society,* ed. Benjamin D. Singer. Scarborough: Nelson Canada.

Fletcher, Frederick J. 1975. "The Mass Media in the 1974 Canadian Federal Election." In *Canada at the Polls: The General Election of 1974*, ed. Howard R. Penniman. Washington, DC: American Enterprise Institute for Public Policy Research.

———. 1981a. "Playing the Game: The Mass Media and the 1979 Campaign." In *Canada at the Polls 1979 and 1980*, ed. Howard R. Penniman. Washington, DC: American Enterprise Institute for Public Policy Research.

———. 1981b. *The Newspaper and Public Affairs*. Vol. 7 of the research studies of the Royal Commission on Newspapers. Ottawa: Minister of Supply and Services Canada.

———. 1987. "The Media and Parliamentary Elections in Canada." *Legislative Studies Quarterly* 12(3): 341–72.

———. 1988. "The Media and the 1984 Landslide." In *Canada at the Polls, 1984*, ed. Howard R. Penniman. Durham, NC: Duke University Press for the American Enterprise Institute for Public Policy Research.

———. 1990. "The Crucial and the Trivial: News Coverage of Provincial Politics in Ontario." In *Government and Politics of Ontario*. 4th ed, ed. Graham White. Scarborough: Nelson Canada.

Fletcher, Frederick J., and David V.J. Bell, eds. 1991. *Reaching the Voter: Constituency Campaigning in Canada*. Vol. 20 of the research studies of the Royal Commission on Electoral Reform and Party Financing. Ottawa and Toronto: RCERPF/Dundurn.

Fletcher, Frederick J., and Daphne Gottlieb Taras. 1990. "Images and Issues: The Mass Media and Politics in Canada." In *Canadian Politics in the 1990s*, ed. Michael S. Whittington and Glen Williams. Scarborough: Nelson Canada.

Frizzell, Alan. 1991. "The Perils of Polling as Exemplified in the '88 Election." In *Politics: Canada*. 7th ed, ed. Paul W. Fox and Graham White. Toronto: McGraw-Hill Ryerson.

Frizzell, Alan, Jon H. Pammett and Anthony Westell. 1989. *The Canadian General Election of 1988*. Ottawa: Carleton University Press.

Frizzell, Alan, and Anthony Westell. 1985. *The Canadian General Election of 1984*. Toronto: Oxford University Press.

Gerstlé, Jacques. 1991. "Election Communication in France." In *Media, Elections and Democracy*, ed. Frederick J. Fletcher. Vol. 19 of the research studies of the Royal Commission on Electoral Reform and Party Financing. Ottawa and Toronto: RCERPF/Dundurn.

Gilsdorf, William O. 1990. "The Organizing Processes of the CBC-TV National Election Unit in the 1988 Canadian Federal Election." Paper presented at the Canadian Political Science Association annual meeting, Victoria.

Gilsdorf, William O., and Robert Bernier. 1991. "Journalistic Practice in Covering Federal Election Campaigns in Canada." In *Reporting the Campaign: Election Coverage in Canada*, ed. Frederick J. Fletcher. Vol. 22 of the research studies of the Royal Commission on Electoral Reform and Party Financing. Ottawa and Toronto: RCERPF/Dundurn.

Graber, Doris A. 1991. "The Mass Media and Election Campaigns in the United States of America." In *Media, Elections and Democracy*, ed. Frederick J. Fletcher. Vol. 19 of the research studies of the Royal Commission on Electoral Reform and Party Financing. Ottawa and Toronto: RCERPF/Dundurn.

Hackett, Robert A. 1991. "Smaller Voices: Minor Parties, Campaign Communications and the News Media." In *Reporting the Campaign: Election Coverage in Canada*, ed. Frederick J. Fletcher. Vol. 22 of the research studies of the Royal Commission on Electoral Reform and Party Financing. Ottawa and Toronto: RCERPF/Dundurn.

Johnston, Richard, André Blais, Henry Brady and Jean Crête. 1991. "Letting the People Decide: Dynamics of a Canadian Election." Typescript of a forthcoming volume based on the 1988 Canadian National Election Study. With permission of the authors.

Kay, Barry J., Steven D. Brown, James E. Curtis, Ronald D. Lambert and John M. Wilson. 1985. "The Character of Electoral Change: A Preliminary Report from the 1984 National Election Study." Paper presented at the Canadian Political Science Association annual meeting, Montreal.

Kettering Foundation. 1991. *Citizens and Politics: A View from Main Street America*. Washington, DC: Kettering Foundation.

Kline, Stephen, Rovin Deodat, Arlene Shwetz and William Leiss. 1991. "Political Broadcast Advertising in Canada." In *Election Broadcasting in Canada*, ed. Frederick J. Fletcher. Vol. 21 of the research studies of the Royal Commission on Electoral Reform and Party Financing. Ottawa and Toronto: RCERPF/Dundurn.

Krashinsky, Michael, and William J. Milne. 1985. "Additional Evidence on the Effect of Incumbency in Canadian Elections." *Canadian Journal of Political Science* 18:155–65.

———. 1986. "The Effect of Incumbency in the 1984 Federal and 1985 Ontario Elections." *Canadian Journal of Political Science* 19:337–43.

LaCalamita, John. 1984. "The Equitable Campaign: Party Political Broadcasting Regulation in Canada." *Osgoode Hall Law Journal* 22:543–79.

Lambert, Ronald D., James E. Curtis, Barry J. Kay and Steven D. Brown. 1988. "The Social Sources of Political Knowledge." *Canadian Journal of Political Science* 12:359–74.

LeDuc, Lawrence R., and Richard Price. 1985. "Great Debates: The Televised Leadership Debates of 1979." *Canadian Journal of Political Science* 18:135–53.

———. 1990. "Campaign Debates and Party Leader Images: The Encounter '88 Case." Paper presented at the Canadian Political Science Association annual meeting, Victoria.

Leiss, W., S. Kline and S. Jhally. 1990. *Social Communication in Advertising.* Scarborough: Nelson Canada.

MacDermid, R.H. 1991. "Media Usage and Political Behaviour." In *Media and Voters in Canadian Election Campaigns,* ed. Frederick J. Fletcher. Vol. 18 of the research studies of the Royal Commission on Electoral Reform and Party Financing. Ottawa and Toronto: RCERPF/Dundurn.

MacDonald, L. Ian. 1984. *Mulroney: The Making of a Prime Minister.* Toronto: McClelland and Stewart.

Maclean's/Decima. 1988. "The Voters Reflect." 5 December, 19.

McQuail, Denis. 1987. *Mass Communication Theory: An Introduction.* 2d ed. Beverly Hills: Sage Publications.

Meisel, John. 1975. *Working Papers on Canadian Politics.* 2d enlarged ed. Montreal: McGill-Queen's University Press.

National Election Study, 1989 (Richard Johnston, André Blais, Jean Crête and Henry Brady, principal investigators). Data provided by Institute for Social Research, York University.

Palda, K.S. 1985. "Does Canada's Election Act Impede Voters' Access to Information?" *Canadian Public Policy* 11:533–42.

Paletz, David L., and Robert M. Entman. 1981. *Media, Power, Politics.* New York: Free Press.

Paltiel, K.Z. 1975. "Campaign Financing in Canada and Its Reform." In *Canada at the Polls: The General Election of 1974,* ed. Howard Penniman. Washington, DC: American Enterprise Institute for Public Policy Research.

Penniman, Howard R., ed. 1981. *Canada at the Polls, 1979 and 1980.* Washington, DC: American Enterprise Institute for Public Policy Research.

Price, Richard G., and Maureen Mancuso. 1991. "Ties that Bind: Parliamentary Members and Their Constituencies." In *Introductory Readings in Canadian Government Politics,* ed. Robert M. Krause and Ronald H. Wagenberg. Toronto: Copp Clark Pitman.

Qualter, T.H., and K.A. MacKirdy. 1964. "The Press of Ontario and the Election." In *Papers on the 1962 Election,* ed. J. Meisel. Toronto: University of Toronto Press.

Romanow, Walter I., Walter C. Soderlund, E. Donald Briggs and Ronald H. Wagenberg. 1985. "The 1984 Canadian Federal Election: A Study of Television News Coverage." Paper presented at the Canadian Communication Association annual meeting, Montreal.

Romanow, Walter I., Walter C. Soderlund and Richard G. Price. 1991. "Negative Political Advertising: An Analysis of Research Findings in Light of Canadian Practice." In *Political Ethics: A Canadian Perspective*, ed. Janet Hiebert. Vol. 12 of the research studies of the Royal Commission on Electoral Reform and Party Financing. Ottawa and Toronto: RCERPF/Dundurn.

Schoenbach, Klaus. 1991. "Mass Media and Election Campaigns in Germany." In *Media, Elections and Democracy*, ed. Frederick J. Fletcher. Vol. 19 of the research studies of the Royal Commission on Electoral Reform and Party Financing. Ottawa and Toronto: RCERPF/Dundurn.

Seidle, F. Leslie, and K.Z. Paltiel. 1981. "Party Finance, the Election Expenses Act and Campaign Spending in 1979 and 1980." In *Canada at the Polls 1979 and 1980*, ed. Howard R. Penniman. Washington, DC: American Enterprise Institute for Public Policy Research.

Semetko, Holli A. 1991. "Broadcasting and Election Communication in Britain." In *Media, Elections and Democracy*, ed. Frederick J. Fletcher. Vol. 19 of the research studies of the Royal Commission on Electoral Reform and Party Financing. Ottawa and Toronto: RCERPF/Dundurn.

Siune, Karen. 1991. "Campaign Communication in Scandinavia." In *Media, Elections and Democracy*, ed. Frederick J. Fletcher. Vol. 19 of the research studies of the Royal Commission on Electoral Reform and Party Financing. Ottawa and Toronto: RCERPF/Dundurn.

Snider, Norman. 1985. *The Changing of the Guard: How the Liberals Fell from Grace and the Tories Rose to Power*. Toronto: Lester and Orpen Dennys.

Soderlund, Walter C., Walter I. Romanow, E. Donald Briggs and Ronald H. Wagenberg. 1984. *Media and Elections in Canada*. Toronto: Holt, Rinehart and Winston.

Spencer, David Ralph. 1991. "Election Broadcasting in Canada: A Brief History." In *Election Broadcasting in Canada*, ed. Frederick J. Fletcher. Vol. 21 of the research studies of the Royal Commission on Electoral Reform and Party Financing. Ottawa and Toronto: RCERPF/Dundurn.

Taras, David. 1990. *The Newsmakers: The Media's Influence on Canadian Politics*. Scarborough: Nelson Canada.

Taylor, Paul. 1990. *See How They Run: Electing the President in an Age of Mediaocracy*. New York: Alfred A. Knopf.

Wagenberg, Ronald H., Walter C. Soderlund, Walter I. Romanow and E. Donald Briggs. 1988. "Campaigns, Images and Polls: Mass Media Coverage of the 1984 Canadian Election." *Canadian Journal of Political Science* 21:117–29.

Warhurst, John. 1991. "Campaign Communication in Australian Elections." In *Media, Elections and Democracy*, ed. Frederick J. Fletcher. Vol. 19 of the research studies of the Royal Commission on Electoral Reform and Party Financing. Ottawa and Toronto: RCERPF/Dundurn.

Williams, Robert J. 1981. "Candidate Selection." In *Canada at the Polls 1979 and 1980*, ed. Howard R. Penniman. Washington, DC: American Enterprise Institute for Public Policy Research.

Wilson, R. Jeremy. 1980–81. "Media Coverage of Canadian Election Campaigns: Horse-race Journalism and the Meta-Campaign." *Journal of Canadian Studies* 15:56–68.

Wolinsky, Leo, et al. 1991. "Refereeing the TV Campaign." *Washington Journalism Review* 13(1): 22–27.

CONTRIBUTORS TO VOLUME 19

Robert Everett	York University
Frederick J. Fletcher	York University
Jacques Gerstlé	Université de Poitiers, France
Doris A. Graber	University of Illinois
Klaus Schoenbach	Academy for Music and Theatre, Germany
Holli A. Semetko	University of Michigan
Karen Siune	University of Aarhus, Denmark
John Warhurst	University of New England, Australia

ACKNOWLEDGEMENTS

The Royal Commission on Electoral Reform and Party Financing and the publishers wish to acknowledge with gratitude the permission of the following to reprint and translate material:

Commonwealth of Australia, Australian Government Publishing Service; Longman Cheshire Pty Limited; Ian Ward, University of Queensland.

Care has been taken to trace the ownership of copyright material used in the text, including the tables and figures. The authors and publishers welcome any information enabling them to rectify any reference or credit in subsequent editions.

Consistent with the Commission's objective of promoting full participation in the electoral system by all segments of Canadian society, gender neutrality has been used wherever possible in the editing of the research studies.

THE COLLECTED RESEARCH STUDIES*

* The titles of studies may not be final in all cases.

ROBERT A. HACKETT,
WITH THE ASSISTANCE OF
JAMES MACKINTOSH,
DAVID ROBINSON AND
ARLENE SHWETZ

Smaller Voices: Minor Parties,
Campaign Communication and
the News Media

EILEEN SAUNDERS

Mass Media and the Reproduction
of Marginalization

VOLUME 23
Canadian Political Parties in the Constituencies:
A Local Perspective

R.K. CARTY

Canadian Political Parties in the
Constituencies: A Local Perspective

COMMISSION ORGANIZATION

CHAIRMAN
Pierre Lortie

COMMISSIONERS
Pierre Fortier
Robert Gabor
William Knight
Lucie Pépin

SENIOR OFFICERS

Executive Director
Guy Goulard

Director of Research
Peter Aucoin

Special Adviser to the Chairman
Jean-Marc Hamel

Research
F. Leslie Seidle,
  Senior Research Coordinator

Coordinators
Herman Bakvis
Michael Cassidy
Frederick J. Fletcher
Janet Hiebert
Kathy Megyery
Robert A. Milen
David Small

Assistant Coordinators
David Mac Donald
Cheryl D. Mitchell

Legislation
Jules Brière, Senior Adviser
Gérard Bertrand
Patrick Orr

Communications and Publishing
Richard Rochefort, Director
Hélène Papineau, Assistant
  Director
Paul Morisset, Editor
Kathryn Randle, Editor

Finance and Administration
Maurice R. Lacasse, Director

Contracts and Personnel
Thérèse Lacasse, Chief

Editorial, Design and Production Services

Royal Commission on Electoral Reform and Party Financing

Editors   Denis Bastien, Susan Becker Davidson, Ginette Bertrand, Louis Bilodeau, Claude Brabant, Louis Chabot, Danielle Chaput, Norman Dahl, Carlos del Burgo, Julie Desgagners, Chantal Granger, Volker Junginger, Denis Landry, André LaRose, Paul Morisset, Christine O'Meara, Mario Pelletier, Marie-Noël Pichelin, Kathryn Randle, Georges Royer, Eve Valiquette, Dominique Vincent.

Le Centre de Documentation Juridique du Québec Inc.

Hubert Reid, *President*

Claire Grégoire, *Comptroller*

Lucie Poirier, *Production Manager*
Gisèle Gingras, *Special Project Assistant*

Translators   Pierre-Yves de la Garde, Richard Lapointe, Marie-Josée Turcotte.

Technical Editors   Stéphane Côté Coulombe, *Coordinator*;
Josée Chabot, Danielle Morin.

Copy Editors   Martine Germain, Lise Larochelle, Elisabeth Reid, Carole St-Louis, Isabelle Tousignant, Charles Tremblay, Sébastien Viau.

Word Processing   André Vallée.

Formatting   Typoform, Claude Audet; Linda Goudreau, *Formatting Coordinator*.

Wilson & Lafleur Ltée

Claude Wilson, *President*

DUNDURN PRESS

J. Kirk Howard, *President*
Ian Low, *Comptroller*
Jeanne MacDonald, *Project Coordinator*

Avivah Wargon, *Managing and Production Editor*
Beth Ediger, *Managing Editor*
John St. James, *Managing Editor*
Karen Heese, *Special Project Assistant*

Ruth Chernia, *Tables Editor*
Victoria Grant, *Legal Editor*
Michèle Breton, *Special Editorial Assistant*

Editorial Staff Elliott Chapin, Peggy Foy, Lily Hobel, Marilyn Hryciuk, Madeline Koch, Elizabeth Mitchell, John Shoesmith, Nadine Stoikoff, Shawn Syms, Anne Vespry.

Copy Editors Carol Anderson, Elizabeth d'Anjou, Jane Becker, Diane Brassolotto, Elizabeth Driver, Curtis Fahey, Tony Fairfield, Freya Godard, Frances Hanna, Kathleen Harris, Andria Hourwich, Greg Ioannou, Carlotta Lemieux, Elsha Leventis, David McCorquodale, Virginia Smith, Gail Thorson, Louise Wood.

Formatting Green Graphics; Joanne Green, *Formatting Coordinator;* *Formatters* Linda Carroll, Mary Ann Cattral, Gail Nina, Eva Payne, Jacqueline Hope Raynor, Andy Tong, Carla Vonn Worden, Laura Wilkins.